AT ALL COSTS!

AT ALL COSTS!

Stories of Impossible Victories

BRYAN PERRETT

*'If we go forward we die. If we go back we die.
It is better to go forward.'* Old Zulu Saying

'Courage is will-power.' Lord Moran

ARMS AND
ARMOUR

Arms and Armour Press
A Cassell Imprint
Wellington House, 125 Strand, London WC2R 0BB

Distributed in the USA by Sterling Publishing Co. Inc.,
387 Park Avenue South, New York, NY 10016-8810.

Distributed in the Australia by Capricorn Link (Australia) Pty. Ltd.,
2/3 Carrington Road, Castle Hill, NSW 2154.

British Library Cataloguing-in-Publication Data: a catalogue
record for this book is available from the British Library

ISBN 1-85409-276-6

Designed and edited by DAG Publications Ltd.
Designed by David Gibbons; edited by Michael Boxall; typeset by
Ronset Typesetters, Darwen, Lancashire; camerawork by M&E
Reproductions, North Fambridge, Essex; printed and bound in
Great Britain by Hartnolls Limited, Bodmin, Cornwall.

CONTENTS

INTRODUCTION

I mplicit in the use of the phrase 'at all costs' is the desperate need to attain an objective or maintain an existing position, for the greater good of the whole. A unit can be set an at-all-costs mission in either an offensive or a defensive context. The common factor is urgency, time being the most valuable commodity on the battlefield. In the majority of cases, of course, while senior officers might decree that an action is to be fought irrespective of cost, comparatively few are pressed to such a conclusion. In those that are, it is usually the junior leaders who have provided the driving force and for this reason alone they are worth examining in some detail. A curious feature of this type of action is that, rare as it is, several can occur in one battle or in successive battles fought within days of one another. This phenomenon has produced what in the British Army would be described as Victoria Cross battles, although examples exist in the histories of all first-class armies.

The key can obviously be identified as motivation, yet in some of the examples studied the units involved were fresh while in others they were close to exhaustion, so clearly their experiences, perspectives and outlooks were different. But I was convinced that a common factor existed and in my search I was drawn to Lord Moran's classic *The Anatomy of Courage*. Moran, who served as a medical officer with an infantry battalion during the First World War, defines courage as willpower. He makes the point that every man goes into action with a credit balance of courage in his moral bank account, and he accepts that the size of the balance will vary according to individuals. Withdrawals from the balance occur when a man is exposed to constant fear and danger, bad living conditions, boredom and failure. Ultimately, if too many withdrawals are made, the balance enters a minus quantity and the man concerned becomes a danger to himself and those around him. Conversely, as Moran says, 'If a soldier is always using up his capital he may from time to time add to it. There is a paying in as well as a paying out.' Some of these deposits in the account are simply the inverse of the withdrawals, but others exist and some can provide an extremely powerful source of motivation.

Moran also stresses the obvious truth that morale is a collective as well as an individual force. It follows, therefore, that any unit receiving a sudden infusion of this kind, from whatever source, becomes a formidable opponent. Fear is suppressed by complete absorption in the work to be done; self-preservation is replaced by the need to destroy the enemy.

The examples I have chosen cover a wide spectrum of modern military history and have been selected because they illustrate the point very well indeed. Some are well known, others less so; many others exist. They take place on widely differing battlefields against a background of expanding weapon technology and firepower, yet the moral factors remain constant throughout.

I have begun with Minden where, as the result of a mistake, six British and three Hanoverian battalions advanced in isolation against the French army. By all the rules they should have been wiped out, but they absorbed the worst the enemy's artillery could throw at them, destroyed his cavalry and chased his infantry off the field. As the French commander was undoubtedly told after the battle, it simply should not have happened.

Balaclava was the archetypal Victoria Cross battle. Logic dictated that the 93rd Highlanders should have been ridden down and the Heavy Brigade destroyed, yet together they removed the threat to the British army's supply line. The Light Brigade was destroyed, although its now legendary courage and discipline further demoralized the beaten enemy.

During the Indian Mutiny it was a moot point whether the small, disease-ridden force of British and Indian soldiers on the Ridge outside Delhi was besieging the much larger force of mutineers within the city, or vice versa. In the end, though fearful risks were taken, it was the fierce motivation of the former that carried the day.

At the battle of Gettysburg the courage of those defending an insignificant hillock named Little Round Top lasted for a few critical minutes longer than that of their opponents. If Little Round Top had fallen the entire Union line would have been placed in jeopardy and the probability is that Lee's Confederates would have won, at the least, a limited victory. There would have been no need for the magnificent tragedy of Pickett's Charge the following day and the course of the war, if not its ultimate ending, might well have been different.

The Franco–Prussian War of 1870–1 had a profound effect upon subsequent European history. Arguably, the result of the war was decided in two consecutive battles, Vionville – Mars-la-Tour on 16 August 1870 and Gravelotte – St-Privat two days later. In both the French came very close to victory and inflicted by far the heavier loss. At Vionville only the self-sacrificial cavalry charge known as von Bredow's Death Ride saved the Germans from a potentially disastrous situation. At Gravelotte – St-Privat the German right was heavily defeated and the outcome of the battle depended on what took place on the left. Here the Prussian Guard Corps sustained no fewer than 8,000 casualties in twenty minutes and was pinned down during an ill-conceived attack. When the moment came, however, the guardsmen stormed their objective and caused the French to retreat.

Today, in less idealistic times, we can view the despatch of the tiny Desert Column to the relief of General Gordon, besieged in Khartoum, as an example of political cynicism at its worst. If the column succeeded, well and good; if it were wiped out, no great harm was done. Against all probability, it survived the desert, beat the dervishes in two pitched battles, advanced to within sight of Khartoum and returned to tell the tale. Just for once, mud was left sticking to political fingers.

On 21 May 1940 not even the most optimistic imagined that the Allied counter-attack at Arras would produce significant results, yet it smashed through the flank of Major-General Erwin Rommel's 7th Panzer Division and induced a panic which spread to the neighbouring SS Division *Totenkopf*. Such was the alarm it generated at the highest command levels that the apparently unstoppable drive of the German armour was suspended for 24 hours. This, in turn, was to have a direct bearing on the success of the Dunkirk evacuation.

'Valiant dust' was the term used by an official historian to describe those British, American and German soldiers who died fighting for possession of Longstop Hill, strategically situated at the mouth of the Medjerda valley in Tunisia. In the end, the most important summit fell to a ferocious bayonet charge by just thirty men of the 8th Argyll & Sutherland Highlanders, almost all that remained of the battalion's rifle companies.

The Anglo–American crossings of the Waal during Operation 'Market Garden' also provided examples of supreme courage and motivation. When the US III/504th Parachute Infantry crossed in assault boats it seemed as though none would survive to reach the far bank. Those that did swarmed ashore and overwhelmed the defence in a series of furious local attacks. In the mistaken belief that the far end of the road bridge was in friendly hands, a troop of tanks from the Guards Armoured Division charged across, knowing that the bridge might be blown at any moment and, against odds, fought their way through to link up with the Americans.

The parachute descent of the US 503rd Parachute Infantry on to tiny and very dangerous drop zones on Corregidor Island required nerves of steel in itself, but subsequently demands of a different kind were made on the men's courage for several days. It was not so much that the Japanese preferred to fight to the death rather than surrender, but rather the knowledge that the island's vast underground bunkers contained huge stocks of ammunition which the enemy would not hesitate to explode if he thought he could take some of the attackers with him. Many Americans were killed in this way, but the pressure was maintained until the island was secure.

Finally, on 28 May 1982 the 2nd Battalion The Parachute Regiment, outnumbered, fought its way through a series of prepared positions in depth on the open terrain of a narrow isthmus to liberate Goose Green settlement and win the United Kingdom's first victory of the Falklands conflict. It was a victory which destroyed the Argentine belief that any prospect existed of winning the war.

Taken together, these episodes refute the suggestion that God is always on the side of the big battalions. Rather, they confirm the saying that in war the relationship of the moral to the physical is in the ratio of three to one. As he considers each one in turn, the reader can decide for himself the source or sources of the motivation involved. For what they are worth, my own conclusions are set out in the Postscript.

ACKNOWLEDGEMENTS

T he incidents I have related in this book span some two and a half centuries of history. It would, therefore, have been quite impossible to complete the task I had set myself had it not been for the many people who so kindly assisted me with their time, advice and interest, as well as the learned institutions which provided generous access to their archives. In particular I should like to express my sincere thanks to: Alastair Campbell of Airds, Chief Executive of Clan Campbell; Mr F. Carpenter, Museums Officer, Doncaster Metropolitan Borough Council; Major A. G. B. Cobbold, Hon Curator of the Suffolk Regiment Museum; Mr John M. Coski, Staff Historian, Museum of the Confederacy, Richmond, Virginia; Colonel J. S. Cowley, Light Infantry Office (Yorkshire); Lieutenant-Colonel C. D. Darroch, Hon Archivist, The Royal Hampshire Regiment; Herr von Gusovius of the Bomann Museum, Celle; Major J. McQ. Hallam, The Lancashire Headquarters, Royal Regiment of Fusiliers; Mr T. J. F. Hodgson, The Buffs Museum Manager; Lieutenant-Colonel C. G. O. Hogg, Regimental Secretary, The King's Own Scottish Borderers; Mr Norman Holme, Archivist of the Regimental Museum, Royal Welch Fusiliers; Oberstleutnant Joh. Kindler, Militärgeschichtliches Forschungsamt, German Army; the Ministry of Defence Library; Oberstleutnant Paprotka of the Wehrgeschichtliches Museum, Rastatt; Paul Riches; Dr A. von Rohr, Historisches Museum, Hanover; Major-General J. Scott Elliot, Lieutenant-Colonel A. W. Scott Elliot, Lieutenant-Colonel A. D. Malcolm and Lieutenant-Colonel Hamish Taylor of the Argyll & Sutherland Highlanders; and Mr John J. Slonaker, Chief, Historical Reference Branch, US Army Military History Institute.

Bryan Perrett, October 1992

1
THE DRUMS OF MINDEN
1 August 1759

Until the outbreak of the French Revolution, the wars of 18th-century Europe were essentially dynastic struggles waged by small professional armies, and were notable for the absence of the fanaticism that characterized the religious conflicts that had gone before and the wars between nation states that were to follow. In much of Europe, and in particular the smaller central states, patriotism as we understand the word today did not exist, although in the larger western states such as the United Kingdom and France there was a growing sense of nationality. By and large populations were little motivated by their rulers' quarrels, unless they were directly threatened, and the latter found difficulty in filling the ranks of their regiments.

Soldiering, in fact, was a despised profession. As Dr Werner Holtfort, the German historian, comments, any man who chose to 'go for a soldier' faced a life of *Angst vor Verwundung, Schmerz und Tod* – fear and wounds, pain and death – but this was only part of the story. Inevitably, strict discipline was required to keep men in line during a close-range firefight in which every detail of the enemy's uniform was visible. Infringements of the disciplinary code, in action or out, could attract varying degrees of retribution, including hanging and flogging. The Prussian Army was noted for painful methods of correction intended to return the offender to robotic obedience, but most armies employed similar if less severe disciplinary systems. 'You're not paid to think!' has been the sergeant-major's traditional rebuke to the private soldier since time immemorial, and in this era it meant exactly what it said. When he was paid, the private received rather less money than a farm labourer, subject to a variety of stoppages.

It would be wrong, however, to judge the brutalities of the 18th century by the standards pertaining on the fringes of the 21st. If the soldier's life was harsh, so too could be that of the civilian. One could be hanged or flogged for very little, or deprived of work and even turned out of house and home, with little or no support being provided by the scant social security systems of the day. Thus, while armies might attract a few genuine volunteers, most of the men had been driven to enlist by the desperate need to support themselves. Other sources of recruits were mercenaries and the pettiest of criminals whom the magistrates had offered enlistment as an alternative to prison; some rulers also resorted to a form of conscription by lottery in which those unfortunate enough to be chosen were permitted, if they could afford it, to employ a substitute to serve in their place.

There was another side to the coin. When a man joined his regiment, usually at a time when his self-esteem was at a low ebb, he found himself in an enclosed society isolated from the civilian community which despised it. Within that society he was accepted at quite a different valuation by his fellows, and from the shared experience of hard times together in the field would grow comradeship, one of the priceless bonds which hold a regiment together in times of crisis. Again, the Duke of Marlborough, recognizing that most of those in the ranks were soldiers only because life offered them no alternative, had ensured that responsibility for his men's welfare became an essential part of an officer's duties. The result was that in British regiments an excellent relationship existed between officers and men, despite the wide social gulf which separated them. Together, these elements produced in the soldier a sense of belonging to a strictly regulated and hierarchical family which none the less accepted him and accorded him the respect he earned. It was, too, a family in whose achievements he could take some personal pride and one which he was unlikely to let down. By the middle of the 18th century, therefore, regimental spirit within the British Army was already well developed and was a formidable factor in itself.

In the summer of 1756 the Emperors of Austria and Russia joined forces with the Kings of France, Sweden and Saxony in an attempt to curb the power and territorial ambitions of Frederick the Great of Prussia. The United Kingdom, already engaged in active hostilities against the French in North America and India, supported Prussia, not least because the kings of England were also kings of Hanover and their continental territories were menaced by the anti-Fredrician alliance. At first British support for Frederick was purely financial, but in 1758 a force consisting of six cavalry and six infantry regiments, with supporting artillery, was dispatched to Germany under Lieutenant-General Lord George Sackville, where it joined a composite Hanoverian–Hessian–Brunswicker–Prussian army under the overall command of Duke Ferdinand of Brunswick.

Ferdinand was pleased by the addition of British infantry to his strength, albeit in such small numbers, for during the previous half-century it had established a reputation it had not enjoyed since the days when the English longbow had dominated the battlefields of western Europe. It was steady in action, its first discipline was excellent and its musketry techniques had recently undergone a major refinement which required the troops to aim at a specific target rather than simply at the enemy line opposite. The firepower of the Royal Artillery, too, had been increased by fitting the guns with a simple breech elevating screw in place of the old wedge, the position of which had to be checked with every shot. Moreover, the British had always got on well with the

Hanoverians, who wore much the same scarlet uniforms as themselves. 'They get drunk very comfortably together,' wrote Sackville. 'And talk and sing a vast deal without understanding one syllable of what they say to one another.'

Sackville was an experienced officer, and in some respects a good one. He was, for example, concerned for his men's welfare and had recently put an end to the practice of stopping fourpence a week from their meagre wages to pay for their tentage. On the other hand, he was moody, stubborn, cantankerous, devious and on bad terms with too many people for them all to be in the wrong. Unfortunately, among those to whom he took a dislike was Ferdinand, maybe because of personal jealousy or perhaps because the Duke was known to have lined his pockets with some of the British subsidies paid to Frederick.

As with other wars of the period, the Seven Years War, as it became known, consisted of long periods of manoeuvring punctuated by infrequent battles. Armies were expensive and difficult to maintain and their commanders were understandably reluctant to hazard them unless victory seemed certain. Even then, whether battles were won or lost, large-scale desertions inevitably followed in their wake. To recount the movements of Ferdinand's army in these circumstances would be very tedious indeed. Suffice it to say that by the end of July 1759 his French opponent, the Marquis Louis de Contades, had forced him back to the line of the Weser near the fortified town of Minden, where he would be compelled to fight a battle if Hanover were not to be overrun.

The problem was that Contades, with some 60,000 men and 162 guns, had adopted an extremely strong position with his right covered by Minden and the river, his centre protected by marshland through which ran a stream known as the Bastau, and his left resting on wooded hills to the south-west. Ferdinand knew that to attack Contades' position with only 45,000 men and 170 guns would be extremely foolish. He decided, therefore, that while a detachment under the Hereditary Prince of Brunswick menaced the French supply route near Herford, he would entice Contades from his position and fight on ground of his own choosing. The bait would consist of another detachment of 10,000 men under Lieutenant-General von Wangenheim, apparently posted in isolation at the ominously named village of Todtenhausen (Houses of the Dead) some two miles down-river from Minden. Contades, sensing a quick and easy victory, would attempt to snap up the prize, little suspecting that the remainder of Ferdinand's army was within striking distance and would immediately close in on his left flank as soon as he moved forward.

Contades almost certainly read Ferdinand's mind, but as the latter had deliberately spread his picquets over a wide area to convey an impression of dispersion, he believed that he could probably overwhelm Wangenheim's detachment before the Anglo–German army could intervene. Ferdinand, having lost so great a portion of his strength, would have to withdraw and the way would be open for the invasion of Hanover. On 31 July Contades, believing that the risks were acceptable, ordered eight bridges to be constructed over the Bastau in preparation for the move forward.

By midnight every detail of his plan was in Ferdinand's hands. The story of how this came about may seem to belong more to the world of the Brothers Grimm than to military history, but it is included in most German and some British accounts of the battle and, as the event itself had a bearing on the conduct of operations, the probability is that its substance is true. Contades, it seems, wished to inform the commander of his depot at Herford of his intended movements, almost certainly to warn him that he was on the point of resuming his advance into Hanover so that the necessary supplies could be dispatched forward when the moment came. However, as we have seen, the Hereditary Prince's troops were active between Minden and Herford and, rather than risk the capture of a regular courier, Contades decided that his message would be carried by a German civilian, who would be offered certain incentives and attract less attention. He sent for a Minden shoemaker named Heinrich Lohrmann and told him to make a sample pair of military shoes. The shoes were delivered and Lohrmann was asked to wait while they were examined. He was then told to walk to Herford in them and present them to the depot commander who would, if satisfied, order several thousand more pairs. Lohrmann understood sufficient French to know that matters were not quite as straightforward as they seemed. He also knew that his work had been tampered with and, examining the shoes at the first opportunity, discovered the plans sewn into the soles. He walked not to Herford but to Ferdinand's headquarters at Hille, which he reached at about midnight.

It was understandable that Ferdinand might suspect Contades was engaged in some game of double-bluff but he could not afford to take the chance. At 01.00 he had the entire army turned out of its tents and stood to, although beyond this there was nothing he could do but await developments. Somewhat earlier, at about 22.00, two figures had approached the picquet at Hartum through the gathering dusk. They had been unable to respond to the challenge 'Albert' with 'And Augsburg,' the night's password and, having been promptly arrested, identified themselves as French deserters from the Régiment de Picardie. For some reason the Prince of Anhalt, commanding the outpost line, did not send them back to Ferdinand's headquarters until 03.30, and they did not reach Hille until 04.00. Here they confirmed that Contades' troops had been crossing the Bastau for several hours and were advancing on Todtenhausen. Realizing that not a moment was to be lost, Ferdinand gave the order to march.

The Duke's preparations for the coming battle had been very thorough. His army had camped in eight columns, the order in which it was to make its approach march, so that, on reaching the edge of the battlefield, the columns merely had to deploy and the line of battle would be formed. First light began to appear at about 04.30 and as the columns neared Minden Heath the smoke of battle could be seen hanging heavily near Todtenhausen. As yet, the thunder of the guns could not be heard because it was being carried away by the same howling wind which had smothered the sound of French movements during the night, although the heavy rain which had accompanied it had now cleared.

Details of Contades' deployment became apparent. He had brought his entire army forward and it was now occupying a semi-circular position with its right on the Weser and its left on the Bastau marshes. Contrary to the custom of the day, his cavalry was massed in the centre of the line and his two wings consisted of infantry, a formation almost certainly adopted because only the firm heathland in the middle of the battlefield offered good going for his horsemen. Ferdinand's deployment, when completed, followed the conventional pattern with cavalry on the wings and infantry in the centre, prolonged on the left by von Wangenheim's detachment, which was experiencing no difficulty in holding its own.

We are concerned only with the part played in the battle by Ferdinand's three columns on the right flank. No. 1 Column, commanded by Lord George Sackville, consisted of fourteen British and ten Hanoverian cavalry squadrons. It was late moving off because Sackville had overslept and, for various reasons, he was now in the foulest of moods. Already irritated by his hurried transit from bed to saddle without so much as a bite of breakfast, he perversely bristled with resentment that Ferdinand had not troubled to consult him during the events of the night for, after all, was he not simultaneously commander of the army's British contingent and commander of the cavalry on the right wing? He was determined to teach Ferdinand a lesson, namely that he was not a man to be taken for granted. Sackville's second-in-command, the Marquis of Granby, who would lead the brigade's second line when it was formed, had also annoyed him. Granby was an honest, straightforward soldier, not in the least given to politicking and plots, and Lord George found such men difficult to understand.

The cavalry brigade was approaching Hahlen in column of squadrons when a messenger arrived from Ferdinand with orders that it should form two lines and await further instructions. Sackville complied and, as a cannon ball thumped into the ground nearby, not unkindly told the brigade chaplain to make himself scarce. Fighting was already taking place in Hahlen, where Anhalt and his Hessians were clearing some French infantry from the village. When this task was completed Captain Foy's British light artillery brigade, equipped with four light 12pdr guns,

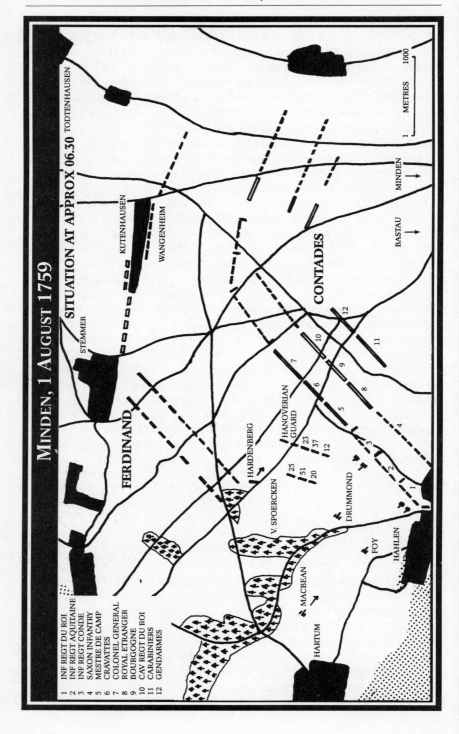

MINDEN, 1 AUGUST 1759

SITUATION AT APPROX 06.30

1 INF REGT DU ROI
2 INF REGT AQUITAINE
3 INF REGT CONDE
4 SAXON INFANTRY
5 MESTRE DE CAMP
6 CRAVATTES
7 COLONEL GENERAL
8 ROYAL ETRANGER
9 BOURGOGNE
10 CAV REGT DU ROI
11 CARABINIERS
12 GENDARMES

TODTENHAUSEN

KUTENHAUSEN

WANGENHEIM

STEMMER

FERDINAND

HARDENBERG

HANOVERIAN GUARD

V. SPOERCKEN

HARTUM

MACBEAN

FOY

HAHLEN

DRUMMOND

CONTADES

BASTAU

MINDEN

METRES

1000

three light 6pdrs and two 5½in howitzers, moved up parallel with the village and began duelling with guns on the left of the French line.

No. 2 Column, on the cavalry's left, was commanded by Major Haase and contained the heavy artillery of the army's right wing. This included a British heavy artillery brigade of ten 12pdr guns under Captain Macbean. In view of the manner in which the battle developed it is worth mentioning that at this stage of its development the Royal Artillery employed neither its own horse teams nor drivers. Both were hired from civilian contractors as the need arose, with the obvious disadvantage that, if the situation turned nasty, the drivers were inclined to take themselves and their horses off the field altogether.

To the left and somewhat in advance of the artillery column was No. 3 Column under Lieutenant-General August Friedrich von Spoercken, consisting of the six British infantry regiments and both battalions of the Hanoverian Guard Regiment, joined by one battalion of another Hanoverian regiment, Hardenberg's from Major-General von Schele's Column No 4, and Captain Drummond's British light artillery brigade, equipped with two light 12pdr guns, three light 6pdrs and four 5½in howitzers. Further firepower could be provided by the infantry's light 6pdr battalion guns, normally issued on the scale of two per battalion, giving a maximum possible total of eighteen. Little is known of the part played by these weapons in the battle, although they were certainly present.

This was the heyday of the proprietorial system, when colonels purchased command of their regiments and were allowed an annual sum by the government to administer them. Each regiment had an official number but was more commonly known by its colonel's name. To avoid confusion arising in the case of the British regiments, therefore, both are set out below, together with the names by which they became known to later generations.

12th (Napier's) – The Suffolk Regiment
20th (Kingsley's) – The Lancashire Fusiliers
23rd (Hulke's) – The Royal Welch Fusiliers
25th (Howe's) – The King's Own Scottish Borderers
37th (Stuart's) – The Hampshire Regiment
51st (Brudenell's) – The King's Own Yorkshire Light Infantry

With the exception of Drummond's guns, which moved forward and to the right to join Foy's in engaging the French artillery, Spoercken's column deployed neatly into two lines in a shallow hollow behind a belt of trees. The first line, commanded by Major-General Waldegrave, was formed, from right to left, by the 12th, 37th, 23rd and the Hanoverian Guard Regiment; the second, under Major General Kingsley, by the 20th, 51st and 25th, with Hardenberg's coming up on the left to fall in behind the Guards. Each regiment was formed in three ranks with the Colours in the centre and the battalion guns on its flanks. Absent were their grenadier companies, consisting of the tallest and best soldiers, which, in accordance with the customs of the time, had already been brigaded into composite regiments and were now fighting hard at Todtenhausen under Wangenheim. A modern observer of Spoercken's line of battle would undoubtedly remark that the size of its men was not impressive; a notable exception was the 23rd which, with an average height of five feet eight inches, is said to have towered above the rest, a tribute to the efficiency of its recruiting sergeants.

At a little after 06.00 one of Ferdinand's aides, a Count Taube, arrived with an order for Spoercken that he would advance *at* the sound of the drum. Drums were the usual method of co-ordinating movement on the battlefield and Ferdinand obviously meant that his own drummers would give the signal; almost certainly, this would not take place before the army's line had been formed to his satisfaction. Spoercken passed on the order to Waldegrave, his leading brigadier, speaking in French, their only common language. The triple translation produced exactly the reverse of what Ferdinand had intended, for Waldegrave interpreted the order to mean advance *to* the sound of the drum. His drummers beat the Advance and the first line moved forward. Kingsley's second line, in which the sergeants were still bustling about with their pikes, attending to the dressing, stepped off minutes later. Taube, horrified, turned about and galloped back to Spoercken. Ferdinand, too, had observed the movement and sent more of his aides spurring to halt it, which they succeeded in doing just short of the trees.

As to what happened next, no explanation has survived, nor can one be offered. The drums began to roll again and both lines set off through the trees and on to the open heathland beyond. Even by the standards of the Age of Elegance they presented a splendid sight with rank upon rank of high white gaiters, scarlet coats and black tricorne hats, all marching steadily in perfect step and with perfect dressing, Colours streaming from their poles in the high wind. Points of light sparkled from bayonets fixed to shouldered muskets, and from the pikes of the sergeants and junior officers. Here and there the drummers, wearing grenadiers' mitre caps and coats of the regimental facing colour or scarlet laced with gold, added an additional splash of brightness to the scene. On they marched, heading straight for the massed ranks of the French cavalry, apparently doomed as they came under fire from the enemy's artillery, supplemented by that of the Regiments of Condé and Aquitaine, delivered at extreme musketry range.

Fortunately, among the preserved accounts of the battle are letters written by two junior officers, Lieutenant Hugh Montgomery of the 12th and Lieutenant Thomas Thomson of the 20th, both of which give vivid accounts of men going into action for the first time.

'On the immediate sight of us', wrote Thomson, 'they opened a battery of eighteen heavy guns which from the nature of the ground, which was a plain, flanked this regiment in particular every foot we marched. Their cannon was ill-served at first, but they soon felt us and their shot took place so fast that every officer imagined the battalion would be taken off [i.e., destroyed] before we could get up to give a fire, notwithstanding we were then within a quarter of a mile of their left wing. I saw heads, legs and arms taken off. My right-hand file of men, not more than a foot from me, were all by one ball dashed to pieces and their blood flying all over me, this I must confess staggered me not a little but, on receiving a confusion in the bend of my right arm by a spent musket shot, it steadied me immediately, all apprehensions of hurt vanished, revenge and the care of the company I commanded took [their] place and I was *then* much more at ease than at *this* time. [He was writing from hospital in Minden nearly three weeks after the event.] All the time their left wing was pelting us with small arms, cannon and grape shot, and we were not suffered to fire, but stood tamely looking on whilst they at their leisure picked us off as you would small birds on a barn door. I cannot compare it with anything as their shot came full and thick, and had one quarter of them taken place [i.e., hit their target] there could not have been a man left.'

Montgomery's experience, described in a letter to his mother, was very similar. 'Now began the most disagreeable march that I ever had in my life, for we advanced more than a quarter of a mile thro' a most furious fire from a most infernal battery of 18-pounders, which was first upon our front but, as we proceeded, bore upon our flank, and at last upon our rear. . . . At the beginning of the action I was almost knocked off my legs by my three right-hand men, who were killed and drove against me by a cannon ball – the same ball also killed two men close to Ward, whose post was in the rear of my platoon. . . . It might be imagined that this cannonade would render the regiments incapable of bearing the shock of unhurt troops drawn up long before on ground of their own choosing, but firmness and resolution will surmount almost any difficulty.'

The reason for this is, perhaps, provided by another, unnamed, subaltern of the 12th. 'The soldiers, so far from being daunted by their falling comrades, breathed nothing but revenge; for my part, though at the beginning of the engagement I felt a kind of trepidation, yet I was so animated by the brave example of all around me, that when I received a slight wound by a musket ball slanting on my left side, it served only to exasperate me the more, and had I then received orders, I could with the greatest pleasure have rushed into the thick of the enemy.'

By now a situation had developed which the Duke of Fitzjames, commanding the French cavalry, could hardly ignore. The 12th were just

100 yards from his front rank, although, as the Anglo–Hanoverian line was oblique to his own, the Guard Regiment was at more than three times that distance. Spoercken had made no attempt to put his men into squares and, deployed as they were in line, they could simply be ridden over by a determined cavalry charge. Fitzjames had 63 squadrons available, drawn up in three lines, but to use them all against such a comparatively small if extremely impertinent force would create overcrowding and, in modern parlance, amount to overkill. He therefore ordered the Marquis de Castries to attack with eleven squadrons from the first line, drawn from the regiment's Colonel-Generals Cravattes and Mestre de Camp.

Hearing the French trumpets and observing the stir in their ranks, Waldegrave halted his brigade in anticipation. While the horsemen increased their pace, the muskets were brought from the shoulder to the aim at the word of command. As the gap closed the tension became unbearable. Not until the thundering squadrons were ten paces (25–30 feet) distant was the order to fire given. We do not know whether the volleys were regimental, grand division (two companies), company, platoon or ranks in succession, but we do know that each round was aimed. A tremendous blast exploded along the front of the brigade and the French seemed to ride into an invisible wall which brought whole troops crashing to the ground in a screaming, kicking welter of horses and riders. Thomson, watching from behind, recalled that the enemy was given, '. . . such a terrible fire that not *even lions* could have come on, such a number of them fell both horses and men that it made it difficult for those not touched to retire'. Only on the extreme right of the British line were the French able to press home their attack, albeit briefly. 'They rode down two companies on the right of our regiment,' wrote Montgomery, 'wounded three officers, took one of them prisoner with our artillery lieutenant and whipped off the tumbrells [i.e., carts containing ammunition for the battalion guns].' Of those who had broken through, five were bayonetted when the rear rank faced about and the rest made off, having caused rather less damage than might be expected. It was clear, however, that the French cavalry was certainly not prepared to let the matter rest, for even as the survivors of their broken first line streamed away a larger body, drawn from the second line, could be seen forming up in preparation for another charge.

This was the moment for Sackville's cavalry to intervene. Ferdinand had already dispatched a Hessian aide with orders for it to be formed into one line and advance to the left in support of the infantry. Sackville had no idea what was going on because his view of the battlefield was interrupted by the same belt of woodland behind which Spoercken had formed his brigades; nor had he taken steps to find out, although the roar of battle had risen to a point that indicated that a crisis was at hand. Once more, the conversation took place in French and, in fairness to Sackville, the aide merely indicated that the cavalry should advance to the support of the infantry. The brigade moved forward to a point near Hahlen then, finding no infantry in the vicinity, halted again. Now desperate to get the cavalry into action, Ferdinand dispatched one aide after another to Sackville who, believing that he had been sent on a fool's errand, was now at his most obstructive and bloody-minded. When one aide referred simply to the British cavalry, Lord George was truly able to vent his spleen. Did His Serene Highness mean only the British cavalry? Were the Hanoverian regiments not required? Or did His Serene Highness really mean all the cavalry under Lord Sackville's command? The aide had better find out and, while he was about it, verify in which direction the advance was to be made. At length one of the aides, in despair, galloped across to Granby who, understanding what was required at once, began to move off in the direction of Spoercken's embattled troops. Sackville brought him up short with a direct order not to advance another foot, and there the brigade remained for the rest of the battle.

Mercifully, officers like Sackville were extremely rare and Spoercken's troops were about to receive assistance from quite another quarter. Macbean's heavy artillery brigade, part of No. 2 Column, had emerged from the forest track on which it had made part of its approach march and, leaving Sackville's stationary cavalry on its right, was nearing the forward edge of the battle line. Once clear of the intervening belt of trees on the left, Macbean was able to take in the whole situation at a glance. Evidently a man of initiative and strong personality, he made the civilian drivers stir their cart-horses into a lumbering trot and brought his ten 12pdr guns into action wheel to wheel on a low spur, between Drummond's and Foy's brigades. Captain Phillips, in overall command of the British artillery, took control of all three brigades, concentrating their fire against the enemy's guns, some 900 yards distant. Contades had allocated thirty guns to his left wing and of these, as we have seen, eighteen were engaging Spoercken's infantry. This enabled Phillips to focus the attention of his guns and howitzers on each of the enemy sections in turn, systematically battering them into silence until, only ten minutes after Macbean had unlimbered, not a French gun remained in action. Heavily engaged though they were, Spoercken's men would receive no further trouble from that quarter and Phillips, relieved of his primary responsibility, was able to switch his fire to fresh targets among the French infantry and cavalry.

Meanwhile, Fitzjames was bringing up troops to mount a second charge against the defiant scarlet rank in front of him. This time the attack would be made with fourteen squadrons of the Régiments Royal Etranger and Bourgogne, drawn from the second line. It was anticipated that the infantry would still be recovering from the shock of the first attack, but, against that, the charge would be made over ground already encumbered with dead and wounded men and horses; likewise, casualties were already being incurred from the first of Phillips' guns, the roundshot and shells of which were slicing obliquely through the ranks as they formed.

The story of the second charge paralleled that of the first. Once again the French squadrons thundered towards the silent, waiting line of redcoats; once again, the latter delivered a series of shattering aimed volleys at point-blank range; and, once again, men and horses went down in heaps. Here and there sheer impetus carried small groups into deadly hedges of bayonets, where they were despatched. Once again, the broken survivors wheeled away to the rear.

Morale in Spoercken's regiments soared. They now felt that they could handle anything the French threw at them and that they were just getting nicely into their stride, but there remained as much work for them to do as they had already done. Contades was now determined to wipe out the small Anglo–Hanoverian force which had inflicted such humiliation on the chivalry of France. His plan was that the infantry to the right and left of Fitzjames' line would wheel forward on to the enemy's flanks while the cavalry reserve mounted a third charge; assailed on three sides, Spoercken's command would be overwhelmed. The idea was sound enough, but the timing of its execution was faulty. The French infantry on the right were checked when Ferdinand, watching the development of the battle closely, pushed forward several Hanoverian regiments from Schele's No. 4 Column, and those on the left either did not receive or failed to act on their orders until the crisis was passed.

The cavalry reserve, commanded by Lieutenant-General the Marquis de Poyanne, was eighteen squadrons strong and consisted of two regiments, the Gendarmes and the Carabiniers, which were formed up on slightly lower ground than the two preceding lines and were hitherto invisible to the British artillery. Their sudden appearance therefore startled Phillips, but he quickly adjusted the lay of his guns. 'They were going to gallop down sword in hand among our poor mangled regiments,' wrote one of Macbean's lieutenants, 'but we clapt our matches to the ten guns and gave them such a salute as they little expected: for we mowed them down like standing corn.'

The casualties sustained did not deter either regiment, for they were the élite of the French cavalry; the Gendarmes, in fact, were part of the Maison du Roi, the King's Household troops, and in their ranks rode many a scion of France's noblest families. Poyanne, observing that the fallen mounts and riders from previous charges lay thickest opposite the right and centre of Waldegrave's brigade, directed the axis of his own attack against the Hanoverian Guard Regiment on its left. For a moment it seemed as though the scarlet ranks were on the point of renewing their advance, but, knowing they were about to be attacked again, they were simply stepping forward a few paces to move clear of their casualties and close gaps.

Poyanne's 1,500 horsemen came sweeping in like a tidal wave, absolutely confident that they could ride down their opponents, to discover in a sudden blast of flame and smoke that the Hanoverian musketry was just as terrible in its effects as the British. Sweeping round the Guards' left, the right wing of the Gendarmes rode straight for Hardenberg's Regiment, only to be shot out of their saddles before they could come to handstrokes. Nevertheless the charge came dangerously close to success. Some squadrons had managed to smash their way through gaps in the front line and for an instant Waldegrave's brigade seemed lost. This, however, was the moment Kingsley's regiments, the 20th, 51st and 25th, had been awaiting, for until now they had been required only to take punishment without handing out anything in return. A blaze of musket fire brought many troopers crashing to ground and others were dispatched in a short but vicious mêlée in which bayonet crossed sabre. Payonne fell, desperately wounded, and the remnants of his regiments fled. Of the 778 Gendarmes who had made the charge, 153 were killed or captured and more than 200 staggered into their own lines with wounds of varying severity.

During the brief pause that followed the Hanoverian Guards picked up six guidons and Hardenberg's Regiment a further two. The Hanoverians also relieved their former owners of eighty gold watches; very probably, expensive timepieces could also be seen dangling from a number of British waistcoats, too.

Contades, dumbfounded, could only remark: 'I have seen what I never thought to be possible – a single line of infantry break through three lines of cavalry ranked in order of battle and tumble them to ruin'. Altogether, 43 squadrons had been destroyed and their survivors were milling around in a disorganized mob. Fitzjames had only twenty squadrons left, but did not dare commit them. For all practical purposes, the French cavalry had ceased to exist and, with it, the centre of Contades' army.

It seems unfair that anything more should have been asked of Spoercken's incredible infantry, but some of them were actually about to embark on the hardest fight of the day. In response to Contades' earlier order, the Count de Lusace had brought forward the French and Saxon infantry on the left wing and this was now bearing down on their right flank. It was, as Montgomery put it, 'a very ugly situation' although Spoercken was equal to the occasion. While the rest of his troops remained facing Fitzjames' routed cavalry, the 12th and 37th Regiments formed smartly to the right and so presented a front to the enemy's leading rank, which consisted of the Régiments de Conde, Aquitaine and du Roi. The ensuing firefight lasted approximately ten minutes during which, as Montgomery says, 'We killed them a good many, and the rest ran away.' His letter continues, 'The next to appear were the Grenadiers of France,' but here he is almost certainly mistaken as this regiment was already engaged at Todtenhausen. They were certainly grenadiers, but were probably drawn from Saxon regiments which, like the majority of the French infantry, wore white coats, so such a mistake is quite understandable. They were, Montgomery says, 'As fine and terrible-looking fellows as I ever saw. They stood us a tug, notwithstanding we beat them off to a distance, where they galled us much, they having rifled barrels, and our musquets would not reach them. To remedy this we advanced; they took the hint and run away.'

The 12th and 37th were at their last gasp when the rest of the Saxons attacked, but by now Spoercken was satisfied that the French cavalry presented no further threat, and Kingsley's brigade was also ordered to form to the right and come in beside the 12th. 'We had a long but not very brisk engagement,' Montgomery recalled. 'At last we made them retire out of reach, when the three English regiments of the rear line came up and gave them one fire, which sent them off for good and all.'

It was during this phase of the engagement that Thomas Thomson of the 20th, who had already been hit three times by spent balls, was seriously wounded. 'This seared me like a red hot iron. I found myself fainting and quitting the regiment after having called for a fresh officer, but found no one to take my place, several being gone off wounded [or] already dead. I had not got four rods in the rear, but I heard the battalion fire which pleased me so much in my agony, that I stood stupefied looking on them. Many poor soldiers praying, begging me to come off [i.e., leave the field], after a few moments I recovered my senses and found I had no further business there and made the best of my way, which was slow enough, over about a mile of common where the balls came as thick as in front. By this time a soldier of the regiment, slightly wounded in the leg, came up offering me his assistance. While supporting me his left leg was carried away by a cannon ball, the wind of which fairly turned me round, but did not hurt me otherwise. The poor man is since dead. The common was strewed with dead and wounded men and horses. On the leeward side of those horses quite dead lay wounded soldiers that could not get any further, to shelter them[selves] from the small shot. The action came on in such a hurry we did not know where to look for surgeons. Captain —— and self walked three miles in this condition before we could get the blood stopped, [and] at last fortunately met with my Lord George Sackville's coach and a surgeon he had in reserve for himself – which he need not have had as there was no danger of his being hurt, as you will soon find by the *Vox Populi*.'

Elsewhere, Ferdinand's German cavalry had charged and routed Contades' right wing. By 09.30 the battle was over and the French were streaming back towards Minden and their bridges over the Bastau. Phillips, whose guns had been hammering away at the French and Saxon infantry, dispatched Macbean and Foy's brigades in a pursuit during which they unlimbered at regular intervals and treated the fugitives to salvoes of case shot. 'Thousands jumped into the water,' wrote the unknown subaltern of the 12th. 'And many were forced into it by the crowds pressing hard behind, and the roads were all strewed with those who lay expiring of their wounds – a dismal sight!'

Had the British and Hanoverian cavalry charged at this moment the French army would, in all probability, have been destroyed. Sackville, suddenly aware of the situation, blandly presented himself to Ferdinand and asked what exactly was required of him. With astounding restraint, Ferdinand merely replied, 'Milord, the moment has passed.' Later in the day, however, he deprived Sackville of his sash and sword, indicating that he had been relieved of his responsibilities – which were assumed by Granby – and that he was under open arrest.

Contades' losses amounted to 7,000 killed and wounded, 5,000 prisoners, 43 guns and seventeen Colours or guidons captured, but his cup of woes was not quite full, for in an engagement at Cohfeld the Hereditary Prince of Brunswick had simultaneously defeated one of his detachments and severed his communications with Herford. He was forced to abandon Minden, the commandant of which surrendered on 2 August, and retired towards the Rhine by the roundabout route of Kassel. Unable to offer any intelligible reason for his defeat, he was dismissed. 'The thought of Minden makes me blush for the French Army,' wrote the Duc de Choiseul, the French Foreign Minister.

Ferdinand's troops sustained the loss of 2,800 killed and wounded, of which proportionally the greater part fell on Spoercken's six British and three Hanoverian regiments. Their strength at the beginning of the action is given below, followed by their casualties.

12th	593	302 killed, wounded and missing
20th	560	321 killed and wounded
23rd	505	217 killed, wounded and missing
25th	564	154 killed, wounded and missing
37th	506	298 killed, wounded and missing
51st	470	102 killed, wounded and missing
Hanoverian Guard	2 battalions	175 killed, wounded and missing
Hardenberg	1 battalion	83 killed, wounded and missing
Total	1,652	

Those involved reacted to the ordeal in their different ways. Thomson, conscientious, serious and obviously well-liked by his men, had been so badly wounded that he did not expect to return to duty before the end of September, and he concluded his letter: 'I don't care who knows my sentiments when I say my curiosity is satisfied and that I never wish to see a second slaughter of my fellow creatures. . . . I hope the nation is now satisfied as there was plenty of blood for their money.' Montgomery, one senses from his letter to his mother, was younger and more resilient: 'I received from a spent ball such a rap on my collar bone as I have [had] frequently from that once most dreadful weapon, your crooked-headed walking-stick. It just swelled and grew red enough to convince the neighbours that I was not fibbing. I got another of these also on one of my legs, which gave me as much pain as would a tap of Miss Mathews' fan. The last and greatest misfortune of all fell to the share of my poor old coat, for a musquet ball entered into the right skert of it and made three holes. I had almost forgot to tell you that my spontoon [light pike] was shot thro' a little below my hand – this disabled it, but a French one now does duty in its room. . . . The noise of the battle frightened our Sutler's wife into labour. The next morning she was brought to bed of a son, and we have Christened him by the name of Ferdinand.'

For some, there were well-earned rewards. Ferdinand was particularly generous to the senior officers of Royal Artillery, presenting 1,000 crowns to Phillips and 500 crowns each to Macbean, Drummond and Foy. Colonels Fitzroy and Ligonier, who carried the news of the victory to London, each received a grant of £500 and promotion. As Horace Walpole recorded, the population went wild with delight: 'I found the town distracted and at night it was beautiful beyond description. Every house is illuminated, every street has two bonfires, every bonfire has two hundred squibs.' Medals in various materials were struck both in the United Kingdom and in Germany, but they were privately issued for distribution to a limited number of individuals, usually senior officers. For the moment, the red-coated infantry who had done so much to win the battle had to be content with a complimentary order of the day and firing a *feu de joie*. In 1773, however, a medal known as 'The Very Honourable Order of the Old Deserving Soldier' was struck by General Sir Eyre Coote, Colonel of the 37th, and issued to the regiment's Minden veterans. On 1 January 1801, some forty years after the event, the Adjutant-General at the Horse Guards wrote to the commanding officers of the six British infantry regiments advising them that they had been granted permission to add the battle honour Minden to their Colours. The surviving artillery batteries had to wait somewhat longer, until 1926 in fact, before receiving their honour titles.

The Battle of Minden, or Thornhausen as it is sometimes called, left a number of loose ends. Sackville, sent home in disgrace, would have done well to take the advice of his powerful friends, who were prepared to gloss over the matter. Instead, with typical pig-headed perversity, he insisted on a court-martial. He was found guilty of wilful disobedience and sentenced to be cashiered, with the rider that he was unfit to serve His Majesty in any military capacity whatever; at the King's order the sentence was read to every regiment in the Army. Incredible as it may seem, Sackville turned to politics and within twenty years had attained high office. As Lord George Germain, Secretary of State for the Colonies, he was to do his country incalculable damage during the War of American Independence.

Sackville's officers and men bore no responsibility whatever for the failings of their leader, but for a year it was difficult for them to look Spoercken's regiments in the eye. Then, at Warburg on 31 July 1760, Granby led them in a brilliant charge which decided the battle. During this Granby's hat and wig blew off, giving rise to the expression 'going for it bald-headed'. The Marquis is often depicted thus on the numerous inn-signs bearing his name; he personally established many of these inns so that the more seriously injured of his soldiers could earn a living in civilian life.

For the descendants of the six British infantry regiments and two surviving artillery batteries that fought at Minden, 1 August is Minden Day, the most important date in the regimental calendar. With the exception of the Royal Welch Fusiliers, regiments and batteries parade with a rose behind their cap badge to honour the men who, against impossible odds, were largely instrumental in smashing Contades' army. An oft-told story is that the regiments went into action with roses in their hats, picked on the way to the battlefield, although the probabilities seem to be against this. There were indeed wild roses in the hedgerows on Minden Heath, but they would have held no interest for soldiers pulled from their blankets on a storm-lashed night, or during the dank first-light approach march. If roses were picked that day, it would have been as the regiments were crossing gardens on the outskirts of Minden during the final stages of the action, but by then the men, looking around their depleted ranks, were probably thinking that, as Wellington said in a later war, a battle won is as sad as a battle lost. In the late 18th and early 19th centuries it was customary for regiments to celebrate the anniversary of their victories by putting a sprig of laurel in their head-dress and some at least of the Minden regiments are known to have done this. The use of roses probably dates from the mid-Victorian era, although the Hampshire Regiment did not receive official sanction for the practice until 1935. Whatever the truth, the achievements of Minden remain unsurpassed and it is entirely appropriate that they should continue to be so commemorated.

2
VALLEYS OF DEATH
Balaclava, 25 October 1854

One day early in 1853 a dispute concerning certain rights at the Church of the Holy Sepulchre in Bethlehem, notably possession of keys and the placing of a silver star in the sanctuary, erupted into violence between Greek Orthodox and Roman Catholic monks. The Turkish police, being Muslims, were unwilling to intervene in so sensitive an area and stood by, with the result that the brawl ended with the death of several of the Orthodox brethren. Such was the unlikely flashpoint which led to full-scale war between Russia on the one hand and Great Britain, France, Turkey and Sardinia on the other.

The brawl itself was merely the excuse which Tsar Nicholas I used to provoke a conflict with the crumbling Ottoman Empire, the latter now spoken of openly as 'The Sick Man of Europe'. Russia desired open access to the Mediterranean through the Bosporus and Dardanelles, and was quite prepared to set about the virtual dismemberment of Turkey to achieve her aim. Within the Ottoman Empire there were fourteen million Orthodox Christians of whom Nicholas regarded himself the guardian, and in this capacity he demanded of the Sultan a number of concessions, some of which no self-respecting sovereign could possibly grant. In July 1853 Russian troops occupied Turkish provinces in Roumania.

Nevertheless, some accommodation might have been reached had it not been for Napoleon III. Ever since the Crusades, France had been the protector of Roman Catholic interests in the Holy Land, although the role was archaic and some rights had been allowed to lapse, including those now contested by the Orthodox Church. This was a mantle that Napoleon willingly resumed, hoping to acquire some of the prestige which had attached to his more able namesake and uncle, Napoleon I, by obtaining renewed confirmation of French status from the Sultan. The British government had little liking for Napoleon, whom it regarded as a devious parvenu, but as its traditional policy had been to support Turkey as a means of reducing the Russian threat to British interests in the Far East, it found itself in reluctant agreement with him; furthermore, it had no intention of seeing the naval balance in the Mediterranean disturbed by the intrusion of a Russian fleet. The dispatch of British and French warships to Constantinople encouraged the Sultan to resist the Tsar's demands and on 4 November 1853 Turkey declared war on Russia.

On land, the Turks did unexpectedly well, but on 30 November the Russian fleet destroyed a Turkish squadron in Sinope harbour. In January 1854 the Anglo–French fleet entered the Black Sea to protect the Turkish coastline and on 28 March the Allies declared war on Russia. Suddenly, the Tsar's military adventure began to turn sour, for in April Austria, supported by Prussia, threatened to intervene unless he withdrew his troops from the Balkans. Despite the humiliation, he complied, although general peace talks foundered when he insisted upon his right to pursue his quarrel with Turkey.

This left the Allies with the problem of finding an objective for the 50,000-strong expeditionary force they had assembled. It was decided, without due consideration of the difficulties involved, that the great Russian naval base of Sevastopol, on the south coast of the Crimea, would be destroyed. On 13 September the troops made an unopposed landing at the inauspiciously named Calamita Bay then, having consolidated their position, began to march south towards Sevastopol, their flank covered by the guns of the fleet. At the River Alma a Russian army of 36,000 men, commanded by Prince Alexander Menshikov, opposed further progress but was driven from its positions after heavy fighting on 20 September and retired into Sevastopol.

It was now apparent that the port would have to be captured by a siege. It was equally apparent that, with winter approaching, the army could not be supplied over the open beaches of Calamita Bay. But there were several small harbours to the south of Sevastopol and it was decided to march round the fortress and secure these. The movement itself was made through difficult wooded country but was completed without serious incident. At one point the troops crossed the tracks of Menshikov's army which, leaving Sevastopol with a strong garrison, had marched out to join forces with the Russian reinforcements who were entering the Crimea.

Arriving south of the city, the British secured Balaclava after a token resistance while the French marched on to capture Kamiesch and Kazatch, farther to the west. The French had much the better of the arrangement, for while their harbours were shallower they were wide enough to permit vessels to manoeuvre, whereas Balaclava was a long, narrow inlet in which ships had to moor stern-on to the wharves on either side, leaving a narrow central channel between. Furthermore, the harbour was hemmed in by steep cliffs through which a gorge gave access to the uplands beyond by means of a single muddy track. This meant that the cramped quays were quickly piled high with stores and equipment that could not be moved efficiently because no one knew where anything was, and the track was always clogged with transport and carrying parties searching for their loads or attempting to find their way out of the chaos into which Balaclava degenerated after a mere fortnight. As if this were not enough, seven miles of bad road separated the harbour form the British siege lines.

Perhaps this would have mattered less if the joint Allied commanders, Lord Raglan for the British and General François Canrobert for the French, had not resisted demands for an immediate assault on Sevastopol, conceding that while it might succeed it would probably cost 500 killed; in the end, this figure was but a fraction of the numbers who would die before Sevastopol. The opportunity quickly passed; by the end of the month the Russians had begun to pour reinforcements into the city through its northern suburbs, which were not under attack, while their chief military engineer, Colonel Franz Todleben, performed prodigies in turning the incomplete southern defences into a series of formidable works. Nevertheless, the Allies remained confident and when their siege batteries opened fire on 17 October it was anticipated that Sevastopol would be reduced to ruins within 48 hours. Three hours after the first shot the Russian counter-bombardment exploded one of Canrobert's ammunition dumps with the result that the French guns were out of action for the next two days. The British batteries, sited beyond effective range and engaging too many targets, continued to fire until, inevitably, they ran out of ammunition. Such damage as they inflicted was made good each night by Todleben's repair parties.

If the performance of the Allied commanders had been uninspiring, so too was that of Menshikov. In addition to the reinforcements which he had sent into Sevastopol, he had acquired a field army of considerable strength which posed a constant menace to the besiegers' open flank. It must have been apparent to him that every musket ball and every mouthful of rations had to traverse the long muddy trail between Balaclava and the British siege lines, and his spies must have informed him of the chaotic conditions within Balaclava itself. He had only to insert a force into the seven-mile gap to achieve a victory either by severing the British line of communication completely, or by compelling the diversion of so large a force from the siege lines for its protection that the siege could not be prosecuted effectively. And, in the fourth week of October, that is what he decided to do, albeit somewhat late in the day.

To understand the battle which followed, it is necessary to consider some aspects of the British Army at that period. It is true that it had not fought a European enemy for forty years, but for all that it was not an inexperienced army, many regiments and individual officers having seen active service alongside the Honourable East India Company's troops in India, most recently in the Sikh Wars of the 1840s, the battles of which had been notable for their sheer ferocity. It was also true that regimental officers still purchased their commissions and promotions, an indefensible practice which would continue until 1871, but the remarkable thing about the system was not that it occasionally placed dangerous fools in positions of power, but that the vast majority of officers were capable professionals; whatever criticisms have been levelled at the British conduct of the campaign, none has ever been directed at the efficiency of the regiments themselves.

The Army's real deficiencies, unfortunately, existed in the critical areas of command, staff and supply. Lord Raglan, its commander in the Crimea, had served on the staff of the Duke of Wellington during the Peninsular War and at Waterloo, losing his right arm during the closing moments of the latter. Until Wellington's death in 1852 he had served as his Military Secretary, then occupied the post of Master General of the Ordnance. His talents were those of the administrator and diplomat, but the Horse Guards, forgetting that he had never commanded troops, let alone on active service, appointed him to the Crimean command because of his long-past experience of war at the higher level, and because of his subsequent association with Wellington. Aged 67, he had become a kindly old gentleman whose natural instinct was to avoid offending others at all costs, and this was simply not compatible with the disciplinary bite essential to a commander-in-chief if he was to keep strong-willed subordinates under control.

Likewise, the Horse Guards had been at pains to demonstrate to the nation that its troops would be going into action under experienced generals, even if the latter might be considered too elderly for active campaigning. Of the commanders of the five infantry divisions, four were in their sixties; the fifth was the Duke of Cambridge, a mere stripling of 35 who, as Queen Victoria's cousin, had received obvious preferment, but who performed well. The Chief Engineer was 72 and some brigadiers had more than forty years' service behind them. Age, of course, is by no means synonymous with incompetence, but the overall effect was that the Army's thinking and reactions were slow.

In the Cavalry Division, which was to play the decisive role in the forthcoming action, two of the three senior officers might have been chosen for the specific purpose of demonstrating the evils of commission by purchase, privilege and influence. The divisional commander was Major-General the Earl of Lucan, who was none too bright and was possessed of a violent temper. At the age of 26 he had purchased the lieutenant-colonelcy of the 17th Lancers for £25,000, exercising command with the zeal of a martinet. He had, however, seen active service, taking part in the Russo–Turkish War of 1828–9 on the staff of Prince Woronzow, where he had demonstrated his courage to such good effect that he was awarded a Russian decoration. More recent years had been marked by wholesale evictions from his estates in County Mayo, coupled with heartless indifference to the fate of those suffering from the repeated failure of the potato crop, with the result that he was cordially hated by his tenants. After the Battle of the Alma he had been nicknamed Lord

Look-on because he had failed to pursue the retreating Russians, although in all fairness he was operating under restrictions imposed by Raglan.

It was the division's misfortune that the officer selected to command its Light Brigade was Brigadier-General the Earl of Cardigan, an overbearing, hot-tempered fool of the most dangerous kind in that he believed that he possessed real ability. His income was not less than £40,000 per annum, an immense sum at that time, and this, together with his position in society gave him, he believed, the right to do as he pleased regardless of the consequences. In 1832 he had purchased the lieutenant-colonelcy of the 15th Hussars for a figure believed to exceed £35,000 but in 1834 he was dismissed for incompetence. Despite this, his influence at Court enabled him to buy the lieutenant-colonelcy of the 11th Hussars for £40,000 in 1836, shortly before the regiment was due to return from India.

Life for a cavalry officer in a home garrison was expensive at the best of times, involving not only heavy outlay for the splendid uniforms of the day, but also maintaining a lifestyle appropriate to the society of the county in which he was stationed. Service in India made fewer financial demands and was therefore popular with officers of limited means. When a regiment returned home it was usual for some of its officers to transfer to an incoming regiment, but many of the remainder, finding their circumstances reduced in England, left the service, which was thus deprived of their valuable experience. From the outset, Cardigan made it clear that he did not like 'Indians', as he called them. It was not a question of professional jealousy, for it would never have entered his head that they might know more about the business than he did. It was neither more nor less than simply snobbery. Such officers, in his opinion, lowered the social tone of the Eleventh, therefore they must go; their place would be filled with fashionable young men quite at their ease in the highest society.

The 'Indian' officers were hounded without mercy. Within the limitations imposed by discipline, they fought back as best they could against a commanding officer who was determined to elevate trivial incidents into matters for complaint to the Horse Guards. There were serious injustices and courts-martial too numerous to mention, all of which were fully reported in the press, as was the Earl's womanizing and a fudged trial in the House of Lords for duelling. For a while Cardigan was the most unpopular man in England, regularly hissed and booed whenever he attended a theatre or concert. Nevertheless, he remained in command of the Eleventh whose mess, in due course, became noted for its exquisite cuisine, French servants and the affected manners of its subalterns.

It was hardly surprising, given their similar temperaments, that Lucan and Cardigan should dislike each other, a situation aggravated by the fact that they were brothers-in-law, Lucan having married Cardigan's youngest sister from whom he had recently separated. Cardigan tended to regard the Light Brigade as an independent command and was strongly averse to taking orders from Lucan who, determined to exert his authority, interfered in the internal workings of the brigade. As a result, the two bickered vociferously and in public over minor details best left in the care of NCOs, thereby attracting the contempt of their peers. An army commander only slightly stronger than Raglan would have sent Cardigan packing at once, but Raglan sought only to preserve harmonious relations between his commanders. Perhaps believing that the two should be kept apart as much as possible, he permitted Cardigan to sleep aboard his private yacht *Dryad*, which was occupying a much-needed berth in Balaclava harbour. This created the absurd situation whereby a brigadier was living in luxury while his divisional commander roughed it with the rest in a tent and, naturally, Lucan resented it.

Fortunately, the Cavalry Division's second major formation, the Heavy Brigade, was commanded by a refreshingly normal officer, Brigadier-General the Hon. James Scarlett who, like Lucan and Cardigan, was in his middle fifties. Scarlett had commanded the 5th Dragoon Guards and had been on the point of retiring from the Army when he was appointed to command the brigade. He was universally liked and respected and was modest enough to recognize that, as he had no experience of active service, he needed the advice of those who had, which meant officers who had served in India. He therefore obtained the services of two thoroughly experienced men whose recommendations he relied upon. The first was a Colonel Beatson, who lacked official status because his appointment had been opposed by Raglan, Lucan and Cardigan, but came along anyway. The second was Lieutenant Alexander Elliot, formerly of the 8th Bengal Cavalry, who had left India for health reasons and was now starting to rebuild his career from the bottom.

Undoubtedly, some of the damage caused by the Army's command problems could have been limited by an efficient staff, had there been one. Facilities for training staff officers existed at what was then known as the Senior Department of the Royal Military College, Sandhurst, but incentives were few and only a handful of men were prepared to leave the mainstream of regimental life for a period of academic study. Consequently, only fifteen of the 221 staff officers in Raglan's army were qualified to perform their duties; the remainder learned their jobs as they went along. At this period, when army commanders usually had the entire battlefield in view, the operations branch of the staff functioned on very simple lines. The general's orders would be scribbled down by his Chief of Staff who would then hand them to an aide-de-camp for delivery to the subordinate commanders named, together with supplementary verbal instructions where appropriate. On arrival the ADC spoke with the full authority of the army commander. In general, verbal orders allowed the subordinate commander some latitude for interpretation, but written orders were mandatory and had to be obeyed immediately and to the letter. For the system to work it will be appreciated that written orders had to be precise and that the ADC should not only have a definite understanding of the army commander's intentions but also be capable of expressing these with absolute clarity. By and large, the system produced the desired results. Unfortunately, it was not foolproof since any mistake in the drafting of orders or in their delivery could result in serious consequences. Given the command difficulties already present in the Cavalry Division, it can be seen that a potential for disaster existed long before the first shot had been fired.

Meanwhile, most minds were concentrated on the supply problem. In addition to the physical difficulties already described, both the Army and the Royal Navy were burdened with a cumbrous system based on the accountability principle, generating a vast paperwork of requisitions, dockets, ledgers, sanctions and signatures, followed by physical checks if the goods could actually be located on the jumbled Balaclava quays. The commissary staff work long, hard and willingly, but the task was beyond them. A commander less considerate than Raglan, or perhaps less steeped in Whitehall bureaucracy, might have torn the tangle apart and imposed something more appropriate to an army at war, but it was not to be.

Raglan, had, however, recognized the potential threat to his lines of communication and the steps he had taken to cover the seven-mile gap between Balaclava and the siege lines were to dictate the course of the battle. From Balaclava the supply road climbed through its gorge to Kadikoi village before swinging away to cross the Sapoune Heights to the north-west. At Kadikoi Raglan stationed the 93rd Highlanders (later known as the 2nd Argyll and Sutherland Highlanders) and one battery of field artillery, under the command of Major-General Sir Colin Campbell, while on the hills above Balaclava and to the east of the track was a further battery of guns manned by Royal Marines. To the north-east of Kadikoi was a plain which extended as far as the Fedioukine Hills, subdivided into the North and South Valleys by a shallow ridge named Causeway Heights because along its summit ran the Woronzoff Road, connecting Sevastopol with the estates of Count Woronzoff to the east. A series of six weak redoubts had been hastily thrown up along the length of the Heights, No. 1 being on a detached feature known as Canrobert's Hill at the eastern end of the ridge, the remainder being sited approximately half-a-mile apart along the crest. No. 1 contained three naval 9pdr guns and was held by a battalion; Nos. 2, 3 and 4 contained two naval 9pdrs each and were held by half a battalion; Nos. 5 and 6 were unarmed and unoccupied. The garrisons were Turkish troops drawn from Tunisia, supplemented by one British artillery NCO in each of the manned redoubts. Finally, at the western end of Causeway Heights were the camps of the Cavalry Division, the patrols of which were in daily contact with the Russians at the River Tchernaya beyond the North and South Valleys.

These provisions were not designed to impose anything more than a check on a Russian advance, buying time in which reinforcements could be brought up from the siege lines. Campbell's little force was regarded as a line of last resort which, it was hoped, would not be needed. Such an appreciation was, at best, optimistic, but Raglan made a further serious error in not designating a sector commander for so sensitive an area; the effect was that while Lucan and Campbell had each other's troops in view, neither had authority over the other.

On 24 October the commander of the Turkish contingent, Rustum Pasha, was informed by one of his spies that the following day the Russians would attack Balaclava with 25,000 men under the command of the recently arrived General Liprandi. The report was remarkably accurate, for in the event 22,000 infantry, 3,400 cavalry and 78 guns were deployed. Rustum warned Lucan and Campbell, who sent a messenger to Raglan's headquarters. As there had already been several false alarms, Raglan merely asked to be kept informed.

The threat was treated seriously in the Cavalry Division. It was Lucan's custom to stand-to an hour before dawn and at first light on the 25th he trotted into the South Valley with his staff to inspect the pickets; with him was Lord George Paget, in temporary command of the Light Brigade while Cardigan still slumbered aboard *Dryad*. As the sky lightened two flags could be seen flying above No. 1 Redoubt on Canrobert's Hill. Only one staff officer recalled that this signalled a general advance by the enemy, but the debate was resolved when the redoubt's guns opened fire seconds later. Simultaneously, a picket came galloping back down the valley to report that three Russian divisions had crossed the Tchernaya; one was scaling the Fedioukine Heights, the second was advancing on Causeway Heights and the third was already attacking Canrobert's Hill. Liprandi, in fact, knew every detail of the British defences and was aware that it would take three hours for reinforcements to reach the scene from the siege lines; in that time he believed that his troops would simply roll over the small force in their path and secure Balaclava, thereby reducing the siege operations to impotence and placing the entire expeditionary force within a virtual trap. For both sides, therefore, the outcome of the battle would be critical.

Once the alarm had been raised Allied troops began to converge on the Balaclava plain. Canrobert dispatched General Pierre Bosquet with two infantry brigades and two regiments of Chasseurs d'Afrique which, because they had less distance to travel, would reach the Sapoune Heights first. Raglan ordered his 1st and 4th Divisions, commanded respectively by the Duke of Cambridge and Major-General Sir George Cathcart, to march from their camps down into the plain. The Duke complied at once, although it took him thirty minutes to set his men in motion. Cathcart, however, was in a cantankerous mood and bluntly informed the aide who had brought the order that it was impossible for his division to move as most of the men had just returned from the trenches; the aide, he suggested, should either join him in some breakfast or return to Lord Raglan and tell him what he had said. It takes courage for a captain to argue with a divisional commander in this mood but the aide stuck to his guns. He had, he said, delivered an order to the 4th Division and he was not leaving until it was carried out. Cathcart knew the rules and reluctantly complied; even so, by the time the division began to march over an hour had elapsed since receipt of the order.

Meanwhile, the fight for the redoubts continued. On Canrobert's Hill the 500 Turks holding Redoubt No. 1 were engaged by no less than thirty guns and assaulted by five infantry battalions with six more in support, but it was not until 07.30 that they were driven out, leaving 170 dead in the defences. This was no mean achievement and cost the Russians priceless time plus an unknown number of casualties. The central Russian division had now reached the eastern end of Causeway Heights and its artillery was shelling Redoubt No. 2, which was quickly abandoned, many of its garrison being cut down by Cossacks as they fled. Lucan and Campbell had sent up their artillery batteries on to Causeway Heights to support Redoubt No. 3, but, outranged by the Russian guns, they began to sustain serious loss and were withdrawn. The Turks, believing themselves deserted, took to their heels, followed by the garrison of Redoubt No. 4, leaving the British NCOs barely time to spike the guns. A few were rallied and fell in on the flanks of the 93rd at Kadikoi, but most paused to loot the camps of the Cavalry Division, which had been struck, and then headed for Balaclava, where their yells of alarm and despondency were rewarded with a series of hearty smacks around the head with a broomstick, delivered by the robust wife of a Scottish soldier.

It was now some time after 08.00. The first French troops had already reached the edge of the Sapoune Heights and were emplacing their guns. Raglan and his staff had arrived, too, as had William Howard Russell, the correspondent for *The Times*. From their vantage point 500 feet above the plain every detail of the unfolding battle was clear. The Turks could be seen running from their redoubts and Russian infantry and artillery had begun to occupy the eastern half of Causeway Heights. Entering the North Valley from the far end were six formations of cavalry, the reflected light glittering from sabres and lance points, followed by some twenty guns, with the main mass of the Russian infantry bringing up the rear. To the right Lucan's Cavalry Division was drawn up to the east of its camp in the South Valley, ready to fall on the flank of any attack directed against Balaclava; farther still to the right was the red splash of Campbell's 93rd, covering the approaches to the port on a knoll near Kadikoi. Raglan, misunderstanding Lucan's intentions, felt that his division was too isolated and dispatched what became known as his First Order to the Cavalry Division. It was written by Brigadier-General Richard Airey, his Quartermaster-General and, like all of Airey's orders during the battle, was dashed off at tremendous speed, incorporated the gist of the army commander's wishes, but was far from specific. It read: 'Cavalry to take ground to left of second line of redoubts occupied by Turks.'

Lucan was annoyed and understandably puzzled. There was only one line of redoubts and the Turks had gone – what did Lord Raglan mean? The aide, a Captain Wetherall, explained that the division should be withdrawn to the western end of the Causeway Heights ridge where it could be covered by the fire of the French guns on the Sapoune escarpment. Angrily, Lucan complied, believing a withdrawal would provoke further sneers of 'Lord Look-on'. The regiments pulled back in good order, watching with impotent fury as the Cossack skirmishers looted the abandoned camp, killing the sick and spare horses in their picket lines. As they reached their new position a brief lull descended on the battlefield and the men were allowed to eat such food as they had with them. Lord Cardigan, clean, well rested and fed, arrived from his yacht to take command of the Light Brigade, wearing his splendid 11th Hussars uniform.

The Russian cavalry in the North Valley was now within range of the French guns and began wheeling left slowly to climb Causeway Heights. It immediately became clear to Raglan that Balaclava was the Russians' objective and that their cavalry would probably be used to screen the right flank of an infantry advance southward from Causeway Heights towards the port. In such circumstances he realized that he had been wrong to interfere with Lucan's original dispositions and issued his Second Order: 'Eight squadrons of Heavy Dragoons to be detached towards Balaclava to support the Turks, who are wavering.' The first part of the order was clear enough, although the second is odd as it was the 93rd Highlanders who were covering the approach to Balaclava and they were certainly not wavering. It would, however, take some thirty minutes for an aide to descend the escarpment and Lucan to execute the order, and in that time much was to happen.

Suddenly four squadrons detached themselves from the main body of the Russian cavalry and trotted over the crest of Causeway Heights. Their task was probably nothing more than to probe across the South Valley and test the strength of Balaclava's defences. At first it must have seemed as though they could ride straight in, for the valley looked deserted and the only signs of activity were Campbell's field guns standing in apparent isolation near Kadekoi. In fact, Campbell and his

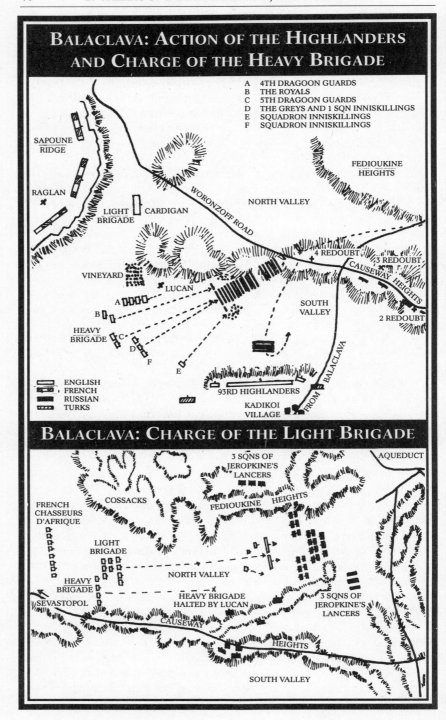

BALACLAVA: ACTION OF THE HIGHLANDERS AND CHARGE OF THE HEAVY BRIGADE

A   4TH DRAGOON GUARDS
B   THE ROYALS
C   5TH DRAGOON GUARDS
D   THE GREYS AND 1 SQN INNISKILLINGS
E   SQUADRON INNISKILLINGS
F   SQUADRON INNISKILLINGS

SAPOUNE RIDGE

FEDIOUKINE HEIGHTS

RAGLAN

LIGHT BRIGADE   CARDIGAN

WORONZOFF ROAD

NORTH VALLEY

4 REDOUBT

3 REDOUBT

CAUSEWAY HEIGHTS

VINEYARD

LUCAN

SOUTH VALLEY

2 REDOUBT

A

HEAVY BRIGADE

B

C

D

F

E

FROM BALACLAVA

ENGLISH
FRENCH
RUSSIAN
TURKS

93RD HIGHLANDERS

KADIKOI VILLAGE

BALACLAVA: CHARGE OF THE LIGHT BRIGADE

3 SQNS OF JEROPKINE'S LANCERS

AQUEDUCT

COSSACKS

FRENCH CHASSEURS D'AFRIQUE

FEDIOUKINE HEIGHTS

LIGHT BRIGADE

NORTH VALLEY

HEAVY BRIGADE

SEVASTOPOL

HEAVY BRIGADE HALTED BY LUCAN

3 SQNS OF JEROPKINE'S LANCERS

CAUSEWAY

HEIGHTS

SOUTH VALLEY

men were still there. Aged 61, Campbell had seen more fighting than any other senior officer in the Army. Like many of his generation, he was packed off into the Army very young and as a 16-year-old Ensign he had been visibly frightened during his baptism of fire at Vimiera. The company commander brought him out and walked him up and down the ranks, talking. Gradually he brought his fear under control, where it had remained ever since. Now, after 46 years' service, he was known as a fierce, fire-eating commander who could exact the last ounce of effort from his Highland regiments, of whom he was extremely proud.

With him he had 400 men of the 93rd, 100 invalids (men recovering from wounds or sickness) who had been hurried up from Balaclava by officers with a greater sense of urgency than Cathcart, and an unknown number of Turks. His little force on the knoll above Kadekoi had already been subjected to the fire of the Russian guns on Causeway Heights and to avoid needless casualties he had ordered the men to lie down on the reverse slope. When the enemy cavalry was within 900 yards they were called forward to the crest and dressed their ranks. Details of the enemy's uniforms became clear, hussars in light-blue and dragoons in grey, approximately 500 of them coming on at a canter that seemed capable of rolling over the negligible obstacle in their path.

Campbell had a poor opinion of Russian cavalry and did not form square; later, he commented that they did not even merit forming fours. Instead, he chose to receive the attack in the usual two-deep firing line, combining firepower with length. Nevertheless, there was no point in minimizing the gravity of the situation. 'Remember, men,' he shouted as he rode along the ranks, 'there is no retreat from here – you must die where you stand!' 'Ay, ay, Sir Colin – we'll do just that!' was the response, amid laughter and ironic cheers. If there was an element of familiarity in the dour humour, it was because an easy, almost family relationship existed between the regiment and Campbell, who still wore a Highlander's feathered bonnet in preference to his general officer's cocked hat.

Those on Sapoune Heights watched the impending clash in total silence. Russell saw the Russian cavalry pause briefly then launch itself across the valley in a headlong charge against '. . . that thin red streak tipped with a line of steel'. At 800 yards there was an ineffective splutter of musketry on the British flanks as the Turks, still shaken by their earlier ordeal, fired a ragged volley then fled towards the harbour. The 93rd remained impassive but brought its muskets to the present. At 600 yards it fired its first rolling volley. It was delivered at extreme range and had little apparent effect, but it gave the men time to reload. While they were doing so the fire of Campbell's field battery and the Royal Marine guns on the hills behind began thudding into the Russian mass. Closing the gaps in their ranks, the enemy came on, their pace undiminished. At 350 yards the 93rd fired its second volley and was astonished by the result.

Some horses and riders went down but the remainder, instead of pressing their attack, reined in and began wheeling to their left.

The inherited instinct of the clan charge, delivered with berserk fury, remains a factor which has always made it difficult, and more often than not impossible, to stop a really determined attack by Scottish infantry and, just at that moment, the Highlanders were more than willing to come to grips. Against expectations they had halted the enemy's attack and now, while he was still milling in confusion, an all but uncontrollable impulse demanded that they should go in and finish him off. The wild eyes, angry muttering and forward movement of individuals were all signs that Campbell recognized. Knowing that if he did not stop them at once they would be gone beyond his control, he summoned all the power in his lungs: 'Ninety-third! Ninety-third! Damn all that eagerness!' The check was sufficient to prevent a breakaway and the mood subsided. It was as well that it did, for the fight was not quite over. The Russian cavalry was moving again and its intention was apparently to ride round the 93rd's right flank. At Campbell's order, the regiment's grenadier company doubled out in their direction, halted and fired a further volley which emptied several more saddles. The Russians turned and galloped back across the valley, disappearing over Causeway Heights; behind they left a few wounded and perhaps a dozen killed. This was not a reflection on the 93rd's marksmanship, for it was later learned from Russian sources that the second and last volleys had caused considerable damage. This was not apparent because even a mortally wounded cavalryman would use all his remaining strength to stay mounted until his horse had carried him out of danger.

Although on a small scale, the affair was significant. The information which the commander of the Russian force was able to pass on to General Liprandi clearly suggested that the approaches to Balaclava were more strongly defended than had been thought. He might have claimed that his troops had ridden into an ambush and, indeed, the sudden appearance of the Highlanders rising from the earth could easily have suggested one. It would have seemed unlikely to him that such a small force of infantry could have remained so steady unless they were supported by a much larger force lying concealed somewhere in the South Valley. All of this may well have given Liprandi food for thought, but for the moment a far more serious development demanded his attention.

The factor which influenced almost every aspect of the Battle of Balaclava was the rolling, broken terrain, which seriously restricted the vision of those on the plain itself. Thus, having passed on Raglan's order that most of the Heavy Brigade should proceed to Kadekoi, it was natural that Lucan should seek a vantage point for himself on the higher ground of Causeway Heights. Before doing so, he was determined to pin down the ungovernable Cardigan with specific orders. 'I'm going to leave you,' he said. 'You'll remember you are placed here by Lord Raglan himself for the defence of this position. My instructions to you are to attack anything and everything that shall come within reach of you, but you will be careful of columns or squares of infantry.'

As Scarlett began to move off, Lucan and his staff rode up on to the ridge, unaware that the North Valley was teeming with enemy cavalry. They arrived in time to see the four detached squadrons cross the crest and commence their attack on Campbell's position. To their left the Russians' main body had started to climb the ridge at a walk, taking a line that would bring them directly on to the flank of the Heavy Brigade. Wheeling round, Lucan galloped down the slope towards Scarlett but by the time he arrived the crest was bristling with lance points and Scarlett, already aware of the danger, had ordered his squadrons to 'Left wheel into line!'

The brigade had been moving towards Kadekoi in two loose columns, with the result that when these turned to face the Russians they were widely extended in squadron groups. On the extreme right was the 1st Squadron of the Inniskilling Dragoon Guards; with Scarlett in the centre were the Inniskillings' 2nd Squadron and one squadron each of the Royal Scots Greys and 5th Dragoon Guards; a little to their left and rear were the second squadrons of the Greys and the 5th; on the left flank were both squadrons of the 4th Dragoon Guards; and, beyond them, the two squadrons of the Royal Dragoons, which had not been detailed to move to Kadekoi.

Surveying the position as the Russians continued to pour over the crest, Scarlett decided that the centre of the brigade would take ground to the right and so avoid having to fight in the abandoned camp or a nearby vineyard, where tents, picket lines, posts and holes would hinder the horses. The Russian commander, General Ryjoff, thought likewise and, halting, took ground to his left until the centres of the two formations were opposite each other. Still not satisfied, Scarlett ordered the five squadrons with him to attend to their dressing with the object of producing as compact a mass as possible when he attacked.

Before this could be completed, trumpets sounded in the enemy ranks and the Russian mass, a block of 3,500 men with a three-squadron frontage, began to move down the slope with a drumming of hooves that shook the ground. Then, unexpectedly, the trumpets sounded again and the mass slowly came to a halt at a dry ditch running across the hillside, its outer wings somewhat forward and presenting a concave front. Just what was in Ryjoff's mind at that moment remains a mystery, for the ditch was no obstacle and the small knot of British squadrons, still dressing ranks with the officers' backs turned in a provocative display of sang-froid, was less than 400 yards distant and apparently on the point of being ridden into the ground. His front ranks opened a popping fire with their carbines and this suggests that, for the moment at least, he was not contemplating any further aggressive movement.

At last Scarlett was able to grunt approval at the lines and placed himself several horse-lengths ahead of them with his aide, Alexander Elliot, his Trumpet-Major, Thomas Monks, and his giant orderly, Sergeant James Shegog. Turning to Monks, Scarlett told him to sound the Charge and the squadrons began to move forward, gathering pace slowly against the incline. Big men on big horses, whose principal role was shock action, they had spent all their years in the service training for this very moment. Many times they had simulated mock charges at reviews and field days, but now the enemy was real and personal, clad in unfamiliar uniform, alien-faced and hard-eyed. Once the charge was in motion there could be no turning out of the moving ranks, and the only alternative was to kill or be killed. Participants later spoke of being impelled forward by a wild, demonic fury which made them more than a match for ordinary men, and of a complete indifference to life; their repeated use of the words sublime and glorious indicates complete possession by the joy of battle.

Elliot had wanted to wear a peaked forage cap, which the regulations permitted, but Scarlett insisted that as a member of his staff he must wear a cocked hat. However, with a contrariness not unknown in even the best-liked senior officers, Scarlett himself wore a dragoon's helmet. Naturally, the Russians took Elliot to be the brigade commander and an officer, ignoring Scarlett, rode straight at him. Elliot avoided his thrust and ran him through to the hilt, dragging the man out of his saddle as he smashed into the enemy ranks just behind Scarlett. Short-sighted and no hand at all with a sword, Scarlett nevertheless laid about him. Immediately behind came Sergeant Shegog, famous for his strength and skill with the sword, who undoubtedly saved his general's life many times, taking strokes intended for him on his own blade and dealing tremendous, skull-cleaving blows in return.

Seconds later the brigade's three leading squadrons crashed into the Russian ranks, the English with a cheer, the Irish with a wild yell and the Scots with a snarl. They had been able to work up very little speed on the slope so that the impact took place at about eight miles an hour, or little more than twice walking pace. Nevertheless, the Russians made the cardinal mistake of meeting the attack almost halted and their leading ranks were broken open. With the arrival of Scarlett's two second-line squadrons, the Russian formation was penetrated to a depth of five files. In the ensuing mêlée the combatants were packed so tightly that even those killed were held firmly in place. It was quickly discovered that the Russian greatcoats were so thick that sabre cuts made no impression and only a few individuals like Elliot were armed with non-regulation weapons which could be used for thrusting. Because of this, attention was concentrated against the enemy's heads using Cuts One and Two, for which additional power could be gained by standing in the stirrups. But not even these could penetrate the tough leather shakos worn by some Russian units and in such cases resort was made to the horizontal Cuts Five and Six, delivered across the face from, respectively, the forehand and backhand. In some cases the enemy were so close that they were dragged out of the saddle by the throat, to be trampled under the stamping hooves. Most vulnerable in this respect were the brown-clad Russian lancers, who were unable either to use their long weapons or defend themselves effectively in the press. However, while the British were the more expert, and certainly the more aggressive swordsmen, the Russians were fighting back hard. Scarlett's helmet was battered in and he received five minor wounds. Elliot was cut on the forehead, across the face and behind the ear, and a final slash cut through his cocked hat. Fortunately, his life was saved by a silk handkerchief he had folded double inside and, while he lost consciousness for a while, he remained locked in the saddle until he came to. Many British lives were, in fact, saved by the bluntness of the Russian sabres.

Far above, the watchers on the Sapoune escarpment could see every detail of the mêlée. Beneath the whirling sword blades, small scarlet groups with burnished helmets or the black bearskins of the Greys were slowly but surely fighting their way forward into the blue, grey and brown mass. The outer wings of the Russian phalanx began to wheel round on to their rear and, for a moment, it looked as though they would be cut off and destroyed. Then the situation changed with dramatic speed. Scarlett had already dispatched his brigade major, Captain Connolly, to bring up the Inniskilling squadron which had been leading the move to Kadekoi. This entered the fray over good going and crashed into the Russians' inward-wheeling left wing at speed, taking it on the vulnerable bridle hand. Horses and riders were bundled sideways and ridden down as the dragoons came to hand-strokes.

On the opposite flank Lucan had sent an aide to order the 4th Dragoon Guards to attack while he galloped on to bring up the Royals, who were, in fact, already heading for the action on their own initiative. The attack of the former was decisive, driving into the enemy's right flank and cutting across the Russian files from right to left. Seconds later the Royals, forming line from column at the gallop, ploughed into the rear of the Russian right wing as it wheeled inwards.

The effect of these repeated hammer blows can be compared to the series of small explosions used to bring down a quarry face or large building. The internal stresses set up within the Russian mass shook it to pieces as it was heaved about and ripped apart from within. Beginning at the left rear, it began shredding away then suddenly turned and bolted up the South Valley, finally recrossing Causeway Heights to obtain the shelter of its own guns. The dragoons carried out a short pursuit before the trumpets sounded Rally. With shouts of 'Fall in, fall in!' the officers raised their swords and the intermingled troopers quickly converged on them to re-form their regiments.

It had taken the Heavy Brigade just five minutes to defeat a force several times its own number, and in the process it had incurred only 78 casualties, of whom most were wounded. Known Russian losses amounted to approximately 200, the great majority being wounded. Raglan sent a personal note of congratulation to Scarlett and the French were loud in their praise of the brigade's remarkable achievement. Over at Kadekoi the 93rd Highlanders, still standing to, had a very personal interest in the outcome of the mêlée; when it was over Campbell, inclined to be clannish, trotted over and singled out the Greys for his praise, causing some annoyance among the more numerous lesser mortals who had also taken part in the charge.

There was, however, one rather more important matter which gave rise to bitter recrimination. Throughout the action the Light Brigade had remained inactive a mere 500 yards away, despite the fact that Cardigan and some of his regiments had a clear view of the fighting. Riding up and down in front of the brigade in a state of suppressed excitement, Cardigan burst out: 'Damn those Heavies! They have the laugh of us this day!' But as the minutes passed, he did nothing. Impatience in the ranks grew and Captain William Morris, an 'Indian' officer with wide experience in the Sikh Wars, now commanding the 17th Lancers, was on the point of committing his regiment when he was brought up sharp by Cardigan. A heated argument ensued in which Morris repeatedly urged the brigade commander to pursue the beaten Russians, or at least allow him to do so with the 17th. Cardigan refused, emphasizing that his orders were for the brigade to remain where it was.

No further orders had come from Lucan, for the simple reason that the divisional commander and his aides were all engaged in directing the Heavies' supporting squadrons into action. Lucan did, however, send his trumpeter towards the Light Brigade, sounding the Charge, which had been repeated twice, without result. The moment passed and the Russians escaped; had the opportunity been taken, perhaps the day might have ended differently. In the end, Lucan contented himself by sending his brother-in-law a curt note reminding him that when his divisional commander was engaged to the front his duty was to support him on the flank.

Although there are some grounds for believing that the Light Brigade's intervention might not have been quite as decisive as some thought at that time, the fact was that Cardigan had been grossly negligent in his duty and should have been sent back to his yacht. His excuse that the Russians had never approached the position he had been ordered to remain in and defend was as lame as it was selective in its recollection, and his denial that any discussion had taken place between himself and Morris was a barefaced lie, for not only had their conversation taken place in full view, but sufficient snatches of it had been audible for the whole to be pieced together. Yet Cardigan was no coward, so what was he playing at? Was he simply a cardboard soldier, good only for reviews and social events, who could not recognize a tactical opportunity when it stared him in the face? Or was he simply being bloody-minded and trying to make trouble for Lucan? The probability is that there was something in both suggestions.

It was now approximately 10.30 and the issue of the day had been decided. The defeat of Ryjoff's cavalry had deprived Liprandi of the screen which was to have protected the flank of his advance on Balaclava across the South Valley and without it he was not inclined to proceed further. The guns which had entered the North Valley with the cavalry had been withdrawn and were now extended across its far end, covering the battered squadrons as they rallied. Infantry were also present in large numbers but their dispositions suggested that no further advance was contemplated. All that remained of the Russians' earlier gains was a thin strip stretching partway along Causeway Heights and it seemed probable that even that would be evacuated in due course; indeed, when the Duke of Cambridge's First Division began to appear in the distance the Russians promptly abandoned Nos. 3 and 4 Redoubts after blowing up the magazines. Raglan had only to wait for his infantry to come up and then commence a steady advance along the Heights to recover the remainder. But another matter was troubling him. For centuries the capture of the enemy's artillery had been regarded as a tangible proof of victory, and although the idea had begun to look a little dated by the middle of the 19th century, Raglan was firmly wedded to the past and only too aware that the Duke of Wellington, his mentor, had never lost a gun in action. Now, his principal concern was to prevent the Russians hauling away the guns they had captured in the redoubts and exhibiting them in triumph. In his view urgent action was required and Airey dashed off his Third Order to Lucan and handed it to an aide for delivery.

What the order said was: 'Cavalry to advance and take advantage of any opportunity to recover the heights. They will be supported by the infantry which have been ordered to advance on two fronts.' However, the copy which Lucan received ended a little differently: '. . . have been ordered: Advance on two fronts.' Neither version was comprehensible enough for a recipient to act upon, but Lucan's copy came close to gibberish. What heights? Where were the infantry that were to support the operation? Why was the Cavalry Division to advance on two fronts? The aide did not know; no one had told him, and he had not bothered to ask. Understandably puzzled, Lucan decided to take no positive action until the infantry arrived and, as the South Valley was now deserted, he moved his division around the end of Causeway Heights into the North

Valley, where the Russians could be seen drawn up behind their guns at the far end. The stage was now set for the last tragic act in the drama.

Raglan's intention was a parallel advance by 1st and 4th Divisions along, respectively, the South Valley and Causeway Heights, screened by the Cavalry Division. While the Duke of Cambridge's 1st Division was about to descend to the plain, however, Cathcart's 4th was still some way behind and Cathcart himself, resenting the fact that his men would probably have some fighting to do while the Duke's would not, was not hurrying them along.

The minutes ticked away without either side making any further move. Then Raglan spotted Russian horse-teams moving on to the far end of Causeway Heights. At this stage the Russians were merely preparing to limber-up their own field artillery, but to Raglan's anxious eyes they were there for the sole purpose of removing the captured guns while Lucan's cavalry stood idly by. From his position on the edge of the towering escarpment Raglan could see everything, but he seems to have forgotten that when terrain features are viewed from so far above they merge and flatten, and that the Russians on Causeway Heights were not only on higher ground than the Cavalry Division but also hidden from Lucan by a series of rolling crests.

At length Raglan's patience snapped and he spoke rapidly to Airey. The latter scribbled furiously and was on the point of handing the order to the next aide for duty when Nemesis appeared in the shape of Captain Lewis Edward Nolan of the 15th Hussars. Nolan, possibly the finest horseman in the Army, had written a history of cavalry and a manual on horse management; he was also opinionated, vain, volatile and openly contemptuous of Lucan and Cardigan, so he was not the ideal choice to deliver Raglan's Fourth Order to the Cavalry Division. Nevertheless, Raglan considered speed to be of the essence and he insisted that Nolan should be the bearer. Disappearing over the edge of the escarpment, Nolan tore down its face along what amounted to little more than a goat track. Reaching the plain he galloped through the ranks of the Light Brigade in a state of high excitement, reining in beside Lucan to hand him the order. This still exists and it is possible to decipher Airey's pencilled scrawl:

> 'Lord Raglan wishes the cavalry to advance rapidly to the front – follow the enemy and try to prevent the enemy carrying away the guns. Troop Horse Artillery may accompany. French Cavalry is on your left. Immediate.

The order was no more intelligible than its predecessor had been and Lucan's request for clarification drew forth a haughty response. 'Lord Raglan's orders were that the cavalry should attack immediately!' That was not what the written order had required and it introduced an altogether new element into the situation. 'Attack, sir? Attack what?

What guns, sir?' demanded Lucan. Nolan's answer was delivered with studied insolence as he flung out his arm in the general direction of the Russian guns at the far end of the North Valley: 'There, my lord, is your enemy! There are your guns!'

Perhaps in other circumstances Lucan might have placed Nolan under arrest, but for the moment he seemed dumbfounded by the enormity of what was required. His division was to attack a battery of guns 1½ miles distant and in the process would cross a natural killing ground covered from the left by Russian artillery on Fedioukine Heights, from the right by more Russian guns on Causeway Heights, and from the front by the battery which was its objective, to say nothing of the fire of the enemy's infantry, or the cavalry massed behind the battery itself. The only possible outcome was the destruction of the entire division. In such a situation he would have been justified in *demanding* clarification, and would have received the support of his brigade commanders had he done so. Yet the written order demanded immediate action and Nolan spoke with all the authority of the army commander. He decided that the divisional attack would be led by the Light Brigade with the Heavy Brigade echeloned to its right rear. Cardigan pointed out the obvious dangers but accepted the situation with a mutter of 'Here goes the last of the Brudenells!'

As finally deployed for the attack the Light Brigade consisted of three lines with the 13th Light Dragoons and 17th Lancers in the first, the 11th Hussars in the second behind the Lancers, and the 8th Hussars and 4th Light Dragoons in the third. Altogether, the brigade's strength amounted to 678 men, including two Sardinian cavalry officers, plus a rough-haired terrier named Jemmy who lived in the 8th Hussars' mess and followed his masters everywhere. Their average age was in the early twenties and, although very few had been in action before, they knew exactly what was being asked of them and that few would return to tell the tale. As Lieutenant Thomas Hutton of the 4th Light Dragoons put it: 'A child might have seen the trap set for us – every private dragoon did!' At 11.10 a quiet descended over the battlefield as Cardigan took his place five lengths ahead of the leading ranks. With a shout of 'The Brigade will advance – first squadron of the 17th Lancers direct!' he wheeled his horse and set off down the valley towards the Russian mass. Bridles jingling and hooves thudding steadily, his regiments followed in their ranks, first at a walk, then a steady trot. Survivors recalled that at this point they were gripped within by cold, crawling fear in all its forms – fear of death or injury, fear of being seen to be afraid, and fear of letting themselves or their comrades down. Assisted by discipline and pride in their regiments, they swallowed it as best they could.

Nolan was riding with his friend Morris at the head of the 17th Lancers. Ever since the event historians have questioned whether he was aware or not of Raglan's real intentions. Alexander Kinglake, whose

Invasion of the Crimea, published between 1863 and 1887, came to be regarded as a semi-official history of the campaign, records that after 200 yards had been covered Nolan, realizing that the brigade was heading straight down the valley instead of wheeling right on to Causeway Heights, spurred diagonally across its front, shouting and pointing with his sword until a Russian shell exploded nearby, killing him instantly. This statement was apparently based on the evidence of a single unnamed officer, but as W. Baring Pemberton points out in his excellent *Battles of the Crimean War*, not only did officers who left otherwise full accounts fail to mention the incident, but 'no such conduct on Nolan's part is (so far as is known) recorded by any who rode in or in front of the first line (whose evidence alone would be of value).' Fortunately, such a record does exist in autobiographical notes prepared by former Sergeant-Major J. I. Nunnerley in 1892. Nunnerley, a steady, honest man with no axe to grind, had left the Regular Army in 1857 and later become drill instructor to a troop of the Lancashire Hussars, a post which he held for 22 years. At Balaclava he was a corporal, riding in the front rank of the 17th Lancers' right squadron, and he recalled that Nolan gave '. . . a kind of yell which sounded very much like "Threes right", and throwing his sword-hand above his head, his horse wheeled to the right and he fell to the rear. As though obeying this death-like order, part of the squadron wheeled "Threes right", and observing their left squadron advancing, with Lord Cardigan in front, . . . Nunnerley immediately gave the order "Front forward" and so brought them into line again.'

'Threes right' would have been the appropriate order to have given if Nolan, attempting to correct the terrible error which had resulted from his cavalier arrogance, had wanted to put the brigade back on its correct axis of advance. Nunnerley was clearly not alone in hearing the words and others thought that he had shouted 'Come on!' It seems, therefore, that Kinglake's version is probably correct. Cardigan, however, either did not hear or chose to ignore Nolan's shouts. During the short briefing prior to the attack, Nolan had made an insulting remark to him and in reply he had bellowed: 'By God, if I come through this alive, I'll have you court-martialled for speaking to me in that manner!' Now, it looked very much as though Nolan was intent on committing a further breach of military etiquette by riding across the front of the brigade commander. Cardigan's rage was so great that he thought of little else throughout the charge.

Shortly after the brigade had ridden over Nolan's body the order was given: 'Draw – swords!' Waves of light flashed along the trotting blue lines as the blades came out. The order, received with a cheer, seemed to break the tension and the men settled into their saddles. For the Russians, the target, growing larger by the second, was an artilleryman's dream come true. Shells from both flanks and ahead were bursting in the ranks, blowing gaps and splattering men and horses with blood and torn flesh. 'Close in! Close in! Close in to the centre!' was the cry as each swathe went down. To the right rear, the Heavy Brigade had also entered the killing ground and had soon sustained more casualties than it had during its earlier encounter with the Russian cavalry. Lucan was riding with them and, horrified by the dreadful wake of dead, dying and maimed men and horses left by the Light Brigade, he reached a decision. 'They have sacrificed the Light Brigade – they shall not have the Heavy if I can help it!' he said to his adjutant, Lord Paulet. His trumpeter sounded the Halt and the Heavies pulled up, then wheeled away out of range. The horse artillery battery had not been committed to the slaughter because the heavy going would have rendered it too slow and vulnerable.

Meanwhile, the Light Brigade trotted on, the focus of an explosive hurricane. Those on the Sapoune escarpment were at first struck dumb by the enormity of the mistake that had been made, and by the appalling scene which was being enacted below. There seemed to be something preternatural, almost superhuman, in the brigade's apparently casual indifference to certain death, and it reduced some to tears. 'My God, what are they doing?' cried one elderly French officer. 'I am old, I have seen many battles, but this is too much!' General Bosquet agreed: 'It is magnificent, but it is not war.' Then, realizing that if any of the Light Brigade survived the attack their chances of returning across the killing ground were equally slim, he ordered the 4th Chasseurs d'Afrique to charge the Russian guns on Fedioukine Heights.

In accordance with Lucan's instructions, Cardigan kept his regiments in hand and would not allow them to increase the pace. Once the brigade came within range of the Russian infantry, however, the horses instinctively opened their stride and suddenly the whole formation was bearing down at a wild gallop. There were dead men riding in the ranks now, held in the saddle by the regular cavalryman's tight thigh muscles. Nunnerley watched the headless Sergeant Talbot, still gripping the reins and with his lance down at the Engage, career on for thirty yards before sliding sideways off his mount. The battery that was the brigade's objective was silent for the moment, but only because the gunners were double-shotting their weapons. At about 50 yards' range the guns belched flame, smoke and flying iron; most of the leading rank went down, including Nunnerley, whose horse had a foreleg blown off. Regiment by regiment, the remnant of the Light Brigade tore into the drifting fog of powder smoke.

Driven by blood lust and the desire for revenge, the 17th Lancers and 13th Light Dragoons speared and cut down most of the gunners in the battery, then charged the already demoralized Russian cavalry behind, driving them back to within sight of the Tchernaya before they halted to rally. Next to arrive were the 11th Hussars and 4th Light Dragoons, sweeping respectively past the left and through the centre of the battery where they killed the remaining gunners and joined in the pursuit of the Russian horsemen. It is a measure of the Russians' alarm that the nearest infantry regiments formed square for their own protection. Finally, the 8th Hussars drove past the now silent battery's right flank and halted beyond, where they formed a rallying point for troops returning from the Tchernaya.

The question in everyone's mind was, having overrun the guns, what was the brigade to do next? Of Cardigan there was no sign, although he had been seen to ride into the battery. Beyond the guns he had found himself surrounded by Cossacks and might have been killed if he had not been recognized by a Russian officer, Prince Radziwill, whom he had met socially in London before the war. Radziwill offered a reward to any man who could take him alive and the Cossacks merely jabbed at him with their lances, pricking his thigh and tearing his pelisse. At this point the remnants of Cardigan's leading regiments arrived and he was able to break free. He had, as he saw it, performed his aristocratic duty by leading his men into battle. The rest, he believed, was up to them and, to his eternal disgrace, he left them without any thought of rallying them or leading them to safety.

That task fell to Lord George Paget, the brigade's Second-in-Command, to such commanding officers as survived, and to individual officers and NCOs. It was not made easier by the fact that the Russians, suddenly realizing that their assailants were so few in number, had faced about and begun to counter-attack in a half-hearted manner. Furthermore, Liprandi had sent a lancer regiment down from Fedioukine Heights to cut off the brigade's retreat. The withdrawal was therefore made obliquely across the valley, so that it was exposed at close range to the fire from Causeway Heights, which caused further casualties. The larger groups cut their way out, but for the stragglers it was a matter of luck. Some, wounded and on foot, were simply speared to death; others were prodded to the rear as prisoners; a few who had remained mounted or had caught loose horses got through. Had not the French Chasseurs d'Afrique charged along Fedioukine Heights, forcing the Russian artillery there to limber up and withdraw towards its infantry squares, only a handful would have regained their own lines.

As each group arrived it was cheered in by the Heavies. The egregious Cardigan, ignoring the look of contempt in the eyes of Paget and other officers, personally acknowledged the cheers. Paget subsequently submitted a formal complaint regarding the brigade commander's conduct, then resigned his commission in disgust. The brigade's return was captured by Lady Butler in her painting 'Balaclava' using soldiers who had taken part in the charge as her models; among them was Nunnerley, shown cradling the mortally wounded Trumpeter Britten across the saddle-bow of a stray horse he had caught. Some men are depicted in deep shock, others reeling in the saddle, others with visible wounds sanitized in the Victorian manner; the horses are shown wild-eyed, broken-winded, plastered with sweat and blood, staggering head down or foundering. Yet, when the artist showed the completed painting to her models their verdict was that the horses were 'too good'. The remnant of the brigade formed up to the sound of the farriers' pistols putting the worst cases out of their misery.

Only 195 men answered the roll-call. The regiments of the Light Brigade had been reduced to the size of troops; all that remained of the 13th Light Dragoons was a little knot consisting of two officers and eight other ranks. 500 horses had been killed or put down. Jemmy, the 8th Hussars' terrier, came back with two shell splinters in his neck but survived and later returned to England. Cardigan, always popular with his troopers, rode along the short line. 'Men, it was a mad-brained trick, but it was no fault of mine!' 'Never mind, my lord, we are ready to go again!' called a voice from the ranks, and no irony was intended. 'No, no, you have done enough!'

At the other end of the valley about forty men, some of them mortally wounded, had been rounded up by Cossacks and were being herded to the rear. Some were beaten and bound, others prodded with lances or dragged along at the tail of a horse, but once they had been handed over to regular units they received decent treatment; one Russian officer was so disgusted when he found that the wounded Private Farquharson of the 4th Light Dragoons had been bound, beaten and dragged through a river by a particularly brutal Cossack that he thrashed the man with his own knout. Many were given vodka and had recovered their morale by the time General Liprandi arrived to interview them. 'Come now, men,' he asked, not unkindly. 'What did they give you to drink? Did they prime you with spirits to come down and attack us in such a mad manner?' Private Kirk of the 17th gave him a dusty answer: 'By God, if we had so much as smelt the barrel we would have taken half Russia by this time!'

Raglan was so shaken by what had taken place that he did not proceed with his plan for an advance along Causeway Heights, although both infantry divisions had now arrived. Neither side made any further move and towards evening the Russians withdrew, taking with them seven of the captured guns. Only then was the Light Brigade stood down. Nunnerley, like the rest, returned to a tent which had been thoroughly looted by Turks and Cossacks. The previous night he had shared it with twelve others; now, he was alone. Detractors later suggested that Cardigan rode off for a hot bath and a good dinner aboard *Dryad*, but this was far from the truth. With the onset of the inevitable physical and mental reaction, he displayed, albeit briefly, an unexpected kindness and sympathy for others, spending the night of the battle among his men, rolled in a blanket beside a campfire.

Recriminations concerning the loss of the Light Brigade had begun as soon as Raglan reached the foot of the escarpment. Cardigan, having simply obeyed the order of his immediate superior, was exonerated at once. Lucan angrily protested that he had simply obeyed the army commander's own order, delivered in such a manner that he was clearly permitted no latitude in the matter. To this Raglan retorted, 'Lord Lucan, you were a lieutenant-general and should therefore have exercised your discretion, and, not approving of the charge, should not have caused it to be made!' While this contains a tacit admission that the order was itself flawed, the point was a telling one. Despite the apparent urgency of the situation, Lucan had been entitled to request absolute clarification before taking an action of which he disapproved; it was, after all, on his own initiative that the Heavy Brigade had been pulled up, and for that none would criticize him. Again, as Raglan pointed out in a private letter to the Duke of Newcastle, the Secretary for War, written shortly after the battle, 'The written order sent to him by the Quartermaster-General did not exact that he should attack at all hazards, and contained no expression which could bear on that construction.' Indeed, the word 'attack' had been Nolan's verbal interjection, altering the entire sense of the written order. Nevertheless, in the final analysis, Raglan, Airey, Lucan and Nolan can all be seen to have contributed to the disaster in their own ways.

The sacrifice of the Light Brigade achieved nothing save possibly further to demoralize the already defeated Russian cavalry. It remains, however, the supreme example of discipline and courage, forming the subject of innumerable books and two major films, and was immortalized by Alfred Lord Tennyson in his poem 'Charge of the Light Brigade'. For a man to have ridden as one of the Six Hundred was to guarantee him the profound respect of his community for the rest of his days.

History has not been quite so generous concerning the three other major events of the day. The stubborn Turkish defence of Redoubt No. 1, which bought priceless time for Raglan, has rarely received the credit it deserved. The determined stand by Campbell and the 93rd Highlanders has fared somewhat better, although Russell's 'thin red streak' has long become a 'thin red line' and has been applied in many different contexts. The defeat of the Russian cavalry by Scarlett's dragoons, the decisive engagement of the battle, has been largely eclipsed by the dramatic fate of the Light Brigade. At the time, however, it was rightly hailed as a brilliant success and was also commemorated by Tennyson in his 'Charge of the Heavy Brigade'. That the poem is almost unknown today exemplifies the Anglo-Saxon trait of celebrating gallant failure rather than victory gained at a modest cost.

On 5 November the Russians again attempted to capture Balaclava, using a 57,000-strong force consisting mainly of infantry. This time their axis was directed southwards from Inkerman, but their advance was slow and unco-ordinated. From start to finish the fighting was confused, brutal and frequently hand-to-hand. It was a soldiers' battle in which the generals played little part. When it ended the Russians had sustained 12,000 casualties and were thrown back into their defences; Allied losses amounted to 3,300, mainly British.

Russell's reports on Balaclava and Inkerman were read eagerly at home. So, too, were his harrowing accounts of the incompetence which led to the deaths of thousands of men from exposure and disease during the subsequent winter. The soldiers, lacking suitable clothing and wood for tent floors or even cooking fires, were permanently wet and cold. Inevitably, pneumonia and cholera decimated the ranks. The remnant of the Cavalry Division quickly ceased to exist. There was fodder in plenty at Balaclava, but there was no means of transporting it and the horses were kept in the forward areas in case the Russians attacked again. The animals starved in wind-blasted, hock-deep mud, gnawing each other's manes and tails until they dropped dead. Those that survived were no longer fit for cavalry use and became beasts of burden. Such was the public outrage that Lord Aberdeen's government fell in January 1855 and conditions improved rapidly. Russell, the world's first true war correspondent, had a long career in which he also reported the Indian Mutiny, the American Civil War, the Seven Weeks War between Prussia and Austria, the Franco–Prussian War, the Zulu War and the 1882 British intervention in Egypt; he was knighted in 1895. His Crimean dispatches remain his greatest monument for, in addition to their immediate results, they initiated a slow but fundamental change in the British public's attitude to the ordinary soldier; there were too many stories of heroism, self-sacrifice and plain decency for the image of the drunken brute to persist.

Raglan, undeniably a good man himself, was broken by the fate of his army and the public's response to Russell's reports, commenting that if he dared to show his face in England again he would be stoned to death. He neither returned home nor witnessed the fall of Sevastopol the following September. He began to suffer from clinical depression and, contracting cholera, died on 28 June 1855.

With the Cavalry Division gone there was no point in its commanders remaining in the Crimea. Cardigan arrived home first, to receive a hero's welcome, a personal audience at Windsor Castle and his appointment as Inspector-General of Cavalry. However, once stories began to circulate that he had abandoned his brigade in action, together with insinuations that he had not even taken part in the charge, he again became unpopular, and was forced to vindicate himself in court. In 1858, following the death of his first wife, he married the beautiful but wild Adeline de Horsey, of whom society heartily disapproved, although she suited him well enough. He died ten years later, having sustained fatal injuries when he fell from his horse after suffering a stroke.

Lucan reached England still seething with rage that he had been held responsible for the loss of the Light Brigade. His demand for a court-martial was rejected but he was consoled with promotion and other honours, dying a field marshal in 1888.

Of all the British senior officers engaged at Balaclava, only Campbell was to distinguish himself in another campaign. Sent to India to quell the Mutiny, he personally commanded the force which relieved the besieged garrison of Lucknow. During this operation he had wished to reserve the honour of the final breakthrough for his beloved 93rd Highlanders and was greatly annoyed when a promising young officer named Garnet Wolseley, mentioned elsewhere in these pages, initiated the decisive attack with other troops. Yet, such things and a tendency to caution apart, in the eyes of Queen Victoria, the general public and his own men, he was a hero and a great man. Elevated to the peerage as Lord Clyde, he ended his days as a field marshal; it was no mean achievement for the son of a Glasgow carpenter.

3
THE WALLS OF DELHI
1857

That an empire should be acquired by accident is remarkable; that it should be administered by a commercial organization is doubly so. When the Honourable East India Company received its first charter from Queen Elizabeth I in 1600 its object was simply profit to be derived from trade with India, and it had begun by establishing trading posts at various points around the coast. In the 18th century, however, England and France were almost continuously at war and it became necessary for the Company to raise its own troops to fight those of its French rivals and their Indian allies. When, following Robert Clive's astonishing victory at Plassey in 1757, the Company consolidated its hold on Bengal, the French cause in India was doomed. In 1765 the Moghul emperor granted the Company the status of a feudatory ruler in recognition of the fact that it had become a power in the land. From then on its influence was steadily extended by intrigue, alliance, annexation and war. It was not, however, entirely master in its own house, for to stave off bankruptcy in 1772 it was forced to borrow £1 million from the British government and in return the latter demanded the right to supervise and regulate affairs within the Company's Indian territories. By the middle of the 19th century the Company had ceased to be a trading organization and instead had become an agency for the civil and military affairs of the greater part of the sub-continent.

Some measure of the stability imposed by the Company's rule can be gauged from the fact that, while the population of India in the 1850s amounted to some 300 million people, spread over a vast area, only 340,000 troops were needed for defence and aid to the civil power. Of these, 300,000 were Indian sepoys of the Company's Bombay, Madras and Bengal armies. These native regiments were led by British officers who received their commissions direct from the Company and were better paid than their counterparts in the British Army, which was known as the Queen's Service in India. Furthermore, Company officers received their promotion by strict seniority within their regiments, whereas Queen's officers were still required to purchase their promotion, although some relaxation of the latter was permitted on active service, when vacancy and merit were taken into account. Ostensibly fairer, the Company system had the disadvantage that officers tended to be older for their rank than in the Queen's Service. The effects of this were most apparent in the senior ranks, where colonels were in their sixties and generals in their seventies, ages at which, the Crimean experience clearly indicated, the majority had long passed their peak of efficiency. For the sepoy, service in the Company's regiments was regarded as honourable, conferring status at home and ultimately a pension, with the prospect of promotion as far as the junior commissioned ranks.

As stiffening, the Company also maintained several intentionally named European regiments, numbering approximately 15,000 men, who also received better rates of pay than could be obtained in the Queen's Service. The majority of the men were British, but other nationalities were present as well. They no doubt had excellent reasons for volunteering for what amounted to lifelong exile with a high risk of death in action or from disease and were regarded as a hard lot. Having nothing in common with the sepoys, yet looked at askance by the Queen's troops, they tended to regard themselves as an élite and invariably fought well.

For additional security the Company also rented Queen's regiments, the rank and file of which found service in India more congenial than at home because plenty of cheap labour was available to make their lives more comfortable in barracks; as one private of the 14th Light Dragoons put it, 'We live like gentlemen here'. The demands of the Crimean War had reduced the number of British troops in India with the result that in 1857 there were only 25,000 of them, the largest concentration being in the recently annexed Punjab in the north of the country, the remainder being scattered in garrisons widely separated from one another.

Over the years the Company's administration had brought many benefits to its territories, including law and order, an efficient civil service, stable trading conditions, improved roads and bridges, the electric telegraph and the beginnings of the railway system. By and large the Company had preferred not to interfere in local affairs, but it had been outraged by the custom of *sati* (the live burning of widows on their husbands' funeral pyres) and the depredations of the secret religious society that practised *thagi* (ritual murder by strangulation in honour of the goddess Kali) and had endeavoured to stamp hard on these evils.

Thus far the Company's interference was accepted, although it made enemies of those with vested interests. But the view of early Victorian society was that since the Almighty had made Great Britain responsible for a large proportion of the world's population, there was a sacred duty to see that the lot of its subject people was improved. In addition to effecting practical measures, the improvers did not neglect the spiritual dimension, which meant extending the spread of Christianity throughout India.

Sincere and well intentioned though the improvers were, they failed to understand that Indian society was conservative by instinct and still thought in feudal terms, and that religion, especially caste, permeated every aspect of Indian daily life. Thus, the passing of a measure permitting widows to re-marry provoked unexpected anger, while the imposition of a land title system where none had previously existed resulted in a widespread feeling of injustice arising from the confiscation of thousands of estates and small-holdings. The princely rulers were divided in their attitude to the Company. Some had alliances with it and had benefited from their association with it; others resented the loss of their former powers and would avail themselves of any opportunity to recover them. Many Hindus, especially the Brahmins, saw in Christian missionary activity a British plot to violate the caste system and so imperil their souls. The year 1857 was in itself also significant, for an old prophesy said that during the centennial of the Battle of Plassey the British would be driven from India for ever. Furthermore, with fewer British troops in the country than previously, and stories of British shortcomings in the Crimea still in the air, the moment seemed to be ripe. Much of India was unsettled, not least by the mysterious passage of *chapattis* between villages in the night. No one knows to this day where they originated or what they meant, but the runner always brought instructions that fresh *chapattis* should be baked and similarly passed on to other villages. To simple minds the implications were that decisive, wide-ranging and probably violent events were about to take place.

Of the Company's three armies, that of the Bengal Presidency was the largest and most experienced. It was also the most seriously affected by the present troubles because its ranks contained a high proportion of Brahmins, high-caste Hindus and Rajputs, recruited mainly in Oudh. In addition to their other grievances, the Hindus objected strongly to a recently introduced regulation requiring them to serve abroad, as this would probably entail a sea passage which, according to their faith, would lose them their caste. Since the Sikh Wars a new generation of British officers had entered the Company's service, including a number who made no secret of the fact that they disliked and despised the sepoys and were therefore quite unsuitable for their appointments. The formerly close relationship between officers and men in the Bengal Army's native regiments had, therefore, become more distant, although there remained contact enough for the more efficient officers to warn their generals that serious trouble was brewing in the ranks. The generals, grown old among the sepoys, were unable to believe that their men would not remain true to their salt and were dismissive of ideas that a mutiny was in the offing.

Although the Company had created a highly volatile situation, it is possible that tragedy could have been avoided if the sepoys had not been pushed beyond safe limits. It had been decided to replace the old Brown Bess musket with the Enfield rifle, which had demonstrated its efficiency in the Crimea. Ammunition for the Enfield consisted of a greased paper cartridge incorporating the powder charge and ball, and it was customary to bite the end off this before ramming it down the barrel. There were agitators at work and it was almost certainly one of these, a workman at Dum Dum Arsenal near Calcutta, who initiated a clever and extremely effective rumour which spread like wildfire. He claimed that the cartridge was greased with a mixture of cow and pig fat. Because the cow was sacred to the Hindus and the pig was abominated by the Muslims, the entire native element of the Bengal Army was suddenly destabilized. Contact with the grease would render the sepoy unclean and he would be forbidden to sleep with his wife until he had been ritually purified. It seemed to the sepoy that he was to be deliberately damned to his own faith as a further step along the road towards enforced Christianity, and the terror he felt conditioned all his subsequent actions. For once, the authorities listened and promised to redress the grievance, but the damage had been done and the troops no longer trusted them.

From January 1857 onwards the unrest began to worsen. Some regiments, including the 19th and 34th Native Infantry and the 7th Irregular Cavalry, refused to accept the Enfield cartridges at any price and were disbanded. On 24 April a Colonel Carmichael Smith, an autocratic, insensitive man, attempted to force the cartridges on his regiment, the 3rd Light Cavalry, during a formal parade at Meerut, a garrison town 36 miles north-east of Delhi. Eighty-five of the troopers refused and were promptly court-martialled and sentenced to a term of hard labour. On 9 May the entire garrison was drawn up, the British with loaded weapons, the Indians without, to witness the convicted men being publicly stripped of their uniforms, shackled and led off to gaol.

The sepoys were now faced with three alternatives. They could accept the cartridges at the risk of losing their souls; they could refuse the cartridges and face severe punishment; or they could mutiny and destroy the system which placed them in such jeopardy. The following day, a Sunday, they chose to mutiny when the British troops were at church parade, and whatever the merits of their case, nothing could justify the frenzied orgy of destruction and slaughter which ensued. British officers were cut down, their wives were violated with burning torches until they died, and their children were slaughtered. Then, having burned the European bungalows and released their comrades from prison, the mutineers set off along the road to Delhi before the stunned garrison commander could organize a coherent response.

The mutineers reached Delhi next day and were joined by the garrison. Once again, British officers, civilians, women and children were hunted down and killed. The news spread quickly and further outbreaks occurred at Ferozepur, Aligarh, Mainpuri, Etawah, Bulundshar, Nasirabad, Bareilly, Moradabad, Shahjahanpur and elsewhere. Prompt disarming of the sepoys at Lahore, Agra, Lucknow, Peshawar and Mardan slowed the progress of the revolt, but could not halt it. Many of the mutinous regiments converged on Delhi, cheered by their comrades as they marched in. At times there was a nightmare quality in their arrival, for the scarlet lines swung along as smartly as ever, proudly carrying their Colours, while their bands played traditional English marches.

Delhi provided a natural focus for the mutineers, for in the crumbling palace known as the Red Fort lived the successor to the once magnificent Moghul emperors, Bahadur Shah II. The line of Timurlane, however, had long since lost its power and Bahadur, now over eighty, was known simply as the King of Delhi. He received financial support from the Company and British officials accorded him the courtesy and respect due to his descent, but his days were passed in surroundings where faded splendour merged with utter squalor, among a host of hangers-on who claimed kinship and intrigued bitterly among themselves. Yet the King provided a figurehead who was acceptable to both Hindus and Muslims and, though by no means in control of the situation, he allowed himself to be proclaimed Emperor of Hindustan and designated his eldest son, Mirza Moghul, commander of his newly acquired army.

During the next few weeks the mutineers, believing that they had already won, made no concerted effort to destroy the remnant of British power in northern India when it was at its most vulnerable. Within Delhi, the situation began to deteriorate. In what was essentially a mercenary army, the primary loyalty of the sepoy was to his regiment, and once the bonds of regimental discipline were loosened he simply became one tiny portion of a vast armed mob, held together by a herd instinct for common survival and the prospect of loot.

News of the first mutinies had been telegraphed to General Headquarters at Ambala, 130 miles north of Delhi, during the afternoon of 11 May. General Sir George Anson, the Commander-in-Chief, was at the hill station of Simla, to which the telegraph had not yet been extended, and he did not receive copies until the following day. He reacted with commendable speed, recognizing that possession of Delhi was the key to the situation, and that once the mutineers had been deprived of their focal point they could be defeated in detail. Unfortunately that was a great deal easier said than done, for not only had he very few troops available, but he was also critically short of artillery, ammunition and medical equipment, and lacked even a supply train, which had to be cobbled together at a moment's notice.

The Delhi Field Force, as Anson's column was known, consisted of the 9th Lancers, 75th (Gordon) Highlanders and two troops of the Royal Horse Artillery from the Queen's Service, the 1st and 2nd Bengal Fusiliers (Europeans), the 9th Light Cavalry, 4th Irregular Cavalry, and 5th and 60th Native Infantry; despite the assurances of their British officers, neither of the native infantry regiments could be relied on and when, some days later, the 60th mutinied and made off for Delhi, the 5th was disarmed.

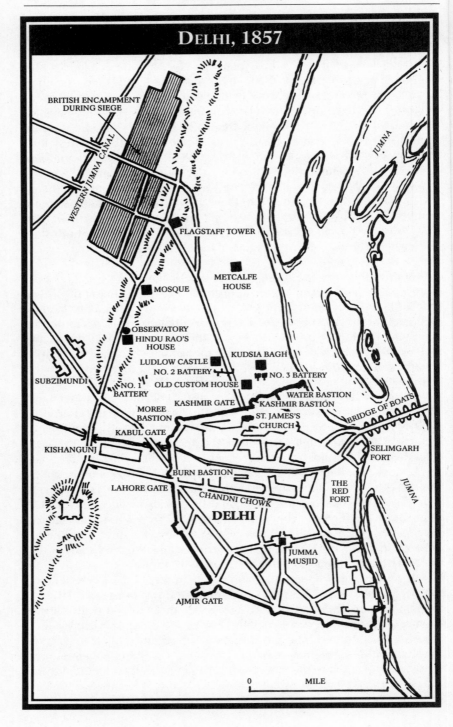

DELHI, 1857

BRITISH ENCAMPMENT
DURING SIEGE

WESTERN JUMNA CANAL

JUMNA

FLAGSTAFF TOWER

METCALFE
HOUSE

MOSQUE

OBSERVATORY
HINDU RAO'S
HOUSE

KUDSIA BAGH

LUDLOW CASTLE
NO. 2 BATTERY

NO. 3 BATTERY

SUBZIMUNDI

NO. 1
BATTERY

OLD CUSTOM HOUSE

WATER BASTION

KASHMIR GATE

KASHMIR BASTION

MOREE
BASTION

ST. JAMES'S
CHURCH

BRIDGE OF BOATS

KABUL GATE

SELIMGARH
FORT

KISHANGUNJ

BURN BASTION

THE
RED
FORT

JUMNA

LAHORE GATE

CHANDNI CHOWK

DELHI

JUMMA
MUSJID

AJMIR GATE

0   MILE

Given the difficulties under which Anson laboured, plus the fact that he was in his 70th year and had last seen action at Waterloo, his achievement in getting his column moving by 17 May, and so restoring the strategic initiative to the British, has received less credit than it deserves. The strain, however, had told on him and on 27 May he died from cholera. Command passed to General Sir Henry Barnard, who continued to march south through Karnaul before halting briefly at Baghpat, where he was joined by the remnant of the Meerut garrison under Colonel Archdale Wilson; this consisted of two squadrons of 6th Dragoon Guards, part of the 60th Rifles (King's Royal Rifle Corps), some loyal Company cavalry and seven guns, including five captured from a rebel force which opposed its crossing of the River Hindon.

At Badli-ke-serai, six miles north of Delhi, Barnard's progress was temporarily halted by the bulk of the mutineer army, some 30,000 strong with thirty guns, in an entrenched position. Barnard, a Crimean veteran, had fewer than 4,000 men available but he was heir to a long tradition of actions in India when British commanders, faced with similar odds, had always attacked without hesitation. He did likewise and after a short, sharp fight the rebels broke and streamed back towards the city. The column, elated by its success, resumed its advance and occupied a two-mile-long feature known as The Ridge, running from north to south, to the north-west of the city walls. Its first act was to burn the mutineers' former barracks as a signal to those in Delhi that ferocious retribution awaited them; in the event, the gesture was short-sighted since it left the British without adequate shelter during the hottest months of the Indian summer. The rebels had thrown bodies into the cantonment wells and, as the waters of the nearby River Jumna were undrinkable, the column established its camp to the west of the Ridge, where the Western Jumna Canal not only provided a better source but also offered protection against attack from the rear.

The Ridge itself was some forty feet higher than the surrounding terrain but consisted almost entirely of rock from which it was impossible to construct fortifications. There were, however, a number of buildings along the crest which were turned into strongpoints, including a large mansion known as Hindu Rao's House, a tower named the Observatory, a ruined mosque and the circular two-storey Flagstaff Tower. Between the Ridge and the city lay a triangular no man's land in which lay two other mansions, Metcalfe House and Ludlow Castle, a summer palace named the Kudsia Bagh, and the Old Custom House. This area was covered with lush vegetation, gardens and walls which provided excellent cover for rebel sorties against the British lines. The defences of Delhi were old-fashioned but still formidable, consisting of seven miles of masonry curtain walls 24 feet high, with bastions mounting artillery at regular intervals, the whole fronted by a ditch 20 feet deep and 25 feet wide save along the two-mile frontage with the

Jumna. Ten gates pierced the walls, the Kashmir, Kabul and Lahore Gates being closest to the Ridge. Within the city the Red Fort, with walls 110 feet high surrounded by a wide, deep ditch, served the dual purpose of royal palace and citadel.

Ostensibly, an absurd situation had developed. A British force of 600 cavalry, 2,300 infantry and 22 field guns, holding a precarious position on a barren ridge, could hardly be said to be besieging up to 40,000 rebels and their allies, equipped with several hundred artillery weapons of various types, holding secure fortifications. Barnard's hopes that Delhi could be recaptured by *coup de main* were clearly ill-founded. Instead, it was the Delhi Field Force which had to fight desperately to maintain its position against frequent sorties; on 23 June, the anniversary of Plassey, the rebels made several determined attacks on the Ridge but were repulsed.

Elsewhere, the mutiny continued to sweep through the garrisons of the Bengal Army. At Cawnpore 300 British and loyal Indian troops, together with 500 non-combatants, mainly families, were persuaded by the rebel leader Nana Sahib to surrender on promise of safe conduct by boat to Allahabad. As they were embarking, the majority were fired on then cut down by cavalry. The few surviving women and children were held prisoner until a British column approached, then slaughtered and thrown down a well. Many rebels continued to converge on Delhi, including, on 1 July, a large contingent from Bareilly commanded by Bakht Khan, an Indian artillery officer with some forty years' service, who wasted no time in prevailing upon the King to appoint him commander-in-chief in place of Mirza Moghul. Naturally the latter, despite his failure to dislodge the British from the Ridge, resented the fact and from this point relationships between the senior rebel commanders were marked by mutual suspicion and recrimination.

Barnard died from cholera on 5 July. His successor, General Thomas Reed, was already an invalid and, a fortnight later, he was forced to hand over to Archdale Wilson, who was granted the temporary rank of major-general. Although, like his opponent Bakht Khan, Wilson had served for forty years in India and the Far East, his career had thus far been unremarkable and few thought highly of his intellect or his military abilities. Now greatness had been thrust upon him and, with it, a fearful responsibility. His first task was to impose a degree of organization into the force on the Ridge and, to everyone's surprise, he succeeded. As to his primary mission, he knew that it was beyond his resources at the time, commenting in a letter to his wife that between 25,000 and 30,000 men would be needed to capture Delhi. His Chief Engineer, Colonel Richard Baird Smith, believed that the longer an assault was delayed the smaller would be its chance of success. It was one thing to attack superior numbers of rebels in the open, however, but quite another to launch an assault on formidable defences which had not been breached by artillery and, given thé small number of troops available, a costly repulse at Delhi could spell disaster for the British cause in India. In the circumstances, therefore, Wilson was absolutely correct in deciding simply to hold his ground.

Reinforcements were reaching the Ridge, but daily wastage was such that the active strength of the Delhi Field Force remained about the same. At the beginning of July it had a nominal strength of 6,600, but in one week's fighting alone during the ensuing month it sustained 400 battle casualties; in the period of a fortnight, 2nd Gurkha Rifles, holding Hindu Rao's House against daily attacks, lost 200 men. Cholera, dysentery and heatstroke laid low as many as did the rebels, often with fatal consequences. The once-lush landscape, now scarred by entrenchments and battery positions, began to resemble semi-desert as its trees were cut down for firewood. Over all hung the sickly stench of death, emanating from the numerous bodies of mutineers decomposing in the fierce sun below the Ridge. Yet, for the rebels, no more dangerous enemy existed in all the world than the ragged, exhausted men of Wilson's command, for this war was quite unlike any other that had been fought in India. It has always been difficult for the British soldier to generate a personal hatred for his enemy, but there are some acts he will never forgive, particularly the massacre of his womenfolk and children, and for this neither those who were in India at the outbreak of the mutiny, nor those who arrived to reinforce them, were inclined to show the slightest mercy to their opponents.

For the time being, as the protracted struggle for the Ridge raged on, there was nothing Wilson could do but take stock. The mutiny continued to spread but the Company's Bombay and Madras armies, though slightly affected, remained loyal. Some princely rulers, notably the Rani of Jhansi, threw in their lot with the mutineers, while others, including the powerful Nizam of Hyderabad, stuck by their treaties and contributed contingents to assist in putting down the rebellion. In the worst affected areas small British garrisons continued to hold out against odds with little prospect of relief until the situation underwent a radical change. At sea, reinforcements were converging on India and a substantial force of Crimean veterans under General Sir Colin Campbell had left the United Kingdom, although it would be many weeks before their presence would make itself felt.

In the meantime, reinforcements were approaching the Delhi Field Force from the most improbable of areas, the Punjab, annexed only nine years previously after two hard-fought wars. The wars had themselves generated a sincere mutual respect between the British and the Sikh population, which held a prominent place among the martial races of India, and the British administration had brought many benefits to the country. In general, the Sikhs tended to look down on the Company's sepoys, but when the mutiny had begun they had stood aside to watch developments. That the mutineers made no headway at all in the Punjab was due to the energetic response of the province's Chief Commissioner, Sir John Lawrence, who had moved quickly to disarm suspect regiments and secure arsenals and important strategic points.

Most notable of Lawrence's deputies was Brigadier-General John Nicholson, the eldest son of a Dublin doctor. An uncle, a director of the Company, had awarded him a cadetship in the Bengal Army and he had subsequently seen active service during the First Afghan and Second Sikh Wars. He disliked India intensely, writing to his mother that he 'would rather go home on £200 a year than live like a prince here'. Self-contained, reserved and humourless, he possessed a dominant personality which immediately impressed itself on those around him. Deeply religious, he would have felt at home in the ranks of Cromwell's Ironsides, for his God belonged essentially to the Old Testament. Nothing gave him greater satisfaction than the pursuit of the wrongdoer and, attached to Lawrence's civil administration with the responsibility of pacifying the Punjab and its borders, he had become a legend among the wild mountains of the North-West Frontier. Once, when his men had been unable to apprehend a particular criminal, he had set off after him personally, met, fought and killed him, then displayed the man's head on his desk as a warning to others. His remoteness, his terrifying reputation and his contempt for the softer things of life combined to make him an object of worship among the tribes.

Under Lawrence, Nicholson commanded a highly mobile force known as the Movable Column, which included a contingent of Multani horsemen fiercely loyal to him. With this he had pre-empted mutinies, dispersed regiments of doubtful loyalty and hunted down rebels in arms. The ringleaders of the last were tied with their backs to the muzzles of cannon and blown apart. Horrific though it was, this decisive action impressed the Sikhs, who volunteered in such large numbers to fight for the British that in August Lawrence was able to send Nicholson to Delhi with the Movable Column, three Punjabi cavalry regiments and seven Punjabi infantry battalions; these were followed by a heavy siege train drawn from the arsenals of Phillaur and Ferozepur, and a corps of Punjabi sappers and miners.

The arrival of Nicholson and his men effectively doubled the size of the Delhi Field Force, but the heavy siege guns, trundling slowly along behind their plodding elephants, were still on the road and Bakht Khan, aware of the fact, sent out a force of approximately 6,000 rebels to intercept the convoy. Warned by his own intelligence service within the city, Wilson dispatched Nicholson with 2,500 men and sixteen guns in pursuit. During the evening of 25 August the mutineers were found drawn up at Najafgahr, some sixteen miles from Delhi. After a personal reconnaissance Nicholson decided to pierce the enemy's centre then roll up the right of his line, ordering his infantry to advance to within thirty yards of the opposing ranks, fire a volley, then charge with the bayonet. In an action lasting an hour the rebels were routed, losing 800 killed plus all their guns and baggage; British casualties amounted to 25 killed and 70 wounded.

British morale on the Ridge soared after Nicholson's arrival and the victory at Najafgahr. Inside Delhi, Bakht Khan, a professional artillery-man, knew only too well that the city's ancient walls could not withstand a prolonged battering by modern siege guns and, for the first time, a profound sense of unease pervaded the counsels of the rebel leaders. On 30 August an envoy arrived in the British camp, offering terms hedged with conditions; he was sent packing without so much as a promise that even the King's life would be spared.

On 3 September the lighter elements of the siege train began to come in, followed by the heavy guns, including six 24pdrs, eight 18pdrs, four 10in and four 8in mortars, the following day. With them were carts carrying 1,000 rounds of ammunition per gun and a corresponding number of charges, the whole forming a convoy which covered more than thirteen miles of road. Wilson, desperately worried by the prospect of failure, was still reluctant to mount an assault. Baird Smith, his Chief Engineer, pointed out that the British strength had now reached its probable peak and that unless an assault were launched promptly disease and the constant attrition would cause it to fall; the Delhi Field Force, in fact, would be unlikely to find itself in as favourable a position again. While the two debated the issue, Nicholson visited every position along the Ridge. Of commanding stature, he radiated such confidence and strength that the troops soon began talking openly of him as The General. This caused some annoyance among older officers who were aware that the 35-year-old John Nicholson's substantive rank was captain, that he was a lieutenant-colonel by brevet only and that his brigadier-general's appointment was temporary and acting; some, because of his long attachment to the Political Service, made scathing references to *Mister* Nicholson. He ignored them, making clear his iron determination that Delhi would be stormed. 'It is absolutely essential that this should be done at once,' he said to the future Field Marshal Lord Roberts, then serving as a subaltern in the Bengal Artillery. 'And if Wilson hesitates longer I intend to propose at today's meeting that he should be superseded.' Roberts remarked that such a course of action would leave Nicholson himself the senior officer with the Force. Nicholson answered that he had not overlooked the fact, but intended proposing someone else for command, under whom he would gladly serve to avoid accusations of personal advancement. Whether he was by temperament capable of serving under a junior in such circumstances remains an academic question, for Wilson reluctantly agreed to an assault, with the reservation that Baird Smith should be answerable if it failed.

Baird Smith was to be responsible for the technical aspects of breaching the walls, while Nicholson was to lead the main attack. The first phase, the occupation of no man's land, was completed without difficulty because, between their attacks, the rebels tended to withdraw inside the city walls. The gabions, fascines, gun platforms and other siege material had been prepared in advance and were brought forward to the battery sites by camels and bullocks, followed by the guns, under cover of darkness. The work of establishing the batteries was carried out under heavy fire which caused severe casualties among the Indian labourers recruited by the Sappers and Miners, but by the morning of 8 September No. 1 Battery, located 700 yards in advance of Hindu Rao's House and the same distance from the Moree Bastion at the north-western angle of the city walls, was in action. The battery was sub-divided into two sections, one with five guns and a howitzer to destroy the Moree Bastion, and the other with four guns to engage the Kashmir Bastion. The mutineers responded with heavy fire from the walls, punctuated with attacks on the battery itself, but were driven off. By the evening the Moree Bastion had been reduced to a heap of smashed masonry and jumbled cannon. No. 2 Battery, sited forward of Ludlow Castle, contained eighteen guns, half to engage the Kashmir Bastion and half to breach the curtain wall between it and the Water Bastion beside the Jumna; No. 3 Battery, positioned only 160 yards from the walls near the Old Custom House, engaged the Water Bastion itself; and a mortar battery, located in the grounds of the Kudsia Bagh, provided supporting fire along the front.

Unable to withstand the sustained hammering, the red walls crumbled, sending hundreds of tons of shattered stone thundering into the ditch below. Nevertheless, the rebels fought back hard, inflicting 327 casualties on the besiegers during the next seven days. On 13 September it appeared that the breaches were wide enough to permit an assault and shortly after dusk two patrols commanded by engineer officers carried out a detailed reconnaissance under fire which confirmed that it would be possible for infantry to scale the steep slopes of jumbled rubble. Wilson decided to stake all on an attack at first light the following morning.

Every man who was not completely incapacitated by wounds or sickness reported for duty with the five assault columns, which were made up as follows:

No. 1 Column (Brigadier-General John Nicholson)
75th (Gordon) Highlanders
1st Bengal Fusiliers (European)
2nd Punjab Infantry
Total 1,000

No. 2 Column (Brigadier-General William Jones)
8th (The King's) Regiment
2nd Bengal Fusiliers (European)
4th Sikhs
Total 850

No. 3 Column (Colonel George Campbell)
52nd (Oxfordshire & Buckinghamshire) Light Infantry
Kumaon Gurkha Battalion
1st Punjab Infantry
Total 950

No. 4 Column (Major Charles Reid)
Sirmoor Gurkha Battalion
Guides Infantry
Dogras and assembled picquets
Total 850 plus 1,000 men of the Kashmir Contingent in reserve

No. 5 Column (Brigadier-General Longfield)
61st (Gloucestershire) Regiment
4th Punjab Infantry
Baluchi Battalion
Rajah of Jheend's Contingent
Total 1,300

During the assault, most of the cavalry and the horse artillery was to form up on the right of No. 1 Battery as a counter to enemy sorties through the Lahore Gate. The Ridge itself and the Camp was held by the sick, a handful of cavalrymen and such artillery as had not been moved forward to support the assault. Nicholson's plan was for No. 2 Column to storm the breach near the Water Bastion while he led No. 1 Column through the main breach at the Kashmir Bastion; No. 3 Column, led by a 'forlorn hope' party which was to blow in the Kashmir Gate, was to penetrate the city as far as the Jumma Musjid mosque. Apart from this, further action was left to the initiative of commanders on the spot, although the rallied Nos. 1 and 2 Columns were to move to their right along the walls and admit No. 4 Column at the Kabul Gate. No. 5 Column was to be committed as necessary. Conscious that a mere 5,000 men were attacking a force still in excess of 30,000, Nicholson did not wish the latter to fight with the desperation of the trapped and intentionally left them a golden bridge along which they could escape through the southern gates of the city.

In darkness the columns marched down from the Ridge and formed up behind Ludlow Castle and the Kudsia Bagh, awaiting the order to advance. Here, shortly after midnight, the last orders were given: the wounded must lie and take their chance where they fell until after the battle, because men could not be spared from the ranks to help them; likewise, no prisoners would be taken as there was no one available to guard them; women and children were not to be harmed; plundering was forbidden, but such items as were acquired were to be added to the common stock for fair division. The officers were required to swear on their swords that they would abide by these orders, and the troops promised to follow their example. Shortly after, the Roman Catholic Chaplain, Father Bertrand, approached Lieutenant-Colonel Herbert, commanding the 75th Highlanders, and received his permission to bless the regiment. 'We may differ, some of us, in matters of religion,' said Bertrand. 'But the blessing of an old man and a clergyman can do nothing but good.' To the ranks of bare, bowed heads it was a comfort to hear the priest invoke the blessing of Heaven on those who would survive and its infinite mercy on those would not, but it was also a reminder that not all of them would return from what would inevitably degenerate into brutal, vicious, close-quarter street-fighting. Not many of them were able to sleep in the short hours remaining before the assault began.

Between 03.30 and 04.00 the columns began moving steadily forward into a wall of thundrous sound and livid explosions created by the covering fire of the siege guns and the enemy's reply. Suddenly, the word was passed for the men to lie down. As the light grew stronger it had become apparent that during the night the rebels had done what they could to close the breaches with sandbags and had replaced some of their damaged guns, so that further time was needed for the siege batteries to blow these new defences apart. The minutes ticked away as the nerves of the waiting infantry were stretched to breaking point, but gradually the firing died away to be replaced by a silence heavy with menace. The sun was now up, and the assault columns were in clear view of those on the walls.

At a signal from Nicholson the columns' skirmishers, 200 men of the 60th Rifles, rose and trotted forward across the open ground towards the ditch. Here and there a man dropped but the remainder did not halt until they reached their firing positions along the upper edge of the glacis, where they began to pick off defenders on the walls. With a tremendous cheer Nos. 1 and 2 Columns surged forward, led by parties with scaling ladders. The enemy's guns had been silenced, but the rebels were standing three and four deep along the ramparts, which were ablaze with musketry. Three-quarters of the ladder parties were shot down, their burdens snatched up by others who ran on towards the ditch. Dead or alive, men tumbled down the counterscarp to the bottom under a fire which one officer described as 'like a hissing sheet of hail'. Then came the horrifying discovery that the ladders were too short unless placed on the berm, which was itself too narrow to hold them. Hundreds died during the frantic minutes it took to pile rubble and the bodies of comrades into heaps on which the ladders could be placed, work carried out under a rain of masonry blocks thrown by those above. The fury of the attackers, however, was not to be denied. Scrambling up the ladders, or crawling hand over hand up the debris of the breaches, they came face to face with the rebels and drove them off the walls in savage hand-to-hand fighting.

Meanwhile, Campbell's No. 3 Column had advanced from Ludlow Castle towards the Kashmir Gate, led by its 'forlorn hope'. This consisted of Bengal Sappers and Miners and was commanded by Lieutenants Duncan Home and Philip Salkeld of the Bengal Engineers, the latter of whom had succeeded in making his escape when the Delhi garrison mutinied in May. The plan was that Home and three men would each place a 25-pound sack of gunpowder against the gate, leaving the fuzes exposed; Salkeld and six men would then tamp down the charges with sandbags and light the fuzes with a portfire. Attached to the party was Bugler Robert Hawthorne of the 52nd, whose task was to sound the Advance for the column as soon as the gate had been blown in.

Few expected any of the 'explosion party', as it was called, to survive. Yet, to a limited extent, luck was with them. As Home's group broke cover, the mutineers on the walls were so taken aback by their sudden appearance that they were able to cross the partially wrecked timber bridge unharmed. By the time Home had dumped his bag, however, the enemy were fully aware of his intentions and opened a heavy fire from above and through a wicket in the main gate, killing Sergeant Andrew Carmichael and seriously wounding Havildar Madho. Sergeant John Smith picked up their charges and put them in place, coolly checking the position of the fuzes.

Salkeld's party were now crossing the bridge with their tamping bags. Salkeld was about to light the fuzes when he was hit first in the leg, then in the arm. Before he fell from the bridge into the ditch, where Home and Hawthorne had already jumped to give his group room to work, he handed the portfire to Corporal Burgess, not knowing it had gone out. Burgess asked Smith for a box of matches but was hit in turn. Havildar Tillok Singh was mortally wounded as he helped him off the bridge and Sepoy Ram Heth was killed. Now the only survivor within reach of the charges, Smith applied a match to a fuze and, observing that it was burning too fiercely, attempted to jump clear. The tremendous explosion blew him into the ditch amid a cascade of shattered timber and broken brickwork, but he escaped with a bruised leg. As the dust and smoke cleared, Home could see that the right-hand door had been blown off its hinges and he ordered Hawthorne to sound the Advance three times.

Some sources suggest that, amid the din of battle, the call was not heard. In fact Colonel Campbell, lying in the cover of a stone wall 100 yards from the gate, was uncertain, but Bugler Johnson, his orderly bugler, ran forward several yards until he could positively identify the notes. The 52nd's leading company, led by Captain J. A. Bailey, quickly rushed the gate, forcing their way through the narrow gap to find that most of the defenders had been killed or incapacitated by the explosion; some lay around a loaded cannon under the archway, clearly intended to blow away the leading ranks with a double charge of grapeshot. The rest of the column followed, including a small party of sappers under Lieutenant George Chesney, also of the Bengal Engineers, which removed the now fallen door and used it as a new deck for the damaged bridge, thereby enabling artillery to enter the city and support the fiercely embattled infantry.

Beyond the Kashmir Gate lay a wide square known as the Main Guard, from which the rebels had fled. In this the three assault columns rallied and were joined by the reserves before moving off through the warren of streets, Nos. 1 and 2 westwards towards the Kabul Gate, No. 3 southwards towards the Jumma Masjid mosque. In every case the advance was bitterly contested by the rebels, who fired from loopholed houses, rooftops and side alleys. In the face of increasingly tough resistance, the euphoria engendered by the early successes began to evaporate. Wilson, watching the assault from the roof of Ludlow Castle, was seriously alarmed by a potentially disastrous situation which had developed on his right, where Major Reid's No. 4 Column was to have advanced through the heavily fortified suburb of Kishengunj to the Kabul Gate. From the start, almost everything possible had gone wrong for Reid. The guns he had been promised to support his advance had not arrived. The raw Kashmiri contingent had launched a premature attack on rebel troops which it believed were fleeing from the city, and had been routed. Encouraged, the rebels began pouring through the Kabul and Lahore Gates to counter-attack the main body of the column. At the critical moment Reid was wounded and his successors issued contra-dictory orders, with the result that the column was driven back in confusion towards the Ridge. For a while a real possibility existed that the enemy might swarm on to the Ridge itself, or swing right across the rear of the columns which had fought their way into the city. They were held in check only by the thin screen of Major Henry Tombs' troop of Bengal Horse Artillery and the cavalry. Tombs' gunners fired until their barrels glowed, but the cavalry, unable to charge because of gardens to their front and unwilling to retire because that would expose the guns to capture, could only sit and endure the hail of musketry and gunfire not only from the rebels facing them, but also from the western city walls. The situation eased somewhat when Jones's No. 2 Column stormed the Moree Bastion and the Kabul Gate from within, but was only brought under control when the Guides' Infantry, followed by the Baluchi Battalion, arrived to push the enemy back. The engagement, which had lasted several hours, cost Tombs 27 of his 48 gunners plus nineteen horses, while among the cavalry the 9th Lancers alone sustained 42 casualties, a quarter of their strength, and lost 61 horses.

Back in the city Campbell's No. 3 Column, much reduced in strength, had fought its way to within sight of the Jumma Musjid only to find that the mosque's gates were closed and its arches bricked up and sandbagged. Lacking artillery or demolition charges, Campbell was unable to mount an assault. There was no news of the other columns and he became worried that his men would be cut off deep within enemy-held territory. With great reluctance he withdrew, first to the Begum Bagh (Queen's Garden), which he held for thirty minutes under heavy fire, then to the area of St James's Church.

Nicholson had meanwhile joined Jones at the Kabul Gate. His next objective was the Lahore Gate, at one end of Delhi's principal street, the Chandni Chowk, but the only way forward lay along a narrow lane passing between the city walls to the right and flat-roofed houses with parapets, held by mutineers, to the left; within the lane itself were two cannon, about 100 yards apart, and beyond this was the Burn Bastion, which mounted several more guns. Twice the 1st Bengal Fusiliers charged into the lane, and twice they were repulsed, losing eight officers and fifty men. The correct street-fighting solution would have been to break through and clear each of the houses on the left in turn, but that would have been a lengthy process and Nicholson was in a hurry. Shouldering his way to the head of the column, he called for another effort. For the moment, however, the exhausted fusiliers had had enough and only the brigade major and a few of their officers followed him, hugging the wall to the left. Finding himself almost alone, Nicholson stepped out into the lane to wave the rest on, and while so doing he was shot in the right side by a sepoy on a roof above. He was quickly pulled into cover and taken to the rear, fully conscious and aware that the wound was mortal.

During the afternoon Wilson moved his command post from Ludlow Castle to St James's Church. This had been thoroughly desecrated by the mutineers, who had used hammers to shatter the marble memorial slabs and had thrown down the bells. It was in this hollow shell, with stained glass shards from the gaping windows ankle-deep on the floor, that senior officers met in sombre mood to discuss the next step. The facts before them were depressing. Reid's No. 4 Column had been defeated, Nicholson was dying, and there was an apparently endless stream of doolie-bearers carrying wounded from the city to the nightmare hospital on the Ridge, where vultures had begun to circle above the growing piles of severed limbs. As far as could be ascertained, about a quarter of Delhi was now in British hands, the cost being 66 officers and 1,104 men killed or wounded, approximately a quarter of those involved in the assault. To Wilson, the obvious projection was that his command would be fought to destruction, and he tentatively raised the subject of withdrawal. Baird Smith and others argued strenuously against the idea. Conscious that the ultimate responsibility was his, Wilson remained silent, thoughtfully stroking his goatee beard until a subaltern handed him a brandy. Draining the glass, the General reached his decision: 'You are quite right – to retire would be to court disaster! We will stay where we are!'

Elsewhere, the attackers had broken into the abandoned stores of the city's wine merchants. After the terrible ordeals of the day it was inevitable that spent men should seek to deaden their torn nerves; it was also inevitable that the process should degenerate into excess, with the result that for 36 hours the entire force was incapable of further action. Some accounts suggest that Bakht Khan and others, understanding the British soldier's fondness for drink, had deliberately placed temptation in his way. If this were true, it was incredible that the rebels, instead of mounting a counter-attack which would have produced excellent results, left their opponents severely alone. Somewhat late in the day, Wilson ordered the destruction of the remaining liquor stocks.

By the morning of 16 September the force, somewhat hung-over, had consolidated its position and was ready to resume its advance. In the main, this was a slow business involving methodical clearance house by house. There were, however, signs that the mutineers' morale had begun to crack. The suburb of Kishengunj, so long a thorn in the side of those on the Ridge, had been abandoned the previous night, and the Magazine, the walls of which had been breached by siege guns brought into the city, was stormed without difficulty; inside was an artillery park containing 171 guns and howitzers and a large quantity of ammunition. Civilians were permitted to leave the city although as a precaution women were required to unveil; a number of the latter were found to be rebels in disguise and given short shrift.

The following day the process continued. Hundreds of bodies lay decomposing in streets, gardens and houses, producing an unforgettable stench that mingled with the smoke of fires that had broken out in several places. Wilson's infantry strength had dropped to about 3,000 dog-tired, hungry, dirty men who were becoming stale. This became evident on the 18th, when troops advancing along a series of winding alleys towards the Lahore Gate were temporarily checked and refused to go any further, knowing that they would be exposed to a heavy crossfire once they reached the Chandni Chowk. Their commanding officer could hardly believe that they were the same men who had fought their way through the breaches a few days earlier. Yet, as James Leasor points out in *The Red Fort*, 'That was the trouble; they were.' They had drawn too deeply on their reserves of courage and required time to replenish them.

On the 19th the Burn Bastion was captured by *coup de main*; the Lahore Gate fell similarly next morning. Jones divided his column, sending half on to the Ajmir Gate and half up the Chandni Chowk to the Jumma Musjid mosque, both of which were taken after a brief struggle. It was now apparent that organized resistance was at an end and, while many rebels remained in the city, most had availed themselves of Nicholson's golden bridge and made good their escape, either to the south or across the Jumna. Wilson turned his attention to the Red Fort, which had been under fire from the siege guns for several days. As a partial reward for his services at the Kashmir Gate, Duncan Home was selected for the dangerous honour of blowing in the palace gate. When the smoke from the blast cleared, the storming parties charged into the courts and halls beyond, killing the few diehards who had chosen to remain. With this the capture of Delhi was virtually complete and a salute was fired from the walls of the palace to signal the fact.

One major act in the drama remained. It consisted of two scenes and in each the principal actor was Major William Hodson, the commander of the famous irregular cavalry unit which bore his name, who was also serving as Wilson's intelligence officer. Like Nicholson, Hodson was a man of action with strong personal convictions and great powers of leadership, but in every other respect the two men provided a complete contrast. The cheerful and high-spirited Hodson, for example, enjoyed fighting for its own sake, whereas the dour Nicholson did so because he believed he was performing God's work. Hodson's agents informed him that Bahadur Shah had declined to accompany Bakht Khan when the latter left the city and had fled with his family to the tomb of the Emperor Hamayun, six miles' distant. Despite this, Wilson was not prepared to leave so important a figurehead at large and on the 21st Hodson was sent out with fifty of his troopers to offer the King his life on condition that he surrendered immediately. The area of the mausoleum was surrounded by thousands of demoralized but dangerous mutineers who closed round Hodson's little group while Bahadur Shah considered the offer. After two extremely tense hours the Queen, Begum Zeenat Mahal, emerged, followed by the King who, having been assured of his safety, handed over his sword. Followed by the sullen mob for most of the way, Hodson escorted the royal party back to Delhi.

He had received further information that the Princes Mirza Moghul, Mirza Kishere Sultanet and Abu Bukht, a grandson of the King's, were also hiding in Hamayun's tomb. All three had actively supported the mutineers and connived at their atrocities, and could easily become the focus of further enemy activity, yet Wilson was curiously indifferent to Hodson's suggestion that they should be apprehended. At length he agreed reluctantly, adding, 'Don't let *me* be bothered with them!' Hodson set off again, this time with 100 troopers and one of the royal nephews who had been promised his life if he co-operated. Having been sent into the mausoleum with a message that the Princes would be taken back to Delhi dead or alive, the man returned after half an hour to ask whether their lives would be spared if they gave themselves up. Hodson retorted that he would accept nothing less than their unconditional surrender. The tension became unbearable as the huge crowd of mutineers began shouting for the Princes to lead them in an attack. The latter, however, had no stomach for a fight and sent out the messenger to confirm that they would surrender.

Shortly after, they emerged in a bullock cart, dressed in their finery. Detaching ten men as an escort, Hodson sent them off along the track to Delhi, drawing up the remainder of his troops across the road to prevent the rebels following. In a colossal piece of bluff, the thin line of scarlet-turbaned troopers faced down the angry crowd in silence, edging forward very slowly until it had been pushed back inside the grounds of the tomb. Then, accompanied only by his Second-in-Command, Lieutenant MacDowell, and four others, Hodson rode up the steps and through the entrance arch, commanding the mutineers to lay down their arms. There was a moment of sullen muttering, during which MacDowell felt that he had never been in greater danger in his life. Hodson peremptorily repeated the order. To MacDowell's amazement ('God knows why, I can never understand it!') the rebels did as they were told.

Hodson was buying time for the cart to get on its way. After two hours spent collecting the weapons, he set off on the return journey to Delhi. Reaching the suburbs, he caught up with the cart not a minute too soon, for it was surrounded by an angry mob bent on effecting a rescue and the escort was in difficulty. This time he knew that bluff would not work and, taking a carbine from a trooper, he shot the prisoners dead. Their bodies were displayed for three days at the spot where some of the mutineers' worst atrocities had taken place. The action aroused deep controversy, largely because it lacked the sanction of the judicial process yet, high-handed as it was, it deprived the rebel cause of its chosen leaders, however decadent they might have been.

From start to finish, the capture of Delhi had cost the Field Force 992 killed, 2,795 wounded and thirty missing, a total of 3,817 which included 1,677 Indian soldiers. It is impossible to say how many mutineers and their supporters were killed during the siege, but the number was far greater; more were tried and executed following the fall of the city. For days Delhi was given over to plunder, yielding everything from the Colours, mess plate and drums of the mutinous regiments to boxes of gold and jewels. By the time the official Prize Agents got to work much of the best had already gone, despite which they managed to amass property valued at £750,000 for ultimate distribution.

Delhi had been a battle which neither side could afford to lose. Much hard fighting remained, including the relief of Lucknow and a hard-fought campaign in Central India, but after Delhi was lost the fortunes of the rebels continued to decline until by the spring of 1859 the last few scattered bands had been eliminated. Bahadur Shah was tried by court-martial and convicted, *inter alia*, of causing the murder of 49 European women and children. He was sentenced to exile and transported to Rangoon, where he died in 1862.

Archdale Wilson was confirmed in his rank, awarded a knighthood and a baronetcy, received the formal thanks of the Commons, the Lords and the East India Company and was granted an additional pension of £1,000 per annum for his services at Delhi. He was present at the capture of Lucknow but left India in April 1858 and did not return.

John Nicholson finally succumbed to his wound on 23 September, knowing that Delhi had fallen; at one period he had seriously considered shooting Wilson if the latter had not continued the attack. His wild Multani tribesmen, who believed that a man who wept should be flogged by women, flung themselves down beside his grave and cried like children. To subsequent generations Nicholson became known as the Hero of Delhi, a title which not even his detractors could deny him since it was he who became the driving force of the siege, he who had seen the siege train safely through and he who led the decisive assault. His statue stood near the Kashmir Gate until, after Independence, the Indian Government proposed to demolish it; instead, it was shipped to Ulster and re-erected in Lisburn where his family had lived and where his memory is still honoured.

A total of 43 Victoria Crosses was awarded for acts of valour during the operations which resulted in the capture of Delhi. Of the 'explosion party' which blew in the Kashmir Gate, Lieutenants Duncan Home and Philip Salkeld, Sergeant John Smith and Bugler Robert Hawthorne all received the award. Home was killed by a premature explosion while demolishing a captured enemy fort at Malagarh, only eleven days after Delhi had fallen. Salkeld never recovered from the wounds he had received and died on 10 October 1857. Smith was commissioned into the Bengal Engineers and continued a successful career, dying in 1864. Hawthorne left the Army in 1861, settled down to family life and was employed as a porter by a reputable banking house in Manchester; on his death in 1879 he was accorded a full military funeral. The surviving Indian officers and soldiers of the party received the Order of British India or the Indian Order of Merit, awards that had been instituted nearly twenty years before the Victoria Cross, and, in appropriate cases, promotion or a grant of land.

The Great Mutiny was a tragic episode in which both sides committed acts of which they have good reason to feel ashamed. Because other interests were involved, it was always something more than a mutiny, but it was never, as some Indian politicians were to suggest in the decade prior to Independence, a national war of liberation. Fully half the troops on the Ridge at Delhi were Indian, and without Indian assistance it would have been impossible to contain the rising elsewhere. In a curious way, however, the old prophesy regarding the centenary of

Plassey was fulfilled. Late in 1857 a measure was placed before Parliament transferring responsibility for the government of India from the East India Company to the Crown and when this was enacted the following year the Company ceased to be a power in the land. As part of the process of reconciliation the Indian Army was reorganized, recruiting its fighting regiments among the martial races of the north. It is a measure of the extent to which the grim ghosts of the Mutiny were laid that during the Second World War more than two million Indians volunteered for service with the armed forces of the Crown. Likewise, in the fifty years since Independence, former British officers visiting their old regiments in India or Pakistan have found that they are welcomed as members of the family; naturally, there have been additions to the mess silver, pictures and furniture, but much remains to remind them of their youth, not least traditions born on hard-fought battlefields long ago.

4
FOR WANT OF A NAIL
Little Round Top, 2 July 1863

T
he belief of both sides in their cause was profound, with the result that the American Civil War lasted from 1861 until 1865 and was fought to the bitter end. That the North, with a population of 22 million, should take so long to achieve victory over the South, with a population of only five-and-a-half million, might seem remarkable since it suggests odds of 4:1; the South, however, was able to field a higher proportion of its available manpower since much of its manual labour was carried out by more than three million slaves, so that the actual odds were 5:2, and generally much closer on the battlefield.

Psychologically, the South was the better prepared for war, although it was vulnerable to attrition not only in terms of manpower but also at the economic level; at the industrial level it could not hope to compete. These factors were in the mind of the US Army's General in Chief, Lieutenant General Winfield Scott, when he devised the strategy which became known as the Anaconda Plan. Scott's record of service to the United States had been long and distinguished. The performance of his grey-clad brigade during the War of 1812 is still commemorated by the grey uniforms worn at West Point Military Academy. In more recent years, Scott had achieved victory in the United States' war with Mexico, a war in which many Civil War commanders on both sides served their apprenticeship as junior officers. In 1861, though now aged 74, his intellect remained undimmed. He believed that the war could only be won by the long-term strategy of raising a 300,000-strong army which, when trained, would advance down the Mississippi to the Gulf of Mexico while the US Navy imposed a blockade on Southern ports. The effect of this, he argued, would be to cut the Confederacy in two and squeeze the major part of it into submission. Such a strategy held no appeal for politicians who wanted quick, easy victories and the only part of the plan to be adopted was the naval blockade. In the end, Scott was proved right and the North only began to make real progress when, in one form or another, his plan was put into effect.

During the war's early years politicians were the bane of the Union army. As the pre-war regular army had numbered only 16,367 officers and men, scattered far and wide in coastal defences and along the western frontier, the Union and Confederate armies alike were forced to rely on militia and volunteer regiments raised by their component states.

However, while the Confederacy wisely distributed its 286 resigned regular officers throughout its army, where they became responsible for training and organization, the Union preferred to keep its remaining regulars within their own units. Thus, the North's volunteer regiments were often commanded by politicians and others who sought personal advancement despite their total lack of experience and, in many cases, ability, some being appointed to the absurdly high ranks of brigade or even divisional commander. When battle was joined a number found the life was not to their liking and discovered urgent reasons for leaving; some fell victim to their own incompetence and were thrown out; others liked the life and possessed sufficient clout in Washington for their shortcomings to be overlooked. As if this were not bad enough, the Washington establishment itself was inclined to intrigue against army commanders who failed or were unwilling to pursue the desired political objectives.

For both sides the task of raising the huge armies required was little short of Herculean. In addition to training large numbers of men in the basics of soldiering, there were entire areas of military knowledge that had to be learned from scratch, and it could not be done overnight. These included the technical aspects of artillery and field engineering, staff duties, communications, logistics and medical services, all on a scale which dwarfed anything in previous American military history. The comment of Count Helmuth von Moltke, the Prussian Army's Chief of General Staff, sitting at the hub of a long-established and well-oiled military machine, that the conduct of operations in America resembled two armed mobs chasing each other round the countryside, might have been appropriate to the early months of the war, but it failed to take into account that improvement would be sustained and inevitable. It was not just that the harsh realities of the battlefield ruthlessly exposed defective training and errors inherent in pre-conceived ideas; equally, the American genius for business and organization also played a major part. With experience came knowledge and with both came confidence. Thus, by the summer of 1862 the Union and the Confederacy had produced armies which, while lacking the spit-and-polish of their European counterparts, were just as capable of doing their job. Again, despite their improvised nature, they were not inhibited by the less positive aspects of European tradition, nor by professional officer corps which were instinctively conservative by nature and, because of this, they were more flexible in their approach and more inclined to be innovative in their tactics and use of weapons. Indeed, some aspects of their operations accurately predicted the manner in which warfare would evolve over the next fifty years.

In the summer of 1863 the conflict showed few signs that it would be resolved quickly. The war was being fought on two principal fronts, with varying fortunes. In the west the Union was winning slowly and had almost secured control of the Mississippi along its entire length; only the fortress of Vicksburg remained to the Confederacy and in May it was besieged by Major General Ulysses S. Grant's Army of the Tennessee. In the east, however, the situation was very different. Much of the fighting had taken place in the area between the two respective capitals of Washington, DC, and Richmond, Virginia. Here, despite repeated changes of command, the Union Army of the Potomac was regularly defeated by General Robert E. Lee's Army of Northern Virginia. In August 1862 Lee had carried the war into the North, fighting the bloodiest battle of the war at Antietam on 17 September before retiring into Virginia. On 13 December he inflicted a serious defeat on the Army of the Potomac at Fredericksburg and, when operations recommenced the following spring, he defeated it again at Chancellorsville in a battle that lasted from 1 to 6 May. At this point the Confederate strategy demanded that he should again invade the North, partly to relieve pressure on the defenders of Vicksburg, but mainly with the object of creating such a furore that President Lincoln's administration would succumb to internal demands for the conclusion of a negotiated peace. Lee's plans included the demolition of the bridge over the River Susquehanna at Harrisburg and extensive destruction along the line of the Pennsylvania Railroad, both of which would seriously disrupt Union communications with the western theatre of war, following which he intended capturing Philadelphia, Baltimore or Washington, depending upon circumstances.

Lee was not in good health. In March he had sustained an attack of pericarditis – inflammation and swelling of the pericardium or membranous sac enclosing the heart – which had incapacitated him for a while. He had recovered sufficiently to command at Chancellorsville, but historians have speculated as to the degree to which the after-effects of the disease, including pain and a general slowing down of the system, might have influenced his conduct of the subsequent campaign; and, since he remained silent on the subject, an answer will not be forthcoming. What is certain is that he believed his army was all but invincible, and this was dangerous given its changed nature since Chancellorsville. The change affected the higher command structure and stemmed from the death of the legendary Lieutenant General Thomas (Stonewall) Jackson, mortally wounded when his own pickets mistakenly fired on him during the evening gloom. The loss of Jackson, whom Lee described as '... the finest executive officer the sun ever shone on', was a severe blow to the Confederacy. After the battle Lee reorganized his army into three corps under Lieutenant General James Longstreet (I Corps), Lieutenant General Richard S. Ewell (II Corps) and Lieutenant General Ambrose P. Hill (III Corps), with none of whom he enjoyed the same mutual understanding which had marked his relationship with Jackson. What Lee could not possibly have foreseen was that his Cavalry Division, which had hitherto served him extremely well under the brilliant leadership of Major General J. E. B. Stuart, would play so negative a role in coming events.

On 3 June the Army of Northern Virginia began leaving the Fredericksburg area, marching north-west to cross the Blue Ridge Mountains into the Shenandoah Valley, then northwards. The task of the Cavalry Division was to screen the right flank of the move, but on 9 June it was surprised in its encampments near Brandy Station by Major General Alfred Pleasanton's Union Cavalry Corps. Hitherto the Confederate horsemen, being natural hard riders with a sense of style and dash akin to Prince Rupert's cavaliers, had repeatedly chased their opponents off the field and consequently held them in little regard. On this occasion, however, they barely succeeded in holding their own in what escalated into the biggest cavalry battle of the war.

For Major General Joseph Hooker, commanding the Army of the Potomac, the battle provided proof that Lee was once again marching north. He informed Washington, where the reaction of President Lincoln and Major General Henry Halleck, the Army's current General in Chief, was that he must conform to the movement, keeping his own army between Lee and the capital.

Meanwhile, Stuart's cavalry screened the passes through the Blue Ridge Mountains while Lee's corps marched steadily up the Shenandoah Valley, destroying a Union force at Winchester on the way. Stuart was still smarting from his near defeat at Brandy Station and was seeking an opportunity to restore his prestige. In June 1862 his division had ridden round the entire Army of the Potomac, causing chaos in the process, and now he suggested something very similar. Knowing that Hooker's troops were already on the move, he proposed harassing their rear then swinging north to rejoin the Army of Northern Virginia by a direct route as it closed in on its objectives. Lee accepted the idea conditionally and three of Stuart's five brigades trotted off to the east. Unfortunately for both Lee and Stuart, the information on which the latter had based his plan was out of date. The Army of the Potomac was spread out over many miles of country so that Stuart was forced into a lengthy detour to the south before he was able to cross its rear. Then, when he turned north, he found that Hooker's troops were setting such an unexpectedly good pace that he was compelled to maintain a parallel route through the heart of Maryland. This prevented him from rejoining Lee, who was thus deprived of his army's eyes and ears at the critical moment.

Concurrently, Hooker was having some problems of his own. Lee's first invasion of the North had revealed that the large Union arsenal at Harper's Ferry was indefensible and now Hooker wanted to abandon it and add its 10,000-strong garrison to his army. When his request was denied he tendered his resignation and, since Washington had never forgiven 'Fighting Joe' for the defeat at Chancellorsville, it was accepted.

On 28 June Major General George C. Meade was appointed the Army of the Potomac's fifth commander within a period of ten months.

Meade had commanded V Corps at Fredericksburg and Chancellorsville and had the reputation of being steady if unimaginative and cautious. Essentially a decent man, he was no place-seeker, nor was he interested in factional politics inside or outside the Army, and perhaps it was for these reasons that he was selected by an establishment which suddenly found itself in serious trouble. He said frankly that he did not want the army commander's job, but it was thrust upon him at a time when a decisive action seemed probable and in the circumstances he could hardly refuse.

The Army of Northern Virginia was now within striking distance of its first objective, Harrisburg. On 28 June Ewell's II Corps, in the lead, had one division at Carlisle and another at York, while Longstreet's and Hill's corps had read Chambersburg, where Lee also established his temporary headquarters. Having heard nothing from Stuart, still moving in isolation far to the east, Lee had no idea of his opponents' whereabouts, but that evening a Confederate spy arrived with two important items of intelligence. The first was that Hooker had been replaced by Meade, which worried Lee not at all, and the second was that the Army of the Potomac had reached Frederick, Maryland, and was still marching north, which worried him a great deal. Frederick was much too close for comfort and it had to be assumed that Meade was being regularly informed of the Army of Northern Virginia's movements both by his own cavalry and the local population. Lee therefore decided that, for the moment, further movement against Harrisburg would be suspended and he ordered his corps commanders to concentrate their troops at Cashtown in preparation for a major engagement.

Eight miles to the east of Cashtown lay the sleepy little town of Gettysburg, set in rolling Pennsylvania countryside. Gettysburg was remarkable only in that it contained a Lutheran seminary and was the meeting place of ten roads. Neither commander intended the town to become the focus of a major engagement, but in the summer of 1863 a totally unexpected factor made it so. By this stage of the war most of the Confederate rank-and-file dressed in hard-wearing homespun, butternut grey or brown in colour, supplemented with odd items of uniform and topped off with a comfortable felt slouch hat. Some men wore boots, others brogues, but such was the shortage of both that many marched barefoot. It was, in fact, following a report that Gettysburg contained a footwear warehouse that a brigade was dispatched from Cashtown on 30 June. As it approached it saw that the town was in the possession of Union cavalry. No engagement took place but at the news that their respective armies were again in contact some 97,000 Union troops and 75,000 Confederates began converging on Gettysburg, the former from the south and south-east, the latter from the west, north and north-east.

The ground over which the decisive actions of the subsequent battle took place lies to the south of the town and consists of two low parallel ridges, approximately two-thirds of a mile apart and running from north to south. The western feature is known as Seminary Ridge and the eastern as Cemetery Ridge. At the northern end of Cemetery Ridge is a hill appropriately named Cemetery Hill and from this the ridge extends southwards, losing height steadily as it does so, until it terminates at a steep-sided valley through which a stream called Plum Run passes on a north-east to south-west axis. Across the mouth of the valley is the Devil's Den, an area of gigantic, tumbled boulders deposited there by retreating glaciers in the remote Ice Age. The southern wall of the valley is formed by two hills named Little Round Top and Round Top. The summit and western slopes of Little Round Top consist of granite outcrops with scattered trees and are reminiscent of the English Lake District; the eastern slopes are densely forested, as is most of the saddle connecting the feature with Round Top, and the whole of Round Top itself. As its name suggests, Round Top was the higher of the two hills, although standing timber denied any view from the summit. From the crest of Little Round Top, however, the whole of Cemetery Ridge was visible and within range, rendering it untenable if an enemy succeeded in establishing himself on the hill. Little Round Top was to become the key terrain feature of the battle, although it was not at first recognized as such, partly because neither the existing maps nor its insignificant appearance suggested that it might be so, but mainly because it played no part in the first serious fighting, which took place on 1 July.

This took the form of an encounter battle between the vanguards of the two armies, fought to the north and east of Gettysburg. Both sides rushed reinforcements into the fight and by evening two Union corps had been pushed back through the town and were occupying positions on Cemetery Hill and the northern end of Cemetery Ridge. More and more troops continued to reach the battlefield during the night until, on the morning of 2 July, the formal battle lines had been established.

The Union position offered a sharply refused right flank and therefore resembled a fish-hook. The extreme right of the line was occupied by XII Corps (Major General Henry W. Slocum), then came I Corps (Major General John Newton) on Culp's Hill with its left extending westwards to Cemetery Hill where it joined XI Corps (Major General Oliver O. Howard). At this point the line turned south along Cemetery Ridge, with II Corps (Major General Winfield S. Hancock) in the centre and III Corps (Major General Daniel E. Sickles) holding the Union left flank. Some distance behind Sickles was V Corps (Major General George Sykes) in reserve. VI Corps (Major General John Sedgwick) was still on the road but would reach the field early in the afternoon.

Meade was satisfied that he was occupying a sound defensive position and he had no intention of attacking his more experienced opponent. Sickles, however, whose III Corps occupied the lower southern end of Cemetery Ridge, was not satisfied with his own position and advanced his troops to somewhat higher ground about 1,000 yards to the west, creating a salient, the left flank of which ran back to the Devil's Den. Meade disapproved of the move but, having been presented with a *fait accompli*, merely indicated his displeasure. It is significant that even at this stage he did not suggest that Sickles should assume responsibility for Little Round Top, nor could Sickles have complied with such an order, so thinly were III Corps' ranks stretched after its re-deployment. In fact, the only troops to take any sort of interest in the hill was a Signal Corps detachment who, needing high ground on which to establish their semaphore station, had climbed to the summit and set up their equipment.

The Confederate deployment paralleled that of the Union army. Ewell's II Corps was facing Culp's Hill and Cemetery Hill; III Corps, under Hill, was in position on Seminary Ridge and Longstreet's I Corps was on the point of entering the battle. Longstreet, observing the strength of the Union position, suggested a march to the south which would place the Army of Northern Virginia between Meade and Washington; Meade would have to respond and Lee could defeat him in a defensive battle on ground of his own choosing. Lee, however, felt that a chance existed to inflict crippling damage on Meade's army before it had completed its concentration, and he rejected this sound advice. Instead, his plan required Longstreet's corps to overwhelm the Union left in a concentrated attack which would also overrun the Round Tops and, at the sound of I Corps' artillery going into action, Hill and Ewell would launch attacks against Culp's Hill and Cemetery Hill. For obvious reasons, Lee wished the attack to begin at the earliest possible moment.

Longstreet left the orders group shortly after 11.00 and by noon his divisions had begun to march south from the Chambersburg Pike. After covering somewhat in excess of two miles his leading division crossed the Hagerstown Road and ascended the high ground beyond. Only 1½ miles, some thirty minutes' steady marching, separated I Corps from its forming-up area, but at this point Longstreet realized that he was in full view of the signal station on Little Round Top. Not wishing to forfeit the element of surprise, he ordered his troops to counter-march, then begin their approach afresh using the dead ground provided by the valley of a stream known as the Willoughby Run, which was further screened by the trees on Seminary Ridge. Given that time was of the essence, and that he had already been within striking distance of his objective, such surprise as was achieved cost the priceless 2½ hours it took to complete the manoeuvre and, since I Corps was unable to mount its attack before 16.00, it can therefore be regarded as a hard bargain.

While Longstreet's men had been winding their way through the countryside, doubtless wishing that the generals would make up their minds, a critical development had taken place within the Union lines. At 15.00 Meade held a brief conference with his corps commanders and during this he told Sykes that his V Corps, presently in reserve, was to be responsible for the security of the Union left, which was to be held 'at all

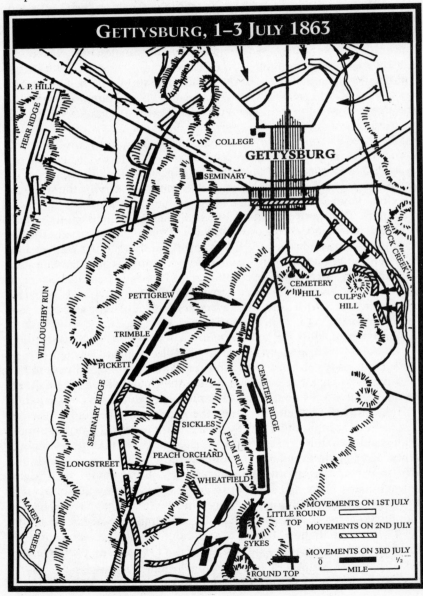

GETTYSBURG, 1–3 JULY 1863

A. P. HILL
HERR RIDGE
COLLEGE
GETTYSBURG
SEMINARY
ROCK CREEK
CEMETERY HILL
CULP'S HILL
PETTIGREW
WILLOUGHBY RUN
TRIMBLE
PICKETT
CEMETERY RIDGE
SEMINARY RIDGE
SICKLES
PLUM RUN
PEACH ORCHARD
LONGSTREET
WHEATFIELD
MAREN CREEK
MOVEMENTS ON 1ST JULY
LITTLE ROUND TOP
MOVEMENTS ON 2ND JULY
SYKES
MOVEMENTS ON 3RD JULY
ROUND TOP
0   ½
MILE

hazards'. Sykes dispatched one of his staff officers with orders that the corps should move into a position behind Little Round Top.

Shortly after the conference dispersed Meade and his staff rode along Cemetery Ridge above the advance positions adopted by Sickles' III Corps. Pausing, Meade pointed out Little Round Top to his Chief Engineer, Major General Gouverneur K. Warren, commenting that he '. . . could hear a little peppering going on in the direction of the little hill off yonder', and asked him to go and investigate. Just then, nothing was going on and the peppering was simply a trick of sound reflecting the fire of the skirmishers who were active between the two armies. Nevertheless, Warren rode to the summit and looked around. In addition to being a qualified engineer, he was an experienced brigade commander and it was immediately apparent that if the Confederates took the hill the whole of the Cemetery Ridge position would have to be abandoned, with disastrous consequences for the Army of the Potomac. At this point the signallers drew his attention to the distant tree line on Seminary Ridge, behind which they suspected enemy movement. Down in Devil's Den, at the extreme left of Sickles' line, was Captain James Smith's 4th Battery, New York Light Artillery. Warren asked Smith to fire a round in the direction of the trees and observed the result:

'As the shot went whistling through the air the sound of it reached the enemy's troops and caused everyone to look in the direction of it. This motion revealed to me the glistening of gun barrels and bayonets of the enemy's line of battle, already formed and far outflanking the position of any of our troops, so that the line of his advance from his right to Little Round Top was unopposed. I have been particular in telling this, as the discovery was intensely thrilling to my feelings, and almost appalling.'

It was now of the utmost importance to get as many troops as possible on to the undefended hill in the little time that was left before the Confederates launched their assault. Warren dispatched one of his staff officers to Meade requesting a division. Meade agreed to the request but then changed his mind when he observed that V Corps was already moving towards Little Round Top. Simultaneously, however, Warren had also sent another of his officers, Lieutenant Ranald S. Mackenzie, to Sickles with a request for a brigade. Sickles hadn't a man to spare, but nearby Mackenzie found Sykes, who was in II Corps' area examining how best to tie in his own corps to its left flank. Sykes, mindful of Meade's instructions, agreed immediately and ordered Brigadier General James Barnes, commanding his First Division, to make the necessary troops available. Barnes promptly ordered Colonel Strong Vincent's Third Brigade on to the hill.

While his regiments marched towards Little Round Top, Vincent rode ahead with his orderly to carry out a detailed reconnaissance. Aged only 26, he was a lawyer by profession and despite his lack of military experience prior to the war he had become a very capable officer who insisted on strict discipline yet retained the liking of his men. He reached the summit as Sickles' artillery began trading rounds with Longstreet's, some of the latter's shells splintering trees as the brigade toiled upward through the woods on the reverse slope. The Confederates had already emerged from the distant line of timber and the signallers were passing details of their advance back to Meade's headquarters. Just below the summit Vincent found a natural terrace on the south-eastern slopes, following the line of the hill round towards the saddle connecting the Round Tops, descending gradually as it did so and ending amid the trees. As his regiments arrived he posted them along this line with the 16th Michigan on the right, the 44th New York and 83rd Pennsylvania in the centre and the 20th Maine on the left. To Colonel Joshua Chamberlain, a former university professor and preacher now commanding the 20th Maine, Vincent emphasized that his regiment must hold its ground whatever the cost. As it reached its position, each regiment pushed forward one company to act as skirmishers. On the right, two companies of the 16th Michigan extended the line loosely down the slope towards Devil's Den, where Smith's battery was already heavily engaged and the 4th Maine, on the extreme left of III Corps, was taking up position.

It was now approximately 16.30. Vincent sent one of his staff officers, Captain Eugene Nash, to the summit of Round Top. Nash could see the enemy advancing across the fields towards Devil's Den but the trees screened all other movement. He reached the top and climbed on to a rock to obtain a better view when suddenly a volley of shots cracked past his ears. On the Round Tops sector the Confederates were much closer than anyone had expected and soon Vincent's skirmishers were engaged along the brigade's front. To the left the 20th Maine's skirmishers, consisting of the regiment's Company 'B' reinforced by a dozen green-clad riflemen from the regular 2nd Sharpshooters, were also climbing Round Top when firing broke out and their commander, Captain Walter Morrill, pulled them back to the saddle and emplaced them behind a stone wall which ran along its length; while this separated the company from the main body of its regiment, it proved to be one of the decisive deployments of the battle.

Some accounts of Gettysburg describe Longstreet's troops as fresh, although the term is relative. They had not been involved in the previous day's fighting, but on 2 July they had marched the 24 miles from New Guilford at a cracking pace and then gone straight into action, so they were understandably tired. However, it was Major General John B. Hood's division which had been detailed to attack the extreme left of the Union line, including the Round Tops, and his division was one of the most formidable in Lee's army. Hood had decided to attack on a two-brigade frontage with Brigadier General Evander M. Law's all-Alabama brigade on the right and Brigadier General Jerome B. Robertson's mainly

Texas brigade on the left. Law was a year older than Vincent, possessed a similar temperament and had also studied law, although he had the advantage of having graduated from a military school. Robertson, aged 48, was a qualified physician but was also a wild frontier spirit who had served in the Texas War of Independence and fought Indians in his youth.

Both brigades formed for the attack in the shelter of Seminary Ridge. Law had five Alabama regiments in line with the 48th on the right, then the 44th, 15th, 47th in the centre and the 4th on the left, giving an approximate strength of 1,500. His scouts had informed him that Round Top was unoccupied and his plan was that, once across Plum Run, the entire brigade would pivot on the 4th Alabama and wheel half-left across the slopes of the hill towards Little Round Top, no easy matter given the broken nature of the slopes and their heavy covering of timber. Robertson's brigade, 1,100 strong, had the 5th Texas on the right, the 4th and 1st Texas in the centre and the 3rd Arkansas on the left; its tasks were to remain in close contact with Law's brigade and to maintain its left on the Emmitsburg Road until the latter had been crossed by McLaw's division, attacking on Hood's left.

In the forming-up area some casualties were incurred from Union artillery fire, but when they moved off both brigades were clearly eager to close with the enemy despite their weariness; this was particularly evident in Law's brigade, which set so rapid a pace that it had to be checked. A 700-yard advance lay ahead, taking the division across open farmland where the only obstacles were two undefended farms and some stone walls and fences which disordered the ranks only briefly while they were negotiated. Both Law and Robertson pushed forward about a tenth of their strength as skirmishers and these men were soon in contact with their opposite numbers from Vincent's brigade, pushing them steadily back.

Luck, however, was not riding with the Confederates at Gettysburg. The Union guns were still blowing gaps in the advancing ranks and Law, identifying the principal source of trouble as Smith's battery in Devil's Den, above which a pall of smoke was hanging, was determined to eliminate it and gave orders that were to affect the course of the subsequent struggle for Little Round Top. His two right-hand regiments, the 48th and 44th Alabama, were advancing towards the southern slopes of Round Top and meeting little or no opposition. He decided, therefore, to shift them to his left flank and direct them into Devil's Den. This could only be achieved by both regiments halting then filing north after the rest of the brigade had passed and meant that, when the moment came, they would make their assault echeloned back to the left. At this point, however, a further factor intervened. Robertson observed that Law's brigade was inclining slightly to its right and, deciding that his first priority was to maintain contact with its left flank, ordered the 4th and

5th Texas to conform. The result of this was to open a gap in the centre of his own brigade as the 1st Texas and 3rd Arkansas continued to advance on Rose's Woods at the southern end of Cemetery Ridge, but into the gap moved the 48th and 44th Alabama, who had just completed their redeployment. The overall effect of these moves, therefore, was inextricably to mix the two brigades just as they were about to strike the enemy position.

At this very moment a shell burst above Hood, riding in the centre of his division. It wounded him so severely that he could not continue and

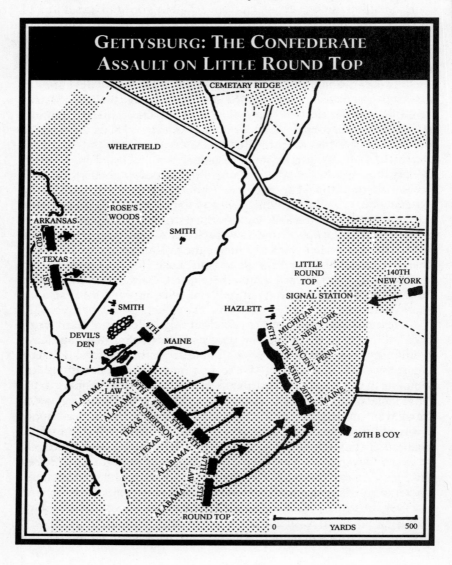

Law, the senior brigade commander, was summoned to replace him. Command of his brigade should have devolved immediately on Colonel James Sheffield of the 48th Alabama, but the better part of two hours were to pass before Sheffield was informed of the fact, and by then the issue had been decided. The situation on Little Round Top was further confused by the intermingling of the two brigades, for the officers of neither had the authority to issue orders to troops from the other. Hindsight might suggest that Law's failure to appoint an overall commander of the troops on the hill was one of the major mistakes of the battle, but this is not altogether fair. If Meade's troops had failed to appreciate the importance of Little Round Top until the final minutes of the eleventh hour, it is unreasonable to expect Law to have grasped the significance of so insignificant a feature at first sight. In Law's eyes, therefore, Little Round Top held a lower priority than Devil's Den, which apparently marked the real left flank of the Union line and, as divisional commander, he naturally diverted greater resources against the latter. Therefore, when the division's supporting brigades came up, Benning's was directed into the struggle for Devil's Den in the wake of the 48th and 44th Alabama, while Anderson's, on the left, was committed to the fighting in Rose's Woods.

The opening of the battle for Devil's Den is described by Colonel William Perry of the 44th Alabama in his report. 'The direction of the regiment after crossing the [Plum Run and the] stone fence [beyond] was such that a march to the front would have carried it to the right of the enemy's position. It was, therefore, wheeled to the left, so as to confront that position, its left opposite the battery [Smith's], and its right extending toward the base of the mountain [Round Top]. This movement was executed under fire and within 200 yards of the enemy. The forward movement was immediately ordered and was responded to with an alacrity seldom, if ever, excelled on the battlefield. As the men emerged from the forest into the valley they received a deadly volley at short range [from 4th Maine], which in a few seconds killed or disabled one-fourth of their number. Halting without an order from me, and availing themselves of the shelter which the rocks afforded, they returned the fire. Such was their extreme exhaustion that I hesitated for an instant to order them immediately forward. Perceiving very soon, however, that the enemy were giving way, I rushed forward, shouting to them to advance. It was with the greatest difficulty that I could make myself heard or understood above the din of battle. The order was, however, extended along the line and was promptly obeyed. The men sprang forward over the rocks, swept the position and took possession of the heights, capturing 40 or 50 prisoners around the battery and among the cliffs.'

Perry's men were greatly assisted by the 48th Alabama, on their right and higher up the slopes of Round Top. Sheffield's progress was slowed by what he described as '. . . the worst cliffs of rocks there could have been traveled over'. At length, the 48th reached the comparatively open boulder field known today as The Slaughter Pen and suddenly found itself just twenty paces from the left wing of the 4th Maine. The latter swung back its flank and in the process some men observed Vincent's brigade moving into position on Little Round Top. The Fourth opened fire first, and Sheffield, whose troops were also taking casualties from Vincent's skirmishers, was forced to pull back part of his line. However, the 4th Maine's centre companies were being raked by the Alabamians' fire and the regiment fell back and re-formed further up the valley.

Shortly after 17.00 Benning's Georgia regiments entered the fray, passing through the 44th Alabama. Wild and savage fighting ensued among the tangled rocks as Union regiments were committed piecemeal to the struggle. Not all of these were of as high a quality as the 4th Maine, and their counter-attacks to recover the lost ground were contained without difficulty. Smith had deployed his battery with two sections forward and one higher up the valley, and he was compelled to abandon the former under intense pressure, taking with him the guns' rammers and sponges; Brigadier General Henry Hunt, Meade's Chief of Artillery, had anticipated the loss and Smith quite properly escaped censure. When the struggle ended the Confederates were not only in firm control of Devil's Den and the lower Plum Run valley, but had also exposed the undefended northern slopes of Little Round Top; unfortunately for Lee, no officer of sufficient seniority or insight was present to exploit the fact.

Farther south, Law's plan of attack had, for the moment, quite literally fallen apart. Here, the 15th and 47th Alabama, which had originally formed the centre of Law's brigade but were now on its right, were under the immediate control of Colonel William C. Oates, the commanding officer of the former. Oates, now aged 29, had spent his early youth brawling, womanizing and gambling but had reformed, studied and become a lawyer with an established practice. His courage was unquestioned, as was his regard for his men's welfare, but he had received his promotion only weeks before Gettysburg and, still slightly uncomfortable with his increased responsibilities, was inclined to be overly cautious. Law had ordered him to wheel left once he had crossed Plum Run and the wall beyond, thus conforming to the movement of the 4th Alabama. However, Oates' attention was distracted when the enemy skirmishers to his front abandoned the wall and retired straight up the western slopes of Round Top. Believing that they were retiring on a much larger force, to which his right flank would become exposed if he wheeled to the left, he pushed both regiments directly up the hill to the summit. Here, hot and exhausted by their long march, advance under fire and steep climb, they halted and lay down. Quite suddenly, the continuous roar of battle from Devil's Den was swelled by a much closer crescendo of firing to their left front, clearly indicating that heavy fighting was taking place on Little Round Top, although the details remained hidden by the trees.

Law, nonplussed by the disappearance of the two regiments, sent his adjutant, Captain Leigh Terrell, to find out what was happening. Terrell, speaking with all the divisional commander's authority, wiped the floor with Oates, who offered the lame excuse that Round Top could and should be turned into a superb defensive position. Ignoring this, Terrell insisted that he must press on without further delay and complete the capture of Little Round Top. Both regiments climbed stiffly to their feet and set off down the slope towards the saddle connecting the two features. On the way Oates, glancing downwards through the trees to his right, saw lines of Union wagons parked behind the Round Tops and detached a company to capture them. The company returned empty-handed after the battle, having been balked either by 20th Maine's Company 'B' or, more probably, the rallied skirmishers and the wagon guard.

The only regiment to conform with Law's original plan was the 4th Alabama. With the 5th and 4th Texas from Robertson's brigade on their left, they wheeled across the shoulder of Round Top, pushing the enemy skirmishers ahead of them. Emerging from the tree line on the saddle between the two hills, they were immediately confronted by the long blue line of Vincent's brigade, 1,000-strong, emplaced among the rocks below the crest of Little Round Top. Pausing briefly to attend to their dressing, all three regiments advanced up the slope, the Texans whooping and yelling. The advance was shredded by a continuous blast of musketry and, their ranks disordered by boulders strewn across the steep slope, the Confederates halted, returned the fire briefly, then retired. Rallied, they attacked again, this time with a sense of grim determination across ground already strewn with their casualties, but were again repulsed.

Concurrently, an unexpected reinforcement had reached the summit of Little Round Top. Captain Augustus Martin, commanding V Corps' artillery, appreciated the significance of the hill and had ordered Lieutenant Charles E. Hazlett's Battery 'D', 5th US Artillery, to take position on the summit. While the guns were being brought forward, Martin and Hazlett rode to the summit where they met Warren, who was dubious about the idea. The passage of the guns up the tree-covered, rocky slopes was difficult to say the least, the crest itself was too narrow to accommodate the entire battery and the guns could not be depressed sufficiently to engage attackers to their front. Undeterred, Hazlett commented that the sound of his guns in action would encourage Vincent's men and discourage the enemy. The arrival of the guns was in itself something of an epic. One of the horse teams actually hauled its burden to the top, but the remainder were forced to halt some way up the slope. Together, gunners and infantrymen pulled, heaved and lifted the guns one by one on to the summit, then went back for the limbers and caissons which they positioned just behind them on the reverse slope. As soon as each gun was ready it opened fire against the numerous targets visible, including the Confederates in Devil's Den.

Warren, observing the battlefield, noted that the enemy was driving in III Corps' salient and had already taken Devil's Den, whence a sniper's bullet grazed his throat. Realizing that pressure would continue to build up against Little Round Top, he rode down the north slope of the hill to bring up more infantry and, by the greatest good fortune, encountered his old brigade. The brigade commander, Brigadier General Stephen H. Weed, was away conferring with Sykes, and in his absence Colonel Patrick O'Rorke of the 140th New York was in command. Warren, who knew him well, shouted: 'Paddy, give me a regiment!' At first O'Rorke demurred, commenting that the brigade was about to move into the line. 'Never mind that!' replied Warren. 'Bring your regiment up here – don't stop for aligning! I'll take the responsibility!' Knowing that the Army Commander thought highly of Warren, O'Rorke needed no further urging and the 500-strong 140th New York, wearing dark-blue zouave uniforms trimmed with red, set off in a trotting column of fours up the hill. Shortly after, Warren met Sykes and the latter agreed that the remainder of Weed's brigade should also be committed to Little Round Top. Then, his self-appointed task completed, Warren rode on to report to Meade.

Meanwhile, back on the hill the situation had developed very much as Warren had feared. Although Vincent's brigade had already beaten off two attacks it had sustained serious casualties in the process. A steady trickle of walking wounded were leaving the line, as were details seeking to replenish the rapidly dwindling ammunition supply. Now, the brigade faced its sternest test as, their regiments at last concentrated, the Confederates prepared to storm the summit. The 48th Alabama, leaving Devil's Den, joined the left of their line and advanced against the 16th Michigan on Vincent's right. Conforming, the 4th and 5th Texas and 4th Alabama renewed their assault on the centre of the Union position. On the Confederate right the 15th and 47th Alabama had crossed the saddle from Round Top and were bringing tremendous pressure to bear on the 20th Maine. The fighting reached a new level of intensity in what became a grim contest of willpower.

The strength of regiments varied enormously during the war. At Gettysburg, for example, the 16th Michigan had less than 140 men in the line. It seems probable that the 48th Alabama's line extended beyond its own and an order seems to have been given with the intention of wheeling back the regiment's right to the crest, so protecting the brigade's flank. This was misinterpreted and caused such confusion that a panicky subaltern ordered the 16th's Colours to the rear, and with them went 45 men, a third of the regiment's strength, thinking the battle lost. Seeing the Union line apparently beginning to break up, the 48th Alabama surged forward, whooping. In a desperate attempt to relieve the pressure Vincent rallied the remnant of the 16th and ordered the 44th New York to fire into the right of the advancing Alabamians, but hardly had he done so than he was mortally wounded. Command of the brigade passed to Colonel James C. Rice of the 44th New York, who was fortunately on the spot.

At this point the 140th New York came streaming across the summit with O'Rorke at their head shouting: 'Down this way, boys! Here they are, men! Commence firing!' While the new arrivals were forming on the right of the shaken 16th the Confederate attack surged on to within forty feet of the Union line and O'Rorke was shot dead. However, in the close-quarter firefight which raged for several minutes the Alabamians were heavily outnumbered. At length some surrendered and the rest retired down the hill into the trees. Once more the Union right was secure.

In the centre, too, the 44th New York and 83rd Pennsylvania succeeded in holding off the 4th and 5th Texas and 4th Alabama, now attacking unsuccessfully for the third time. Around the shoulder of the hill, however, Colonel Joshua Chamberlain's 20th Maine was fighting for its very life against Oates' two regiments. Of these, the 47th Alabama presented the lesser threat, and its poor performance is reflected in the report prepared by its acting commanding officer, Major James Campbell: 'There was some confusion, owing to the fact that in the charge the lieutenant colonel expected the colonel to give all necessary commands, and the colonel remained so far behind that his presence on the field was but a trammel on the lieutenant colonel'. Fired at frontally by the 20th Maine and raked by the 83rd Pennyslvania from the left, the regiment sustained casualties amounting to one-third of its strength, including the lieutenant colonel seriously wounded, and withdrew across the saddle to Round Top.

The attack of the 15th Alabama, however, was handled very differently. Oates attempted to turn Chamberlain's left, causing the latter to extend his line and bend it back until it presented a right angle; this stretched the 20th Maine so far that it was reduced to a single rank, often with several paces between the men. Theodore Gerrish, who served as a private soldier in the 20th and later became a clergyman, has left a vivid account of the battle.

'Our regiment was mantled in fire and smoke. I wish that I could picture with my pen the awful details of that hour; how rapidly the catridges were torn from the boxes and stuffed in the smoking muzzles of the guns; how the steel rammers clashed and clanged in the heated barrels; how the men's hands and faces grew grim and black with burning powder; how our little line, baptized with fire, reeled to and fro as it advanced or was pressed back; how our officers bravely encouraged the men to hold on and recklessly exposed themselves to the enemy's fire – a terrible medley of cries, shouts, cheers, groans, prayers, curses, bursting shells, whizzing rifle bullets and clanging steel . . . The air seemed to be alive with lead. The lines at times were so near each other than the hostile gun barrels almost touched. As the contest continued, the rebels grew desperate that so insignificant a force should hold them so long in check. . . . Our line is pressed so far that our dead are within the lines of the enemy. . . . Our ammunition is nearly all gone and we are using the cartridges from the boxes of our wounded comrades.'

Others remember the smoke hanging so thickly between the lines that the enemy could only be seen by peering beneath it. At one moment even the immediate roar of battle was drowned by a rising crescendo of musketry round the shoulder of the hill, but neither side could spare men to find out what was happening: this almost certainly marked the 140th New York going into action against the 48th Alabama.

The fight between the 20th Maine and 15th Alabama was too fierce to last without the will of one or the other giving way. Both regiments were losing men fast and their ammunition was running low. As the 47th Alabama had already retired, Oates sent to the 4th Alabama for help, only to be told that this regiment had also left the fight. At about this time he was informed that a body of Union troops, estimated to be some 200 in number, was in position to his right rear, behind the wall running the length of the saddle. This was the 20th Maine's detached Company 'B' which, it will be recalled, had been acting as skirmishers and retired there when they were driven in, although its strength was far below the Confederate estimate. Oates therefore decided to withdraw and passed instructions to his company commanders that when the signal was given their men were simply to turn about and run across the saddle to Round Top and re-form on its summit. It does not seem as if the signal was ever given.

Chamberlain also observed signs that his own men, now down to their last few rounds, were becoming unsettled. Only two choices were open to him – he could withdraw, or he could counter-attack. He chose the latter, gave the order to fix bayonets, and told his left wing to initiate the move, wheeling to the right until it was in line with the rest of the regiment, which would then charge as a body. When the moment came the opposing ranks were some thirty yards apart and Gerrish recalled that Lieutenant Melcher, commanding the Colour company, ran forward waving his sword shouting: 'Come on! Come on! Come on, boys!' The Colour-party itself followed and then the entire regiment launched itself down the slope with a wild yell.

Taken completely aback, the 15th Alabama gave ground. At this point Captain Morrill's Company 'B' fired a volley into their flank, leapt

MINDEN **Above:** Painting by Gordon Mills showing the 25th Regiment (later the King's Own Scottish Borderers) beating off the charge by the Gendarmes (French Household Cavalry). (Courtesy of The King's Own Scottish Borderers) **Below:** One of Lieutenant-General von Spoercken's six British infantry regiments in action against French cavalry at Minden. Although the artist has shown the regiment's grenadiers in their distinctive mitre caps, all the British grenadier companies had been detached from their parent regiments and were engaged on another part of the field near the village of Todtenhausen. (National Army Museum)

Top: The 93rd Highlanders defeat the Russian cavalry probe towards Balaclava harbour. (National Army Museum) **Above:** A staff officer's sketch made from the rear of Lord Raglan's position. The mass of Russian cavalry is crossing Causeway heights from left to right and is about to be charged by the Heavy Brigade. The British cavalry camp can be seen to the rear of the Heavy Brigade's squadrons. The sketch emphasizes the altered perspective of terrain viewed from above; Causeway Heights seem much lower than is in fact the case. (National Army Museum) **Above right:** The Charge of the Heavy Brigade, showing the leading squadron of the Scots Greys about to strike the halted Russian cavalry. It was this action which decided the outcome of the battle, although it has been

somewhat eclipsed by the subsequent Charge of the Light Brigade. (National Army Museum)
Above: A watercolour sketch of the Charge of the Light Brigade by William Simpson. Save for one or two details, the sketch is accurate. The brigade's leading two lines were actually a little closer to the viewpoint than shown, and by this stage of the attack the ranks of the leading regiments had been decimated. The

Heavy Brigade and horse artillery battery are not shown but were halted near the extreme right centre of the picture. Beyond the Light Brigade is Causeway Heights on which two of the redoubts can be seen. (National Army Museum)

DELHI Left: A sketch by Eyre Crow, ARA, showing the 'explosion party' at the Kashmir Gate. (National Army Museum) **Below:** The storming of the Kashmir Gate after the explosion. (*Illustrated London News*)

GETTYSBURG Top right: Little Round Top from the north-west. Round Top, more impressive but of less tactical importance, is on the right of the picture. (Mollus Collection/US Army Military History Institute) **Centre right:** Union artillery in action. (Mollus Collection/ USAMHI) **Below right:** Pickett's Charge nears Cemetery Ridge. (Mollus Collection/USAMHI)

DESERT COLUMN **Top left:**
A panorama of Abu Klea
showing various incidents in
the battle. Pegging down the
camels just inside the firing
lines provided a bulwark that
prevented the square being
broken. Within the square a
reserve company doubles
towards the threatened front.
(National Army Museum)
Below left: Hand-to-hand
fighting at Abu Klea. The
Dervish attack struck the
Desert Column's cavalry contingent which, despite its un-
familiarity with the bayonet,
held its own. (National Army
Museum)

ARRAS **Above:** Only by
deploying all his divisional
artillery, including this medium battery, was Rommel
able to halt 1 Army Tank
Brigade's counter-attack at
Arras. (IWM) **Right:** German
soldiers examine one of 7th
RTR's Matilda IIs, broken
down and abandoned during
the retreat to Dunkirk. At
Arras the Matilda II was the
most formidable tank on the
battlefield; in North Africa it
was to play a major part in
the defeat of the Italian army.
(RAC Tank Museum)

Longstop Hill seen from the mountains to the north-west. Djebel Ahmera is on the right and Djebel Rhar on the left; the ravine between the two is clearly visible. Beyond lies the Medjerda valley. (IWM)
Below left: The 2nd Coldstream Guards pass through the US I/18th Infantry to assault Djebel Ahmera. (IWM) **Below:** Churchill tanks (Mk III left and Mk I right) of the North Irish Horse with infantry on Longstop Hill. (IWM)

NIJMEGEN **Top left:** Assault boats of the type used by the US III/ 504th Parachute Infantry in its supremely courageous crossing of the Waal at Nijmegen. (IWM) **Above:** Shermans of the Guards Armoured Division, including a Firefly armed with a 17pdr gun. North of Nijmegen the terrain prevented the tanks leaving the road and the Germans were able to halt the advance on Arnhem. (IWM) **Below left:** The rail bridge at Nijmegen after the attack by German frogmen, with the road bridge in the background. A motorized raft ferries vehicles back from the northern bank; in mid-stream is a DUKW amphibious cargo carrier. (IWM)

CORREGIDOR **Above:**
The crowded drop zones on
Corregidor's Topside into
which the US III/503rd Para-
chute Infantry jumped on 16
February 1945. (USAMHI)
Right: C-47 aircraft make a
low-level re-supply drop to
American troops on Correg-
idor. (USAMHI) **Top right:**
'Old Glory' climbs the flag-
pole again as the 503rd Para-
chute Infantry parades on
Topside after the battle for
Corregidor. (USAMHI)

GOOSE GREEN **Right:** The terrain over which the battle for Goose Green was fought offered the attackers little or no cover at times. For the British, helicopter lift was severely restricted from the outset. (Crown Copyright)
Below: 105mm Light Gun of the type used by 8 Battery to support 2nd Bn The Parachute Regiment's attack on Goose Green. For both sides, the effect of artillery fire was reduced by the soft peaty soil which absorbed much of the explosive force of shells. (Crown Copyright)

the wall and joined in the charge. Routed, the Confederates were pursued across the saddle and partly up the slopes of Round Top before Chamberlain halted the 20th Maine and led it back to its position. His regiment had started the action 386 strong and lost 135 killed or wounded. Oates reported his loss as seventeen killed, 54 wounded and 90 missing; of the last, most were killed or wounded and captured, some fifty bodies being left on Little Round Top. In total, Law's brigade sustained 496 casualties in its attempts to capture the hill, and to this figure must be added the proportionally heavy losses of the two Texas regiments from Robertson's brigade.

The crisis on Little Round Top was over. The remainder of Weed's brigade (91st Pennsylvania, 146th New York and 155th Pennsylvania) arrived to extend the line on the right of the 140th New York. No further attacks took place, although the hill remained under the fire of snipers who made senior officers their special target. Weed, talking with Sykes near Hazlett's battery, fell mortally wounded; Hazlett, kneeling beside him, was shot through the head. Shortly after, deepening dusk put an end to the firing on both sides.

Elsewhere on 2 July Sickles' III Corps was driven from its salient in bitter fighting which left names like The Peach Orchard and The Wheatfield etched for ever in American military history. During this Sickles lost a leg and Major-General David Birney assumed command of the corps. Longstreet's troops pursued their disordered opponents as far as Cemetery Ridge, although by then they were too exhausted and the day was too far gone for the success to be exploited. To the north, the Confederate holding attack directed at Culp's Hill and Cemetery Hill was made without adequate reconnaissance as well as being unco-ordinated and badly timed. The fighting, while desperate at times, continued until after dark but made little impression on the Union lines and did not prevent Meade moving troops from this sector to support his threatened centre.

That night Meade held a council of war with his corps commanders. All those attending were shocked by the number of casualties incurred, amounting to an approximate total of 9,000. On the other hand, no ground of vital importance had been lost and the Union position was actually stronger than it had been when the day began, both Round Tops now being securely held. It was decided, therefore, that the Army of the Potomac would remain on the defensive the following day. As the conference dispersed Meade predicted that Lee's next major attack would be directed at the right-centre of his line.

There seems to have been little doubt in Lee's mind that the battle should continue, although his thoughts were those of a tired man and lacked the spark of imagination. It was true that his troops had gained ground during the previous two days' fighting, but it was also true that these gains were of no tactical value. None of his senior officers had set foot on the summit of Little Round Top and he probably did not realize until much later that only the capture of this insignificant feature could have dislodged the Union army from Cemetery Ridge on 2 July. Now this one opportunity to achieve a clear-cut victory had gone.

Despite this, he retained confidence in his men's ability to deliver a knock-out blow. The question was, where should it be delivered? Both Union flanks were held in strength so, he reasoned, Meade's weakness must lie in his centre. Furthermore, his own troops on the flanks were exhausted after their efforts on 2 July, but fresh formations were available in the centre of the line so that was the place for the attack, to which 15,000 men would be committed. There were, of course, no logical grounds for assuming that Meade's centre was weak and Longstreet, aware that the attackers would have to cross a mile of open fields in the teeth of the enemy's fire, was convinced that they would be repulsed, and bloodily at that. Instead, he proposed manoeuvring against Meade's sensitive left but Lee, encouraged by the arrival of Stuart's cavalry from Carlisle, would have none of it. The attack would go in as planned and, simultaneously, Stuart's troopers would penetrate the enemy's rear areas beyond Cemetery Ridge, compounding the chaos that would ensue when Meade's line was broken.

The morning of 3 July began with the elimination of a Confederate lodgement on Culp's Hill by the Union XII Corps. Elsewhere, the troops detailed for the assault on the centre of Meade's line began assembling behind the trees on Seminary Ridge. From Longstreet's corps came Major General George E. Pickett's division, consisting entirely of Virginians, which had been employed as wagon guards during the previous two days. To Pickett's left the line was continued by troops drawn from Hill's corps who had not been in action since 1 July; these, consisting of regiments raised in the majority of the Confederate states, included Major General Henry Heth's division, now commanded by Brigadier General James Pettigrew, two brigades from Major General William Pender's division, now commanded by Major General Isaac Trimble, and one brigade from Major General Richard Anderson's division under Brigadier General Cadmus H. Wilcox.

Concurrently, the Confederate artillery was being massed into a grand battery of some 130 guns which, under the direction of Colonel E. Porter Alexander, would prepare the way for the assault. Responding to this obvious movement, Meade's Chief of Artillery, Brigadier General Henry J. Hunt, effected a concentration of 80 guns on Cemetery Ridge. Beginning at 13.00, the artillery duel lasted for two hours. Some damage was done to the Union batteries, but not enough to count. Most of the Confederate fire, in fact, was aimed a little too high, passing over the prone ranks of the infantry on the ridge and, to their glee, bursting among the staff and supply troops beyond; Meade's headquarters, located in a small wooden farmhouse below the reverse slope, was hit repeatedly. At about 15.00 Hunt, anticipating that the Confederate attack could not be long delayed, ordered his gunners to slacken their fire and so conserve the ammunition with which to meet it. Opposite, Alexander may have thought that he had succeeded in suppressing the fire of the Union artillery, but his own guns had all but expended their ammunition and, believing that the time had come for the attack, he sent Pickett a message to that effect. Pickett trotted over to Longstreet, saluted, and announced his intention to advance. Longstreet, unwilling to sanction something of which he so wholeheartedly disapproved, nodded silently.

What followed has become universally known as Pickett's Charge and is generally regarded as the most dramatic episode in the entire battle. Rank upon rank, the Confederate regiments emerged from the trees and began to march steadily across the open fields of the shallow valley. Their uniforms might be nondescript but their dressing was perfect, their Colours were to the fore and mounted officers were controlling the direction of the advance as though on a formal parade. For a little while the spectacle evoked sincere admiration in the waiting blue lines on Cemetery Ridge. Then, from Cemetery Hill to Little Round Top, Hunt's artillery commenced its work of deadly destruction. Gaps were blown in the butternut lines, but these were promptly filled and the advance continued without pause. As the range closed the gunners began double-shotting their weapons with canister, blasting even larger gaps, but still the Confederates came on, knowing they had yet to endure concentrated musketry fire which soon began flaring along the ridge to their front. A Vermont brigade under Brigadier General George J. Stannard wheeled out from the Union line and began raking the right of Pickett's division. By now the neat ranks had disintegrated and the attack had become a mass of men pressing forward with supreme courage and determination, the focus of every weapon that would bear. An officer with a Michigan regiment wrote of this phase of the attack: 'On they went, too much enveloped in smoke and dust now to permit us to distinguish their lines of movement, for the mass appeared more like a cloud of moving smoke and dust than a column of troops'. Repeatedly the head of the column was shot away. Inevitably, the Colour-parties became particular targets, but whenever a Colour went down it was picked up and carried forward until none was left to raise it again; later, no less than twenty Colours were found in the space of 100 square yards on the slopes of Cemetery Ridge. Eventually, the ordeal became more than normal men could stand yet, even as the survivors began shredding away singly and in small groups towards their own lines, some 150 Confederates led by Brigadier General Lewis Armistead gained the crest. In their fury they drove through II Corps' battleline, overrunning the wreckage of a battery, but Armistead was mortally wounded and his men were surrounded and forced to suřender by Union regiments which converged spontaneously on the penetration. Today the same spot, now known as the High Water Mark, is marked by a handsome memorial.

Pickett's Charge never stood the slightest chance of succeeding and should never had been mounted. Pickett's Division had gone into the attack with 22 officers of field rank, and of these only Pickett and one other remained; of the rank and file who had stepped off so bravely, just three men in every ten answered the roll-call. Overall, the attack had incurred casualties amounting to approximately half their strength. Lee, horrified by the enormity of his mistake, rode out to meet the survivors as they came in. To Pickett and other senior officers he encountered he said much the same thing: 'All this has been my fault. It is I that have lost this fight and upon my shoulders rests the blame.' Nor was there any comfort to be gained from Stuart's cavalry, who had once more been fought to a standstill by their Union opponents in a fierce contest to the east of the main battlefield. Prominent among the latter was a young, dashing, impetuous and so-far lucky brigade commander named George Armstrong Custer.

Old soldiers' lore at the time had it that heavy artillery fire disturbed the atmosphere sufficiently to cause rain. That certainly seemed to be the case on 4 July, when both armies simply remained in their positions during a torrential downpour. The Battle of Gettysburg was over. It had cost the Army of the Potomac 3,155 killed, 14,529 wounded and 5,365 missing, a total of 23,049. The Army of Northern Virginia had lost 3,903 killed, 18,735 wounded and 5,425 missing, a total of 28,063. That was more than the slender manpower resources of the South could afford and Lee decided to withdraw to Virginia. That afternoon he sent off his wounded in a jolting wagon train of agony which covered seventeen miles of road, following during the night with the rest of the army. Meade did not attempt to pursue.

So high did Lee stand in his men's affections that there were times when they refused to obey his orders unless he retired out of danger. They would forgive him the critical mistakes he made at Gettysburg, which were greater than in any other battle he fought. Many sought to fix blame for the defeat on Longstreet, and indeed it is difficult to justify his meandering approach march on 2 July. Nevertheless, on other issues such as the vulnerability of the Union left flank and the strength of Meade's centre on 3 July, he was undoubtedly right and Lee was wrong.

On 4 July those in Washington had more to celebrate than Independence and Lee's withdrawal from Gettysburg, for from the western theatre of war came the news that Vicksburg had surrendered the same day. The war had reached its turning-point, although 22 months of hard fighting remained before the Confederacy accepted final defeat. It would, therefore, be absurdly simplistic to say that the cause of the South received its death blow at Gettysburg, let alone on Little

Round Top. Yet, so goes the old saying, for want of a nail the shoe was lost, and so in turn the horse, the rider, the battle and the kingdom.

Today, visitors to Little Round Top come suddenly upon a figure wearing a general officer's frock coat and broad-brimmed hat. It stands upon a large boulder, staring westwards to the point where a shot from Smith's battery crashed through the trees on Seminary Ridge and the glitter of Longstreet's approaching bayonets became apparent. To the right lies Devil's Den and the expanse of Cemetery Ridge. The statue portrays Major General Gouverneur K. Warren, Meade's Chief of Engineers, without whose rapid appreciation of the situation the battle would have followed a different course.

VON BREDOW'S DEATH RIDE
Vionville – Mars-la-Tour, 16 August 1870
and
THE PRUSSIAN GUARD AT ST-PRIVAT
Gravelotte – St-Privat, 18 August 1870

Although the American Civil War had provided clear indications as to the way in which expanding technology was changing the nature of warfare, the full implications did not become apparent until the Franco–Prussian War of 1870–1. This conflict had become inevitable after the Prussian defeat of Austria during the Seven Weeks War of 1866, and was cynically triggered by Bismarck's support for the candidature of a Hohenzollern prince to the vacant Spanish throne, given in the knowledge that France would never tolerate a situation in which she found two of her frontiers permanently menaced by potentially hostile powers. As he anticipated, Napoleon III, Emperor of the French, promptly rose to the bait and, supremely confident in the abilities of the French Army, declared war on Prussia and her German allies on 15 July 1870.

In so doing he seriously under-estimated his opponents. A decade earlier few would have considered Prussia to be the continent's leading military power, although in those ten years much had happened. Her defeat of Austria in a remarkably short war caused considerable surprise, but was attributed to superior infantry weapons and the fact that the Austrian Army also had its hands full in northern Italy. Yet by 1870 Prussia had quietly produced an army which was unequalled anywhere in Europe for its efficiency.

The Prussian Army was based upon universal conscription and, thanks to an effective mobilization system, could be rapidly expanded in time of war. Its infantry was armed with the Dreyse 'needle-gun', a breech-loading rifle which could be loaded and fired lying down. It had inflicted serious casualties on the Austrians, who were equipped with the muzzle-loading smooth-bore musket which could only be loaded standing and which had only one-third the rate of fire. This had given rise to some complacency, for the Dreyse had some dangerous defects. These included the fragility of the long 'needle' firing-pin and the poor sealing of the breech mechanism. The latter was particularly serious, as it meant that the user received a painful back-blast of burning gas in his face and was inclined to be shy of the weapon; it also meant that while the weapon could be used at a range of 700 yards, the wastage of propellant gas limited its accuracy to 200 yards. In the field of artillery the Austrians had been the better equipped and the Prussians had responded so quickly to a painful lesson that by 1870 their artillery batteries had been re-armed with rifled breech-loading guns.

It was, however, in the intangibles of war that the Prussian Army excelled and for this its Chief of General Staff, Count Helmuth von Moltke, was responsible. Moltke, utterly dedicated to his profession, worked tirelessly to produce three areas of excellence within the Army. Only a limited number of the best intellects within the officer corps were selected annually by competitive examination to undergo the staff course at the War Academy. The course itself was extremely demanding, but the result was that a uniform pattern of thought was established in staffs at various levels so that it was often possible to anticipate orders from above and plan accordingly. Moltke was also well aware that railways conferred the ability to mobilize quickly and to maintain larger armies in the field than had hitherto been possible, a development which was confirmed by the American Civil War. The Railway Department of the General Staff was therefore of critical importance, for Moltke took the view that the army which completed its mobilization first could also strike the first blow and that once the enemy had been deprived of the initiative he was unlikely to recover it. The Railway Department's plans had been put into effect in 1866 and found to work, with the notable exception that while the trains left for the front on time there were insufficient unloading facilities for them when they arrived. By 1870 this difficulty had been largely, if not completely, solved.

It was, however, in his operational planning that Moltke excelled. At the highest level this meant that the armies of Prussia and her allies would advance along separate routes, then converge on the battlefield itself in overwhelming strength with the object of entrapping the enemy within an iron ring reminiscent of Cannae. This, with one or two anxious moments, had resulted in the Austrians being decisively defeated at Königgratz. In 1870 Moltke planned to destroy the French armies in the same way, then lay siege to Paris.

The French Army was very different in style and character from the Prussian. Its men were also conscripts, but they were drawn from only a quota of the annual class and served for much longer than their Prussian counterparts. It was also an experienced and self-confident army, having seen active service in the Crimea, in northern Italy against Austria in 1859, more recently in Mexico, and almost continuously in North Africa, although much of this experience consisted of counter-insurgency or colonial warfare and would therefore be of only limited value against regular troops. Unfortunately for the French their mobilization system bordered on the chaotic, with the result that some reservists were still actually in transit to their regiments when the most important of the French armies surrendered. Worse, the Army's second line, the recently constituted Garde Mobile, lacked arms, equipment, uniform and discipline as well as being heavily politicized. Again, staff training was not as thorough as in the Prussian service and the layout of the French railway system was less suited to the requirements of a general mobilization.

In some respects, however, the French Army was better equipped for war than the Prussian. The effects of the Dreyse rifle in 1866 had been duly noted and by 1870 the French infantry was armed with a much superior breech-loading rifle designed by a M. Chassepot. This had none of the drawbacks of the Dreyse, had twice the range and was actually sighted up to 1,600 metres. The general feeling within the Army was that the Chassepot's firepower, combined with French élan and experience, would be more than a match for the Prussians. But, having spent 113 million francs on the Chassepot, the French government declined to spend the further thirteen million requested for the re-equipment of the artillery, which would have to make do with the same rifled muzzle-loading cannon that had given good service during the 1859 campaign in Italy, a decision difficult to justify given the number of reports confirming that the Prussians' new Krupp guns possessed not only longer range but also increased accuracy. In general terms, therefore, the contest would be between French rifles and German artillery.

On the other hand, the French possessed a secret weapon which should have made a significant contribution to the fighting. This was the *mitrailleuse*, a simple machine-gun or, more specifically, a rapid fire system originally devised by a Captain Fafschamps of the Belgian Army, subsequently improved and manufactured by Joseph Montigny. The standard *mitrailleuse* used the same ammunition as the Chassepot and consisted of 25 barrels within a central tube. All barrels were loaded simultaneously with a steel plate containing the rounds, behind which the breech-block was closed. By using a crank, the barrels could all be fired at once or singly in rotation. After firing, the plate was removed by hand and the empty cartridge cases were knocked out. The weapon had a range of 2,000 metres and, using several prepared plates in succession, it could achieve a rate of fire of 150 rounds per minute.

On mobilization the French could field 190 *mitrailleuses*, but were immediately faced with the problem of how they were to be employed. So secret had been the project that no training with the gun had been permitted, and thus no doctrine for its use had been evolved. A further question was whether it should be classed as an artillery or an infantry weapon. With the benefit of hindsight we can see that its best application lay with the infantry, but in 1870 such technology was new to the battlefield and, having decided that the *mitrailleuse* was an artillery weapon, the French fitted it with an artillery carriage and limber and deployed it in clearly visible batteries. These, of course, were far outranged by the Prussian artillery and were quickly smashed up as soon as they were identified. On the few occasions when they were employed correctly they gave a good account of themselves.

By the end of July Prussia and her allies had concentrated 475,000 men on the common frontier. These were organized into three armies: the First, under General Karl von Steinmetz, the Second under Prince Friedrich Karl, and the Third under Crown Prince Friedrich Wilhelm. King Wilhelm I of Prussia was nominally in overall command, but the real power was exercised by Moltke, serving as his Chief of Staff, whose aims, as already stated, were perfectly clear.

The French had not completed their mobilization and were only able to field 224,000 men, collectively known as the Army of the Rhine, organized in eight corps under the overall command of Napoleon and his Minister of War, Marshal Edmond Leboeuf. This arrangement was too unwieldy to work well and on 2 August Napoleon formed the three southern corps into the Army of Alsace under Marshal Marie Mac-Mahon, and designated the remaining five corps as the Army of Lorraine under Marshal Achille Bazaine. Neither army possessed a staff as such, so that both commanders had to improvise and were therefore working under an immediate disadvantage. Nor, beyond the popular clamour *à Berlin*, had either been set any firm objectives.

During the next week the French were worsted in the opening battles of the war, although often it was the Germans who incurred the heavier casualties. MacMahon withdrew to regroup at Châlons and Bazaine fell back on the fortress of Metz. Moltke dispatched the Crown Prince's Third Army after MacMahon and followed Bazaine so closely with the First and Second Armies that he penetrated the area between the two French commanders and began to threaten the latter's communications.

On 12 August Napoleon, suddenly grown old and ill, recognized that he was fighting a new type of war which he did not understand. He relinquished command in favour of Bazaine, who was instructed to withdraw his army to Verdun where it would either operate in conjunction with MacMahon's rallied troops or counter a possible German thrust on Paris.

Superficially, Bazaine might have seemed a popular choice for the post of commander-in-chief. Aged 59, he had a long and honourable military career behind him. Of humble origins, he had enlisted in a line infantry regiment as a private in 1831, transferred to the Foreign Legion a year later, quickly risen through the ranks and been commissioned in 1833. He had served in Spain, Algeria, the Crimea and Italy and as commander-in-chief of the French troops in Mexico had conducted a successful counter-insurgency campaign. He was known to possess courage and had the ability to remain cool under fire. But there were a number of reasons why he was unsuitable for the job. Painfully conscious of his roots, he felt a misfit. He had, of course, nothing in common with the former Bourbon aristocracy, and very little with the

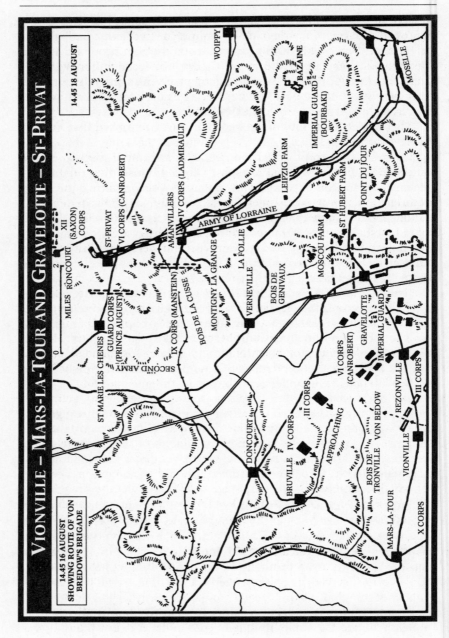

VIONVILLE – MARS-LA-TOUR AND GRAVELOTTE – ST-PRIVAT

14.45 16 AUGUST
SHOWING ROUTE OF VON
BREDOW'S BRIGADE

14.45 18 AUGUST

Bonapartist. Alone of his generation of senior officers, he had never been asked to serve as an Imperial aide-de-camp. He felt surrounded by envy and was uncomfortable giving orders to those from more privileged backgrounds. Despite this, he was still driven by his ambition and had gone to war fully expecting to be given command of an army. In addition to, or perhaps because of, these conflicting psychological pressures he was already suffering from clinical depression and, on leaving Paris for the front the previous month, he had presciently remarked that France was heading for a disaster.

In the past, with all his troops in sight and under his immediate control, Bazaine had shown himself to be a capable divisional commander. That did not necessarily mean that he would make a competent corps, let alone army commander, where the demands on his intellectual resources were different and command was exercised indirectly and beyond view. That he continued to think like a divisional commander, personally siting batteries and allocating regiments their position, was symptomatic of promotion beyond his abilities. Perhaps if he had enjoyed a good relationship with an efficient staff this deficiency might have been partially corrected, but he did not and tended to issue orders directly to his corps commanders without considering the administrative implications for the army as a whole. The essence of Bazaine's difficulties was expressed by Marshal Canrobert during the subsequent court-martial of the army commander: 'Not everyone can command an army a hundred and forty thousand strong; it is difficult to manage when one isn't used to it.'

On 15 August Bazaine fought a successful rearguard action at Borny, east of Metz, and for a while it seemed as though he would manage to turn the tide. But even this modest achievement worked against him, for while he was fighting Steinmetz's First Army to a temporary standstill, the German Second Army under Prince Friedrich Karl was crossing the Moselle to the south and advancing in a north-westerly direction which, at some stage, would interdict the French line of retreat from Metz to Verdun. By evening, in fact, German cavalry had one of the major axes of withdrawal under direct observation.

At dawn on 16 August the Emperor left for Verdun, escorted by two brigades of cavalry, leaving Bazaine to continue with the withdrawal. Two parallel routes were available, the northern through Doncourt, and the southern through the villages of Rezonville, Vionville and Mars-la-Tour, approximately one mile distant from each other. The problem was that these routes did not separate until they reached Gravelotte, so that the whole army and its 5,000 supply wagons had first to travel along a single road from Metz, the centre of which was itself already congested with troops. Such was the tangle that the staff were unable to cope. Some corps, already encamped in the area of Rezonville and Gravelotte, were ready to march, but others were not. Bazaine, already disturbed by reports of German cavalry in the vicinity, postponed the move until the afternoon.

The battle began at about 09.00 when the artillery of Major General von Rheinbaben's 5th Cavalry Division opened fire on the French cavalry camp at Vionville. Rheinbaben has sometimes attracted criticism for his lack of drive, but he knew that he was confronted by the entire French Army and was probably wise not to press his attack, knowing that Lieutenant General Konstantin von Alvensleben's III Corps was moving up on his right. At first Alvensleben believed that he had only the French rearguard to deal with. Once the truth became apparent, however, he decided that as his corps was in a position to halt the French withdrawal he would mount a sustained holding attack until the rest of Second Army arrived.

The overall situation was that III Corps had cut the Metz–Verdun road between Rezonville and Vionville while, to the north-east, the French held an arc of downland with their left on Rezonville. As the day wore on, both sides marched to the sound of the guns and the lines were prolonged to the west, parallel with an old Roman road running between them. Bazaine, however, was more anxious to preserve his communications with Metz rather than re-open the road to Verdun and, ignoring the golden opportunity to encircle and destroy an entire German corps before help could reach it, be reinforced his left wing rather than his right.

Although the Germans succeeded in capturing the villages of Flavigny and Vionville, their infantry attacks were halted with crippling loss by the storm of Chassepot fire. Cavalry attacks by both sides foundered in a hail of bullets or were driven back by counter-charges which in turn ended in bloody ruin. During one such incident Bazaine, personally siting a battery, was surrounded and almost cut down by German cavalry before being rescued by his escort and hurried off to the rear. Inspiring though such displays of courage were, they were not the business of an army commander.

By 13.00 the German advance had been stopped and the battle had become an artillery duel. Alvensleben had committed all his infantry reserves, his ranks had been decimated, his men were running short of ammunition, and his left wing was being battered to pieces by the French guns. He had, however, been assured that Lieutenant-General Voigts-Rhetz's X Corps was approaching and that this would enter the line on his left, so his troops must hang on at all costs. It was a dry, extremely hot day and he could see heavy dust clouds moving westwards beyond the French line, indicating that his left flank would soon be turned. Furthermore, there were signs that the French troops opposite, belonging to Canrobert's VI Corps, were about to take the offensive. Unless something were done quickly he would be forced to retreat or be destroyed where he stood. Only the cavalry could now save the situation, but the only troops Rheinbaben had available were Major-General Friedrich von Bredow's 12th Cavalry Brigade, presently positioned in a hollow to the south of Vionville.

Bredow belonged to an old Prussian military family and had spent much of his service with the Guard Hussar Regiment. He had commanded a cavalry brigade during the 1866 war with Austria and so distinguished himself that he had been promoted and decorated on the spot. Now aged 56, he had a reputation for steadiness and methodical preparation. His brigade consisted of two regiments, the 7th Magdeburg Cuirassiers under Colonel Count von Schmettow, and the 16th Lancers under Major von der Dollen. Both were under strength and had taken the field with only three squadrons instead of the usual five.

Rheinbaben's aide reached Bredow at about 14.00 and delivered orders to the effect that he was to break the enemy infantry opposite. As the infantry was ranged behind a line of batteries this was quite contrary to accepted practice. 'That infantry?' asked the brigade commander, in some surprise. 'The fate of the day hangs upon it!' the aide replied. There was no mistake.

While the regiments formed up Bredow detached one lancer squadron to guard his open left flank and studied the ground ahead. To mount a direct attack in the face of massed artillery and Chassepot fire would be tantamount to suicide, but by inclining slightly to the left the brigade would enter a shallow re-entrant, hardly more than a wide depression, that led almost to the crest of the rolling downland; and at the head of the re-entrant was a wide fold in the ground leading directly to the enemy's right flank. Together, the re-entrant and the fold would provide limited cover from view and some cover from fire while the brigade made its approach. His plan complete, he formed his regiments into column of squadrons and led them out of the hollow at 14.30.

As the column trotted by Tronville Wood it passed the headquarters of the 6th Cavalry Division. The divisional commander, Major-General von Buddenbrock, had evidently not been informed of the situation by Rheinbaben and, understandably, he believed that Bredow was need-lessly placing his troops in jeopardy. He therefore sent an aide galloping after the brigade with a message sufficiently garbled to rival those that had sent the Light Brigade to its doom at Balaclava, the gist of which was that even should an occasion for an attack present itself, no attack was to be permitted. The aide, Lieutenant von Kalckreuth, was a good horseman who, four weeks earlier, had won the Army point-to-point on his thoroughbred mare Linda. He caught up with Bredow north of the main road and delivered his message exactly as it had been given to him. Far from being confused, Bredow merely replied that he had already received General von Rheinbaben's orders to attack and was on the point of carrying them out. Kalckreuth asked for permission to ride with him and when Bredow did not reply he joined the brigade staff.

At the head of the re-entrant the squadrons turned into line with the cuirassiers on the left and the lancers on the right. At Bredow's order the trumpeters sounded the Advance, followed by the Trot. The brigade was now moving in an easterly direction, parallel with the main road and, because of the rolling ground and battle smoke hanging in the warm air, its approach so far remained undetected. Suddenly the French flank appeared and the Charge was sounded. Long, straight swords extended, the cuirassiers worked their mounts into a thundering gallop while, to their right, the leading rank of lance points dropped to the Engage. Kalckreuth, now riding with a lancer squadron, was aware of solid infantry lines rising from the ground and a blast of Chassepot fire cracking past his ears. Then the enemy, infantry and artillerymen alike, broke and fled in an unruly mob as the lancers rode over them.

The cuirassiers overran a battery, the captain of which was cut down by Schmettow. A French artillery officer, General Henry, recalled the incident some years after the battle: 'Where in the world had these cuirassiers come from? All of a sudden they were upon my guns like a whirlwind and rode or cut down all my men save only one. It was only by the skin of my teeth that I myself escaped as the mass of furious horsemen swept past me, trampling down or sabring the gunners. But it was a magnificent military spectacle, and I could not help exclaiming to my adjutant as we rode away, "*Ah! Quelle attaque magnifique!*" '

The brigade, now the focus of concentrated artillery, *mitrailleuse* and rifle fire, swept on, losing men and horses with every yard covered. Schmettow's brass helmet was pierced twice by bullets and his adjutant went down. Some 500 yards ahead lay more infantry and a second line of guns, some apparently limbering up. 'With a cheer we charged towards them,' recalled Kalckreuth. 'The horses strained, knowing what was required of them. Soon we reached them, stabbing and slashing the riders from their horses. One gun remained in our hands.' It was, of course, too good to last. Bredow's brigade had reduced much of Canrobert's front to wreckage, but the cost had been heavy and its horses were blown. Now retribution appeared in the form of the French 1st and 9th Dragoons and 7th and 10th Cuirassiers, which charged downhill into the German flank. Kalckreuth gave his surviving lancers the order to abandon the captured gun and withdraw. 'There were only twenty or thirty men – all the rest were dead or wounded – and we were cutting our way out with difficulty when enemy infantry nearby opened fire on us. My horse, immediately hit in the neck and foreleg, carried me for another 200 paces then we ploughed into the ground together.' Kalkreuth was severely injured and taken prisoner, as was Major von der Dollen, whose horse was also shot under him, but was exchanged two weeks later.

Nearby an incident was taking place which might have sprung from the pages of G. A. Henty, since its hero was a Second-Lieutenant Edmund Cambell of Craignish. Campbell's father, a British infantry officer, had died three months after his son was born, but a godfatherly interest in the family was maintained by General Sir James Kempt, who had commanded a brigade at Waterloo. In 1853 Kempt acted as sponsor for Edmund's elder brother Ronald when he joined the Honourable East India Company's army. Edmund may have wished to follow in Ronald's footsteps but the Company's army had ceased to exist some years before he was old enough to join. However, his mother had been resident in Hamburg for some time and in 1866, aged 18, he enlisted as a private in the Prussian 24th Infantry Regiment and served in the war against Austria. He transferred to the 7th Cuirassiers the following year and after a probationary period was appointed *Fahnrich* (ensign), a rank which has no precise equal in the British or US armies, but is the equivalent of a senior NCO with officer potential. He received his commission in February 1869.

Now, assailed by enemy cavalry, Campbell found that he was engaged with his opposite numbers, the French 7th Cuirassiers. He spurred his way directly at their standard-bearer, cut him down and siezed the standard in his left hand. The French, desperate to recover the trophy, crowded round him, hacking and stabbing. His hand was shattered by a shot from an officer's pistol and he was forced to drop the standard. He would undoubtedly have been killed had not Sergeant-Major Seding noticed his predicament and led a charge which broke through the circle of his assailants. The furious combat which raged around the trampled banner is known as 'The Battle of the Standard' to German military historians and was remarkable for the contrasting styles of swordsmanship used by the two sides, the French directing the point against cuirass joints and beneath the helmet guard while the Germans preferred the cutting edge of their weapons. At length Bredow, seeing more French cavalry closing in and recognizing that his remaining men and their tired mounts would be overwhelmed if they remained, ordered Schmettow to retire. Schmettow grabbed the first trumpeter he could lay his hands on and told him to blow the Rally. At some stage a bullet had passed through the trumpet so that it produced an ear-splitting metallic shriek which nevertheless produced the required result.

The remnant of the 7th Cuirassiers, like that of the 16th Lancers, had to pass through the fire of the French infantry before it reached safety. Of the 500 men Bredow had led into action, only 104 cuirassiers and 90 lancers regained their own lines. The charge, subsequently referred to as 'von Bredow's Death Ride', nevertheless achieved its objectives, having simultaneously removed the threat to Alvensleben's III Corps and seriously disrupted Canrobert's VI Corps, which was already short of artillery and, above all, of trained gunners. It was also the only cavalry charge of the entire war that produced decisive results, largely because the terrain had been used to full advantage. Succeeding generations of cavalrymen were to cite it as a complete justification for the retention of their arm, ignoring the numerous charges that had been shot to pieces by the rapidly expanding firepower of the defence, with the result that all the major European armies entered the First World War with a large and expensive cavalry element for which little use could be found after the first clashes.

Bredow was promoted and received decorations from most of Germany's royal houses. He became one of the Army's most respected figures and in 1889 the Emperor Wilhelm II honoured him further by naming the 4th Dragoon Regiment 'von Bredow's'. On the same occasion Campbell, who had remained in the Prussian Army, rising to the rank of major, was created a baron.

The arrival of Voigt-Rhetz's X Corps on Alvensleben's left in the aftermath of von Bredow's attack was matched by the arrival of fresh French troops on Canrobert's right, so that the battle was prolonged to the west. It concluded with a huge and indecisive cavalry mêlée, the last in western European history, near Mars-la-Tour. Prince Friedrich Karl reached the battlefield at about 16.00 but was unable to initiate any fresh tactical move until the leading elements of Steinmetz's First Army arrived, when an attack was mounted on the French left near Rezonville at 19.00. This gradually petered out as darkness put an end to the fighting.

Technically, the Battle of Vionville—Mars-la-Tour ended in a draw, although both sides had some cause for satisfaction. The Germans had succeeded in halting the French withdrawal to Verdun, and for this most of the credit must go Alvensleben's corps, which had fought in isolation for several hours. This, however, had been achieved at the cost of almost 16,000 casualties and some units had virtually been destroyed; for example the 24th Infantry, Campbell's old regiment, lost no less than 1,000 men and 52 officers.

The French had lost approximately 14,000 officers and men, although they could claim to have held all their ground and were quite ready to renew the contest the following day. Bazaine, however, had no such intention. Hopelessly unsure of himself, he decided that his first priority lay in maintaining secure contact with Metz rather than in attempting to reopen the route to Verdun. At midnight he ordered his corps commanders to fall back to a position closer to the fortress, pivotting on Gravelotte so that their new line faced west rather than south. The order was executed throughout the 17 August by bemused and resentful troops who were not only compelled to burn such of their supplies as could not be transported, but also to abandon some of their wounded.

Strategically, Bazaine had played straight into Moltke's hands by allowing himself to be so trapped. In fairness to him, however, his new position offered definite tactical advantages, and the defensive firepower available should have enabled him to inflict a costly reverse on his opponents. The new French line occupied a ridge running from north to south. The southern half was fronted by a steep wooded ravine carrying the Mance stream southwards towards the Moselle, an obstacle which would itself disorder the close formations in which the Germans made their attacks; above the tree line the crest offered long fields of fire dominated by the fortified farms of Pont du Jour, St Hubert, Moscou and Leipzig, connected by trenches and lines of emplaced batteries. The northern half of the line, beyond the point where the Mance rose in the Bois de Genivaux, extended through Amanvilliers to St-Privat la Montaigne, but was different in character in that the slopes were gentler but offered even longer fields of fire with no protection whatsoever for an attacker and, perhaps for this reason, the French had constructed fewer field works. Bazaine's headquarters was located in the uncompleted fortress of Plappeville, two miles behind his left wing and four from St-Privat, with the Imperial Guard in reserve nearby.

On the morning of 18 August some 188,000 Germans with 732 guns, under the personal control of Moltke, confronted 113,000 Frenchmen with 520 guns in the first set-piece battle of the war. Moltke's plan was that Steinmetz's First Army would mount heavy holding attacks against the French left while Prince Friedrich Karl marched north with Second Army and turned Bazaine's right.

What transpired, in the event, were two battles and in that at Gravelotte the Germans sustained an undoubted defeat. Here, the French commanders had begun siting their *mitrailleuses* in concealed positions among the infantry, adding to the fearful punishment inflicted by the rapid fire of their Chassepots. Throughout the day Steinmetz brutally flung in one assault after another until the Mance ravine had become a densely packed shambles of infantry, cavalry and guns mingled with dead and wounded, under constant fire from the enemy's artillery. As each attack fell back from the French positions its survivors retired to the ravine until the congestion was such that units attempting to advance lost their cohesion and became intermingled with others to make confusion complete. By 17.00 Steinmetz has used up all but a fraction of his reserves and, seeing Lieutenant-General von Fransecky's as-yet uncommitted II Corps approaching the field, he by-passed Moltke and appealed directly to the King for permission to use it. Moltke made no comment at the time but later regretted his silence.

Shortly afterwards the nerve of those in the Mance ravine finally snapped. They came streaming out of the narrow valley in a blind, infectious panic which not even the King and his staff, using the flat of their swords, could bring under control. Careering through Gravelotte, where their progress was illuminated by the flames of burning buildings, the torrent of wild-eyed infantry, horsemen and gun teams did not stop until it reached Rezonville. At one point serious consideration was given to escorting the King off the field altogether.

The effect of this flood of fugitives on the morale of II Corps can well be imagined. Both of Fransecky's divisions, somewhat shaken and now coming under fire, descended into the valley, now empty save for the grisly debris of what had amounted to a massacre. Crossing the stream, they climbed the slope beyond and, emerging from the trees in the fading light, opened fire on an indistinctly seen line of troops ahead, believing them to be French. They were, in fact, Germans who had not succumbed to the general panic and had formed a tenuous front; for them, this assault from the rear was the last straw and they bolted, leaving II Corps to take over their position.

The King, Moltke and their staff had retired to Rezonville where, as they gloomily stood around a camp fire, doubts were expressed that the troops were capable of another such day's fighting. Furthermore, although the sound of intense firing from the north had indicated that Second Army had also been very heavily engaged, no word had been received from it for several hours, and that was ominous. To Moltke, however, it was significant that, even at the worst moments of the rout, the French had not counter-attacked to complete the destruction of First Army, the reasons being that Bazaine was personally unaware of the collapse and that he had left the battle in the hands of his corps commanders with strict instructions that they should remain on the defensive. Moltke, therefore, as was his prerogative, insisted that the King should sanction a renewal of the attack the following day, although the form this would take was not decided. At about midnight an aide arrived from Friedrich Karl with the unexpected news that his army had won a victory, albeit at frightful cost, and that on his sector the French were withdrawing into Metz. If the mood lightened a little it fell far short of elation, for the losses in both armies had been too heavy for that. The King, in particular, was deeply grieved by reports that his Guard had come close to being annihilated in an ill-conceived attack.

Second Army's advance northward that morning had been made in echelon of corps, with the Hessian IX Corps under von Manstein on the right, the Guard Corps under Prince August of Württemberg in the centre and the Saxon XII Corps, commanded by Crown Prince Albert of Saxony, on the left; Alvensleben's III Corps and Voigt-Rhetz's X Corps, which had borne the brunt of the fighting on the 16th, followed in reserve. A French counter-attack into the flank of this unwieldy mass would almost certainly have thrown Moltke's master plan out of gear but Bazaine declined to avail himself of the opportunity.

Friedrich Karl believed that the French right was at Amanvillers and at 10.15 he ordered Manstein to wheel right through Verneville and attack the enemy beyond while he, with the Guards and Saxons, moved against what he imagined was the enemy flank. By the time he realized his mistake IX Corps was already in action and he was compelled hastily to re-plan the battle. The Guard Corps would mount a frontal attack on

St-Privat, where the real flank lay, but only in conjunction with an attack from the north by the Saxons, who were to be sent on a wide enveloping march to secure their start-line at Roncourt. The irony is that this plan too would have failed if Bazaine had not been so shy of his distinguished subordinates. Unhappy that his right flank seemed to be hanging in the air, he had that morning sent an order to Canrobert telling him to abandon St-Privat and take up a stronger position to his rear. The effect of this would have been a refused right against which the Saxons could only have mounted a frontal attack. As expressed to Canrobert, however, the order probably seemed more of a suggestion and it was not acted upon.

For the Germans, the principal difficulty was that a great deal of time would be required to execute Friedrich Karl's amended plan. The first task was to prepare the ground for the attack. This involved clearing the French from a strong outpost they held in the village of Ste-Marie-les-Chênes. Here the attack, delivered with ample artillery support, was delayed until a Saxon brigade arrived and did not take place until 15.00, much to the disgust of Major-General von Pape of the 1st Guard Division, who felt that his men could easily have carried out the task without the assistance of their allies. After thirty minutes' fighting Ste-Marie was in German hands and Friedrich Karl redeployed the Saxon artillery to the north of the village and the Guard artillery to the south, while that of Alvensleben's III Corps was brought forward between the Guard and IX Corps on its right. Altogether, some 180 guns were concentrated against the enemy positions at St-Privat, their fire directed at the opposing artillery or the village itself, leaving the French infantry relatively unharmed.

Prince August of Württemberg had commanded the Guard Corps since 1858 and would continue to do so for the next 24 years, despite the appalling mistakes he made at St-Privat. At about 17.00 the return fire of the French guns began to slacken and he drew the unsubstantiated conclusion that this was the result of an ammunition shortage and that the Guard should therefore attack, with or without the Saxons. Various suggestions have been offered in explanation for his behaviour. One is that he was fiercely jealous of the Guards' prestige and did not want the Saxons to share in the honours of the day; another that the Saxons would be late arriving, as they had been at Ste-Marie; and a third that, because of a misunderstanding between the two corps' liaison officers, he believed the Saxons to be much closer than they were. What is certain is that he was under some pressure from Friedrich Karl, who was becoming increasingly impatient at the long delay. At that precise moment the army commander was some distance away and personally unfamiliar with the situation at the northern end of the line, but he accepted August's assessment and, because of the urgency involved, sanctioned his attack.

In the German service, where members of the various royal families commanded armies or corps, the custom was that a skilled professional would serve as their chief of staff. If mistakes were being made, it was the duty of the chief of staff to correct his commander, as bluntly as was necessary, just as Moltke did with the King. In his instance the Guard Corps Chief of Staff, Lieutenant-General von Dannenberg, was not a lot of help. He agreed with the unproven assumption that the French in St-Privat were weaker, but his diagnosis was that troops were being transferred to Amanvillers for a counter-attack on IX Corps. He did, however, emphasize that the assault should be supported by the Guard artillery, although the commander of the latter, Prince Kraft zu Hohenlohe-Ingelfingen, subsequently testified that no orders to that effect had been received. Von Pape objected strongly to the attack on the grounds that he could see the Saxon columns and it was obvious that they would not be ready to launch their attack for at least another hour, and that the French infantry positions had been left largely untouched by the earlier bombardment. August brushed him aside and gave orders for him to advance immediately. At this point a horrified junior staff officer remarked to a senior colleague that surely the correct thing would be to wait for the neighbouring corps and advance with full support from the artillery. His superior regarded him for a moment then remarked dryly, 'If we were to follow your methods we should all live far too long!'

Thus the infantry of the Guard Corps was committed in isolation to a massive frontal attack across open terrain without the support of its guns. It formed up in assault columns behind a line of skirmishers, with mounted field officers at the head of their units. Then, colours flying and drums beating, it moved forward. It had an advance of 3,000 yards to make and the men had been taught during maneouvres that in the attack it was the combination of speed and weight which counted. They therefore expected to cover most of the distance in quick time then, about 100 yards from the objective, break into double time and charge with bayonets levelled.

At first their advance resembled one of the grand Potsdam reviews in which they had taken part so often, but after they had covered 1,500 yards the French lines suddenly erupted in flame and smoke. The battalion of the Guard Rifle Regiment, which provided the skirmish line, simply melted away under the sustained impact. Its commander was killed instantly, as were most of the company commanders. In attempting to sustain the firefight all the battalion's remaining officers were killed or wounded and command devolved upon the senior rank present, a young *Fahnrich*.

Now it was the turn of the assault columns, the close formation of which made heavy casualties inevitable. The front ranks were shot away time and again but still the advance continued into the teeth of the enemy fire, leaving a long trail of bloodstained blue in its wake.

Observers noticed that the men were leaning forward, heads bowed, as though they were forcing their way into a strong wind. The simile was apt, as it has been calculated that in any one minute they were the target of 40,000 Chassepot rounds, producing a crescendo of sound never heard before on a battlefield. Luckily, much of the fire passed overhead because, from enthusiasm or lack of training, many of the French infantry were simply firing from the hip as rapidly as possible rather than taking deliberate aim. The columns struggled on, but 800 yards from the objective and still beyond the effective range of their own weapons they lay down and not even their renowned discipline could get them moving again. In the twenty minutes since the attack began the Guard Corps had sustained more than 8,000 casualties, including more than 2,000 killed. Scarcely one of Prussia's noble families would remain unaffected by the tragedy. Proud regiments of Foot Guards, Guard Grenadiers and Guard Fusiliers, now with sergeants commanding some of their companies, were pinned to the ground, flayed by rifle and artillery fire. Nevertheless, there was neither panic nor spontaneous movement towards the rear; after the action only 179 men were reported missing from the entire corps. Instead there was a fierce desire to revenge not only their fallen comrades but also the humiliation which they, the cream of the Prussian Army, were being forced to endure. That moment would come when the Saxons arrived and, in the meantime, further encouragement was being provided by Hohenlohe-Ingelfingen who, having observed the catastrophic results of the attack, had brought his guns into action and was already beginning to punish the French.

The Saxons began to make their presence felt at about 18.00. Canrobert, suffering from an ammunition shortage after the previous hour's prodigal expenditure, could spare very few men to hold them off and by 19.00 it was clear that, under pressure from two sides, he would have to abandon St-Privat. He sent back a request that General Bourbaki should cover his withdrawal with the Imperial Guard and attempted to buy a little time with a cavalry charge. The latter barely covered 50 yards before it was broken. The French fire slackened as Canrobert began thinning out and the Guard Corps, interpreting this correctly, charged into the village from the west while the Saxons closed in from the north. Some French units bolted but others fought a determined rearguard action in the streets so that it was not until 20.30 that St-Privat was securely in German hands. No pursuit was attempted.

Bourbaki had already received a request for help from General de Ladmirault, commanding the French IV Corps on Canrobert's left. Ladmirault believed that he was more than holding his own against Manstein and that the arrival of fresh troops would tip the scales in his favour. Bourbaki, all too conscious of the Napoleonic tradition that the Imperial Guard's role was to administer the *coup de grâce* to a beaten enemy, set off for Amanvillers with one division. Arriving in view of the battlefield at about 19.00, he could see troops streaming away from the heavy fighting at St-Privat, while stragglers were leaving Ladmirault's line in increasing numbers. He might have attempted to retrieve the situation on the right wing, and even have achieved a degree of success as the Prussian Guard was in no condition to sustain further serious action. Instead, seeing the vision of *La Gloire* vanishing before his eyes, he began to behave like a frustrated prima donna. 'You promised me a victory,' he screamed at the aides who had brought Ladmirault's request. 'Now you've got me involved in a rout. You had no right to do that! There was no need to make me leave my magnificent positions for this!' As if this tantrum were not enough, he then turned his Guardsmen round and marched off. Not for the first time the French, believing that the retreat of the Imperial Guard signified a battle irretrievably lost, abandoned their positions and dissolved into retreat.

Altogether, the Germans had sustained more than 20,000 casualties during the day, while the French loss amounted to approximately 13,000. Yet the battle, together with that fought two days earlier, decided the war in Germany's favour and was to have a profound effect on subsequent European history.

Bazaine retired into Metz where, freed of the crushing responsibility of commanding a large army in the field, he tamely allowed his troops to be besieged. MacMahon's reorganized Army of Châlons, accompanied by Napoleon, was therefore compelled to march to his relief but on 1 September it was encircled at Sedan and bombarded into surrender. The Second Empire collapsed within days and by 19 September Paris was itself under siege. The leaders of the new Third Republic, unable to accept France's defeat in the field, raised fresh armies of mixed quality which, despite a few local successes, were unable to influence the course of events. Bazaine surrendered Metz on 27 October and when Paris capitulated the following January the war was effectively over.

France had initiated the war and it was naive to expect that Chancellor Bismarck's peace terms would be anything other than punitive although, in the event, they were not unduly so. Alsace and part of Lorraine, the populations of which contained a high proportion of Germans, were to be ceded to Germany, and France was to pay an indemnity of five billion francs, pending which German troops would remain on French soil; the payment was not completed until September 1873. Yet many Frenchmen, already chagrined by the unbelievably rapid defeat of their armies, saw in these terms a further cause for national shame. The desire for *La Revanche* was never far below the surface and was an element in creating the circumstances which led to the European catastrophe of the First World War.

As for Marshal Achille Bazaine, the blame for France's defeat was laid squarely at his door. Hoping to clear his name, he returned from voluntary exile in Switzerland to demand a court-martial, a request which the authorities were only too pleased to grant. He was found guilty of gross negligence, stripped of his rank and sentenced to death. Because of his earlier services to France, MacMahon, now President of the Republic, commuted the sentence to life imprisonment in a fortress. In due course Bazaine escaped; lonely, embittered and defamed, he lived out his last days in Spain.

6
MARCH INTO INFINITY
The Desert Column, Gordon Relief Expedition, 1884–5

Even today, time is a dimension which has little meaning in Egypt. Almost every aspect of the country's history, reaching back over 56 centuries, is recorded somewhere in stone and preserved for posterity by a hot, dry climate. Near Aswan, between the Old Dam and the modern High Dam, is the beautiful Temple of Isis which, between 1972 and 1980, was painstakingly removed, block by numbered block, from its old site on Philae Island and re-erected with infinite care on the higher island of Agilqiyyah to prevent its being lost forever beneath the waters of the Nile. Within, there is a wealth of mural art depicting the Pharaohs and their gods, defaced here and there with early Christian graffiti. Ostensibly, all belongs to the remote past until, on an exterior wall, one encounters a carved inscription which is in neither hieroglyphic nor classical Greek script, but the solid Victorian interpretation of Roman capitals, recalling one of the most impossible missions that soldiers have ever been asked to perform. The preamble reads:

IN MEMORY OF
9 officers & 92 NCOs & men
of the
HEAVY CAMEL REGT
WHO LOST THEIR LIVES IN THE SOUDAN
1884–5
KILLED IN ACTION/DIED OF DISEASE

Below, in two columns, the casualties are listed by their parent regiments (1st and 2nd Life Guards, Royal Horse Guards, 2nd, 4th and 5th Dragoon Guards, 1st Royal Dragoons, Scots Greys, 5th and 16th Lancers), although only the officers are named. Of the total, three officers and thirty other ranks died of disease, the balance of the loss falling most heavily on 4th Dragoon Guards (two officers and nine other ranks), 5th Dragoon Guards (one officer and ten other ranks), 1st Royal Dragoons (one officer and thirteen other ranks), Scots Greys (one officer and twelve other ranks) and 5th Lancers (one officer and seven other ranks). From these figures it is only possible to deduce that, in whatever battle was fought, the men remained grouped in their regimental origins within the composite unit, and that some contingents were more heavily engaged than others.

In other respects the inscription is a puzzle to the majority of visitors. Some, affecting a too-literal translation into their own language, speculate on the nature of a heavy camel. Others, more used to English and the military idiom, are understandably curious as to why camel-mounted elements of ten British cavalry regiments were active in the Sudan a century and more ago, and the question merits an answer.

It could be said that the story began with a bungled internal security operation, mounted in August 1881 to secure the person of an ascetic holy man named Mohammed Ahmed. It was said that he was numbered among the *Ashraf*, or Descendants of the Prophet, and no one has ever questioned his piety or his simple lifestyle. What he preached was a return to the purest values of Islam, and in so doing he openly despised the ways of the Egyptians, whose rule of the Sudan since 1819 had been marked by exploitation, slavery, corruption and casual indifference to the needs of its inhabitants.

Like most oppressed people, the Sudanese believed that one day a man would appear who would deliver them from their troubles. He would be known as the Mahdi, or Expected Guide, and he could be recognized by a gap in his front teeth and a blemish on the right cheek. Mohammed Ahmed was so marked and, when challenged, he admitted that he was indeed the Mahdi. Soon, as might be expected among a people with nothing to lose, he had attracted a large following.

In the meantime, some effort had been made to put the Sudan's affairs in order. In 1874 a Colonel Charles Gordon of the Royal Engineers had been appointed Governor of the Equatorial Province. Gordon had served in the Crimea and in China during the Second Opium War, and it was at the request of the Chinese government that he had assumed command of a privately financed and somewhat dubious force known as the Ever Victorious Army, led by an American soldier of fortune named Frederick Ward until his death in 1862. With this unpromising material Gordon had finally subdued the long and costly Taiping Rebellion, but, ever a man of principle, he had resigned when the Chinese government executed prisoners who had surrendered to him in good faith.

Returning home, Gordon devoted all his spare time and considerable energy to charitable work. In particular, he fed, housed, clothed and found work for destitute boys, often at his own expense. As devout a Christian as Mohammed Ahmed was a follower of Islam, he detested slavery and on his arrival in the Sudan he set about destroying the huge vested interest in the trade. Forming units from liberated slaves, he pursued the traders without mercy, making numerous enemies but many more friends. In 1877 he was appointed Governor-General of the Sudan, a post which he held for the next two years. His combination of courage, drive, incorruptibility and decency was beyond the experience of the Sudanese in their rulers and they found him a man to wonder at, to admire, to respect and to fear. There was, however, no other legacy from his period in office, and Gordon himself recognized the fact.

During this period Gordon and Mohammed Ahmed were each aware of the other, although in their separate spheres. The Mahdi continued to preach that the Sudan's ills could only be cured by the expulsion of the decadent Turks, as the Egyptians were known, and unrest began to grow. At first Gordon's successor as Governor-General, Raouf Pasha, was disinclined to regard the threat as serious, but at length he sent a messenger to Abba Island, where the Mahdi lived with his principal followers, summoning Mohammed Ahmed to justify his actions in Khartoum. Angrily the Mahdi refused, commenting that he was now master of the country, then declaring a Holy War against the foreigners, a war in which those who fell would find their reward in Heaven.

It was not a challenge Raouf Pasha could ignore. During the dusk of an August evening in 1881 a government steamer landed two Egyptian infantry companies on Abba Island. Promotion had been promised to the commander of the company that captured the Mahdi, with the result that co-operation was replaced by competition. Thoroughly keyed up, both companies approached the Mahdi's village by separate routes through the darkness. As they converged, each opened fire into the other's ranks, believing them to be the enemy. At this point the Mahdi and his followers swarmed out of the village to set about the survivors, driving them back towards the steamer, the captain of which refused to put in and take them off; only those few able to swim out to the vessel lived to tell the tale.

The story that the Mahdi and his men, unarmed, had inflicted a defeat on the government's soldiers spread like wildfire throughout the Sudan. Nevertheless, the Mahdi's principal Khalifa (Successor), Abdullahi ibn Mohammed, an altogether more political animal and a better tactician than Mohammed Ahmed, foresaw inevitable retribution unless the party abandoned Abba Island and withdrew to a remote area of the country. Even so, the retreat became more of a triumphal progress after a second government force, consisting of 1,400 men under Rashid Bey, was wiped out in an ambush near Fashoda on 9 December. Hundreds flocked to the Mahdi's Standard and the government reacted by sending Yusef Pasha with a 4,000-strong army to put down the revolt; contemptuous of his foes, Yusef did not even bother to post sentries and his troops were massacred to a man when the Mahdists broke into their zareba at dawn on 7 June 1882. Southern Kordofan was now firmly under the Mahdi's control. When the rising quickly spread to the provinces of Sennar and Darfur it became clear that the entire Sudan would be engulfed in a tremendous explosion. Everywhere, small government posts were overwhelmed and only the larger garrisons survived in isolation.

To a large extent, these developments in the distant Sudan were obscured from the world by events in Egypt itself. The Khedive (Viceroy) Ismail had attempted to modernize the country but in so doing he had incurred foreign debts which Egypt was unable to repay. As a result, the economy was managed by British and French advisers and the British government purchased Ismail's holdings in the recently completed Suez Canal. In 1879 Ismail was deposed and replaced by his son Tewfik. Naturally, many Egyptians resented the extent of foreign influence and discontent finally surfaced under the leadership of Achmet Arabi Pasha in February 1881. In June 1882, after some 50 Europeans had been killed during riots in Alexandria, a British squadron bombarded the city's defences into surrender and then restored order with landing-parties. Elsewhere, however, Arabi remained intransigent and, since an unstable Egypt clearly presented a threat to the Suez Canal, now Great Britain's principal sea route to her Imperial possessions in the Far East, a 25,000-strong army was put ashore at Ismailia with the object of restoring a more acceptable government.

In command was Lieutenant-General Sir Garnet Wolseley, who had seen active service in Burma, the Crimea, the Indian Mutiny and the Second Opium War, as well as commanding the Red River Expedition in Manitoba, Canada, in 1870 and the punitive expedition against the Ashanti in the Gold Coast, now Ghana, in 1874. During the Zulu War he had been appointed commander-in-chief after Lord Chelmsford's un-promising start to the campaign, but, to his disappointment, only reached the theatre of operations after Chelmsford had won the decisive victory at Ulundi.

The hallmark of Wolseley's operations in remote areas of the world was thorough forward planning based on an appreciation that terrain and climate were often as formidable opponents as the enemy. Nothing was left to chance and attention to detail was of paramount importance. The saying 'All Sir Garnet' was used throughout the Army to denote efficiency, and it was of Wolseley that Gilbert and Sullivan were thinking when they drew the character of 'The Very Model of a Modern Major-General' for *The Pirates of Penzance*. Disraeli described him as 'our only general', although the view was not shared by supporters of Lieutenant-General Sir Frederick Roberts, who had recently performed similar prodigies during the Second Afghan War. It was, however, typical of Wolseley that, although his troops had been assembled so quickly that they would have to fight in their traditional uniforms of scarlet or blue, albeit with the addition of sun helmets, they were issued with anti-glare goggles and insect veils; it was also typical of soldierly perversity that these items were hardly used at all, presumably because they were considered 'soft'.

Wolseley had decided to disembark from the Canal itself, partly because he did not wish his troops to become tied down among the waterways of the Nile Delta, and partly because, having established his beach-head at Ismailia, he would be able to strike directly at Cairo. After being worsted in skirmishes at Kassassin, Arabi withdrew his troops to a well-constructed line of entrenchments at Tel-el-Kebir, blocking further progress towards the capital. During the night of 12/13 September, Wolseley's army executed a brilliant approach march and drove the Egyptians from their trenches in a dawn attack. Arabi surrendered the following day when the pursuing British cavalry reached Cairo, and was sent into exile in Ceylon. Leaving 10,000 men to safeguard British interests, Wolseley returned home to receive a hero's welcome, promotion to full general and a peerage. He little realized that, for the Army, his brief campaign marked the beginning of 70 years' continuous presence in Egypt, for although there was at the time no thought of so continuous a commitment, a succession of necessities ensured that it was maintained, and the first of these was the troubled state of the Sudan. There, the major Egyptian garrisons continued to hold out, and on 2 September 1883 that of El Obeid actually inflicted a sharp reverse on the dervishes, as the Mahdi's followers had become known. When, some weeks later, starvation compelled the Egyptians to submit, Mohammed Ahmed had the Governor dismembered as a warning to others who still defied him. With the fall of the town, the dervishes acquired 6,000 rifles, modern artillery and machine-guns and thus became a formidable force.

In Cairo, it had been decided to mount a further expedition to restore order. A force of 9,000 men, most of whom had fought for Arabi Pasha, was assembled at Khartoum under the command of Colonel William Hicks, a retired Indian Army officer who had been appointed the Egyptian Army's Chief of Staff. Hicks' mission was to relieve the garrison of Darfur and at first he made good progress. By 3 November, however, his army had dwindled to 7,000 and at Sheikan, twelve miles from El Obeid, it was surrounded by 20,000 well-armed dervishes and destroyed in two days' fighting.

Once again, the dervish victory had dramatic consequences. Darfur surrendered and the Arabs of the eastern Sudan, between the Nile and the Red Sea, threw in their lot with the Mahdi, attacking Egyptian garrisons on the coast. It was now apparent to Sir Evelyn Baring, the British government's senior representative in Cairo, that further efforts to recover the Sudan would simply be a waste of military and economic resources. The Egyptians agreed, but were anxious to secure the safe evacuation of their remaining garrisons and the survivors of their civil administration. The British government offered Gordon's services to help achieve this aim, but because of the religious nature of the rising the Egyptians at first declined. Instead, they proposed appointing Zubeir Pasha, a former slave-trader whose power Gordon had curbed and who was now living in virtual house arrest in Cairo. Zubeir still enjoyed immense prestige and influence in the Sudan and, in Winston Churchill's opinion, the probability was that, had he been permitted to return immediately as its nominated ruler, and properly supported with arms and funds, he would have brought the Mahdi under control. Baring approved of the plan but in London ministers, comfortably remote from the scene of events, declined to contaminate themselves by dealing with such a man. In the circumstances, therefore, the Egyptians had little alternative other than to accept Gordon as the next most suitable candidate for the job. Baring, well aware of Gordon's mercurial temperament, strongly opposed the appointment on the grounds that if a British general got into trouble in the Sudan, British troops would be required to extract him, but he was forced to give way under combined pressure from the Egyptians, the Foreign Office and an enthusiastic British public.

Gordon described his appointment as the greatest honour he had ever received, but the truth was that he had been handed the slimier end of a very dirty stick. He left London on 18 January 1884, paused briefly to pay his respects to the Khedive and Baring in Cairo, and reached Khartoum on 22 February. During the journey south it became apparent to him that the Sudan had changed beyond recognition since his departure four years earlier, and he recognized that, alone, his chances of completing a successful evacuation were negligible. Zubeir, he knew, was the key to the situation and he telegraphed Cairo repeatedly on the subject. Baring supported him, but the Foreign Office would have none of it; nor would it permit the Egyptians to employ him. Gordon suggested numerous alternatives, including a formal Mandate from the Sultan of Turkey (Egypt then being nominally a province of the Ottoman Empire); the dispatch of 200 British troops to Berber, some 200 miles downstream, or even to Aswan, well within the Egyptian frontier, to demonstrate the government's firm intent; reinforcement with Muslim regiments from the Indian Army; and even a proposal that he should attempt to reach a personal accord with the Mahdi. All his requests were denied.

To what extent Gordon could, at least, have initiated an evacuation remains an open question, for the Mahdi, taken aback by his arrival, expected a substantial force to follow in his wake and paused to await developments. What is certain is that Gordon decided to stay put in Khartoum at a very early stage, driven by a sense of honour that would not allow him to desert those placed in his charge. Denied the assistance of Zubeir and much else besides, he was determined to place William Gladstone's administration in a situation where it was compelled to mount a relief expedition, like it or not. In early March, Gordon offered to resign his commission; the offer was not accepted. On 15 March the telegraph line was cut by the dervishes north of Khartoum. Thereafter his dispatches, routed through the sympathetic Baring, ranged progressively through the insubordinate to the insulting. That of 8 April is almost incoherent with rage: 'I leave you [i.e., the British government] the indelible disgrace of abandoning the garrisons. . . . I feel sure, whatever you [Baring] feel diplomatically, I have your support, and that of every man professing himself a gentleman – in private.'

He was wasting his time. Although they had in no small measure been responsible for creating the problem, Gladstone's philanthropic Liberals were instinctively averse to further military ventures abroad and they were not to be moved either by threat or appeal. In May, the dervishes stormed Berber, leaving Khartoum utterly isolated and under siege by 60,000 men equipped with captured Egyptian artillery. Unimpressed, Gordon fought the battle of his life. He had arrived to find a 7,000-strong garrison, demoralized and indifferently officered, together with 30,000 civilians, many of whom were, if not actually Mahdist supporters and spies, untrustworthy, defeatist or, at best, apathetic, and by sheer force of personality he held them together. He strengthened the city's fortifications, of modern construction but ancient design, strung barbed wire and laid mines, although as a professional military engineer he knew that the defences were inherently weak. He made regular destructive sorties and used his small flotilla of steamers to mount raids deep into enemy-controlled territory. It was Gordon and not the dervishes who held the initiative for much of the time, but he knew that his resources were finite and that unless help arrived the end was inevitable. From time to time he managed to slip a messenger, heavily disguised, through the enemy lines. Day by day he stood on the roof of the Governor-General's palace, his telescope searching the shimmering horizon to the north for some sign that relief was on its way; and day by day the instrument revealed nothing but the dervish encampments with the empty river beyond, reaching into the infinite desert.

At home, the public knew little of the details, but it did know that Gordon was holding out and its sense of fair play was outraged by the government's failure to help him. Together, the Conservative opposition and the press waded into the Gladstone administration at every opportunity. In the Commons, the matter was pressed to a vote of censure from which the government emerged with a seriously reduced majority. The controversy raged on during the Parliamentary summer recess until at length Gladstone, scenting electoral disaster for his party, finally gave way at the beginning of August and sanctioned the dispatch of a small relief force. At first he was prepared to release only one brigade, but his military advisers convinced him that a brigade was neither large enough nor tactically suited to the task in hand and he finally agreed to a force of 10,000 men to be selected from the entire Army.

Wolseley was appointed commander of the expedition and reached Cairo on 9 September. He was aware that the chances of success were diminishing daily, but was prepared to make every effort to break through to Khartoum, although the physical difficulties were immense. Two routes presented themselves. Of these, the shorter lay through Suakin on the Red Sea, across the Desert of the Belly of Stones to Berber and thence upstream. This he rejected not only because substantial dervish elements were in virtual control of the Suakin hinterland, but also because there were too few wells along the desert route and the transportation of water in the quantities required by the force was a logistic impossibility. The longer Nile route offered both advantages and disadvantages. In Egypt itself the railway system and river steamers enabled a base to be established quickly at Wadi Halfa on the Sudan border. On the other hand, the relief force would be operating at the time of year when the river was falling, exposing the series of rapids known as cataracts, six of which existed betwen Aswan and Khartoum. Passage of these was difficult, time-consuming and dangerous, but Wolseley had encountered similar problems during his Red River Expedition and ordered some 800 boats to be shipped out from England immediately. Some sources mention whalers, which were undoubtedly present, but there were also a large number of specially constructed Canadian *bateaux* with flat bottoms, which drew less water and were therefore better suited for the passage of the cataracts. To man the latter, 300 Canadian *voyageurs* were recruited, some of whom reached Egypt dressed for a campaign within the Arctic Circle.

While the troops and their mountains of stores were being assembled, there were numberless matters to attend to before the expedition could proceed further, not least of which was the purchase of thousands of camels. Having given his preliminary orders, Wolseley left his capable staff to cope and made a personal foray by camel to Dongola, hoping to learn something of Gordon. There he was met by his Arabic-speaking intelligence officer, Major Herbert Kitchener, who had gone ahead. The tale Kitchener had to tell was not encouraging. Gordon, believing that a relief force *must* be on the way, had dispatched one of his few British officers downriver in a steamer to urge speed as the situation in Khartoum was deteriorating. Though pursued, the steamer had fought its way beyond the besiegers' grasp and made good progress until its bottom was torn out on rocks near the Fourth Cataract. Those aboard were enticed ashore by an apparently friendly sheik who promised them camels and an escort to Dongola, then murdered them. Gordon's dispatch was now undoubtedly in the Mahdi's hands and, with it, the knowledge that the defence of Khartoum was faltering.

Slowly, the relief force moved south to concentrate at Korti, where Wolseley made his headquarters. Whenever possible, the boats were towed in lines by steamers. Otherwise, they were hauled up the cataracts with ropes or rowed. The work was heavy and continuous, but the result was that when the men reached Korti they were hard and superbly fit, if a little ragged. To encourage progress, Wolseley had offered a prize of £100 to the first regimental contingent to complete the journey; it was won by the Royal Irish Regiment.

On 17 November Wolseley received a message from Gordon, written two weeks previously, expressing doubts that he could hold out beyond 14 December. Given the physical impossibility of reaching Khartoum in that time, a more cautious commander might have abandoned the entire enterprise, but Wolseley was determined that every effort would continue to be made until the issue was decided one way or the other.

A glance at the map shows that anyone travelling up-river from Korti is actually moving in a north-easterly direction, *away* from Khartoum, as far as Abu Hamed, where the course becomes south-easterly to Berber, then south-westerly; furthermore, in negotiating this great arc, the Fourth, Fifth and Sixth Cataracts have to be navigated before Khartoum is reached. However, a track through the Bayuda Desert cut across the chord of the arc, connecting Korti with Gubat, south of Metemmeh, only 96 miles from Khartoum, and along this there were sufficient wells to support a small force. Wolseley therefore decided to adopt a daring and extremely dangerous plan in which the main body of the expedition would continue up-river while a flying column was sent across the desert to Gubat, where arrangements would be made for Gordon's steamers to be waiting. The object of the operation was not Gordon's relief but the reinforcement of the Khartoum garrison by the flying column to the extent that it would be able to hold on until the spring, when the Nile rose and Wolseley would be able to complete the relief. It says much for Wolseley's forethought that he had anticipated that something very like the present contingency, demanding long-range desert mobility, would arise. He had formed a Camel Corps, under the command of Brigadier-General Sir Herbert Stewart, with detachments drawn from cavalry regiments and men with mounted infantry experience, and it was this, suitably reinforced, which would undertake the apparently impossible task of crossing the Bayuda and breaking through to Khartoum.

The word expendable was not then in common military usage, although as a matter of course generals calculated the probable cost of achieving their objectives. On one side of Wolseley's balance sheet was the slim chance that the Desert Column, as it became known, would actually produce the desired results; it was, in fact, the only chance he would be offered. On the other was the possibility that the column, the size of which was strictly limited by the anticipated water supply, would sustain a serious defeat and be unable to continue its advance. In the overall context the loss of life would not be great as, in the nature of things, the farther it marched the more troops it would have to detach to protect its lines of communication and, in the event that the spearhead was wiped out, most of these men could be withdrawn. This was the worst possible scenario, but if it happened Gordon could neither be sustained nor relieved in time and the expedition would have to withdraw. Stewart was fully aware of the implications and also that his little force, once committed, would receive no support from the main or River Column, which would also have its hands full.

The Desert Column consisted of the Heavy Camel Regiment, drawn from heavy cavalry and lancer regiments, details of which have been given above; the Light Camel Regiment, with detachments from the 3rd, 4th, 7th, 10th, 11th, 15th, 18th, 20th and 21st Hussars, which was to be employed on escort and lines of communication duties; the Guards Camel Regiment, consisting of detachments from the Grenadier, Coldstream and Scots Guards and Royal Marine Light Infantry; the Mounted Infantry Camel Regiment, drawn from the Somerset Light Infantry, Royal Scots Fusiliers, Cornwall Light Infantry, South Staffordshire Regiment, The Black Watch, Essex Regiment, Royal West Kent Regiment, King's Royal Rifle Corps, Gordon Highlanders, Connaught Rangers and The Rifle Brigade, most of the men having served previously in South Africa or Egypt; 400 men of the Royal Sussex Regiment and one company of the Essex Regiment; one squadron of 19th Hussars, mounted on horses; a half battery of Royal Artillery with three 2.5in 'screw-guns', which broke down into convenient pack loads; a Royal Navy detachment with one Gardner machine-gun; a Royal Engineer detachment, a portable field hospital and transport details.

Altogether, the strength of the column amounted to 2,000 men, plus 300 locally recruited camel drivers, interpreters and guides. With the exception of the naval detachment, which wore its tropical landing-party rig, the troops were dressed in lightweight grey serge tunics with a leather 50-round bandolier worn over the left shoulder, leather waistbelt with 20-round expense pouch and sword bayonet, haversack slung over the right shoulder, khaki breeches with blue puttees and brown boots; sun helmets, normally white, had been dyed khaki with coffee or, in the case of 19th Hussars, tobacco juice. For reasons which will become apparent, some thirty Guardsmen took their scarlet tunics along in their baggage. On the camel was a leather bucket for the single-shot .45in Martini-Henry rifle, 100 rounds stowed in the saddlebags with personal kit, large water-bottle, six-gallon water-skin, blanket, tentage and corn bag.

The camel regiments had ridden up from Aswan to Korti, so that by the time they arrived they were familiar with the cantankerous ways of their haughty, spitting, belching mounts. Less so were those who joined the column at Korti, including the naval detachment, which caused much mirth as it attempted to master the new skills. Amusing as the results were, Stewart decided that several more days' training were required if they were to keep and control their mounts in the desert.

On 30 December Stewart set out with the Guards and a supply convoy on the first phase of the operation, which involved securing Gakdul, approximately 100 miles along the track, and establishing a base there. The next day a message from Gordon reached Korti; it had been written on 14 December and confirmed that Khartoum was still holding out, but the messenger also delivered an ominous verbal request that Wolseley should come quickly. Stewart returned on 5 January and completed his preparations for the departure of the main body of the Desert Column. After being reviewed by Wolseley, the column set off into the unknown during the night of 9 January, watched by those who pondered its chances of survival, let alone success.

'It was a strange sight,' wrote one, 'to see the 3,000 camels with their necks stretching out like ostriches, and their 6,000 pairs of long legs moving along in military array, until the rising dust first blended desert, men and camels in one uniform grey hue and finally hid them from the sight of those who remained in camp.'

There was little sound as spongy feet plodded through the sand at the steady rate of 2¾ miles per hour, the best that nature would allow. To the west, the moon outlined the shape of the hills which paralleled the track for much of the way: Djebel Magaga, Djebel Gilif and Djebel es Sergain. Shortly after dawn on the 10th the column reached the wells at Hambok and, finding them almost dry, was forced to march on for a further nine miles to those of El Howeiyat. Here the alarming discovery was made that these had also been drained by the supply convoy on its way up to Gakdul. In theory, each man had set off with three days' water, but some of this had been consumed and more had been lost from leaking skins. The risk of dehydration had suddenly become very serious for here, even in January, the midday temperature soars above 100 degrees, the sun beating down from above and reflected by the burning sands underfoot with a glare that bores through the eyes into an aching skull. Some water was oozing muddily back into the wells but it was a slow process and although, from time to time, it was possible to let some men drink by companies, others were rationed to one pint in the morning and another at night, the animals receiving nothing at all.

Late in the afternoon the march was resumed. After dusk, however, difficult going was encountered and the column was forced to bivouac. Next morning it reached the wells at Abu Halfa, where the water supply was better but still inadequate. The engineers dug fresh holes and these began to fill quickly; in the meantime, the thirst-maddened animals had to be held in check until they were ready. For the remainder of the day the men were allowed to rest and drink their fill.

Gakdul, lying in a wide, rocky depression, was reached during the morning of the 12th. Here the Guards had occupied their time to good purpose, building two stone forts and laying out a camp complete with signboards and paths. There was, too, fresh, clear, cold water in abundance. 'We gratified our eyes as well as our throats and stomachs, and had the unaccustomed luxury of splashing and tubbing,' wrote one desert-weary officer. Time, however, was of the essence and during the early hours of the 14th the column set off again, detaching part of the Royal Sussex to hold the wells.

Every step beyond Gakdul was a step deeper into enemy territory. The Mahdi, of course, was well aware of the column's progress and purpose, but he did not regard it as a serious threat. If the much larger army of Hicks Pasha had been so easily destroyed, then Stewart's impudent force could be exterminated without the slightest difficulty. A large body of dervishes under selected emirs was detached from the siege lines at Khartoum and sent north to Metemmeh where it was joined by the Ja'alin tribe. Approximately 12,000 men were ready to fall on Stewart, but their orders were to let him advance to a point from which no escape would be possible once he had been defeated. No time would be wasted in providing Gordon with physical proof of the Desert Column's destruction and, recognizing that his last hope had gone, he would cease his futile resistance. All in all, the appearance of the Desert Column could be seen as a blessing which delivered the enemies of the Mahdi into his hands.

Stewart's next objective was Abu Klea and its wells. On the 15th the cavalry scouts found plenty of hoof marks and a discarded rifle, while several camel riders were seen in the distance, shadowing the progress of the column. Obviously a dervish force was somewhere nearby and the night was spent in a defensive zareba near Djebel es Sergain. Next morning the 19th Hussar squadron was sent on ahead to secure Abu Klea but quickly returned with the news that it was held by the enemy in strength; many banners and a large tent had been seen and, while riflemen opened a distant but ineffective fire, native drums called the dervishes to arms. Stewart gave orders for the construction of a zareba, consisting of thorn bushes, baggage and boxes, in which the column spent a restless night, galled by sniper fire which was drawn to any source of light. Casualties were slight, but the effect, coupled with the continuous beating of drums, was to deprive the men of sleep, which was the dervishes' intention.

Few were sorry when the pre-dawn stand-to was sounded. After sunrise skirmishers were sent out to disperse the snipers on the hill to the north. Some dervish cavalry hovering to the south turned and rode out of range after they had been treated to a few shells from the screw-guns. When it became clear that the main body of the enemy, while closer, had no immediate intention of attacking, Stewart decided that he would bring matters to a head by attacking them. Leaving sufficient men to hold the zareba, the column formed square outside, this being the usual tactic in desert warfare when the enemy's superior numbers would enable him to turn the flanks of any other formation. With the square went the three screw-guns, the Gardner machine-gun and, in the centre, camels carrying water, ammunition and medical supplies; the remainder of the camels were left behind in the zareba.

The Mahdi's emirs could hardly have believed their eyes when the tiny square, containing just 1,500 men, began to advance against them. Yet, in the final analysis, it was the only option available to Stewart, who was relying on firepower and discipline to see him through. Progress was slow and halts to dress the ranks were frequent as the camels would not be hurried and bulged out the rear face of the square. Here and there a man or an animal dropped from the sniper fire which the Mounted Infantry skirmishers and 19th Hussars, on the left of the advance, were unable to contain, although they were pushing the dervish riflemen back.

The square had reached a point some 500 yards from the line of enemy banners, and had again halted to dress its rear face, when the dervishes attacked. About 5,000 of them surged forward behind their mounted emirs, covering the ground at a tremendous pace and heading for the left-front corner of the square. The screw-guns, which formed part of the front face, went into action at once, their shells sending up fountains of dirt as they burst among the charging ranks. Simultaneously, the Guards and Mounted Infantry commenced volley-firing. It seemed to have little effect until the range closed to within 100 yards, when the heavy .45in slugs began slamming home to produce a mounting pile of dead and injured. Completely fearless, the dervishes immediately changed the direction of their attack, streaming past the left face of the square, the fire of which was inhibited as the skirmishers ran in. It was clear that the enemy's intention was now to smash through the left-rear corner, and the Naval Detachment was pushed out with the Gardner to meet the threat.

At this period, the Army was less enthusiastic about machine-guns than the Navy, partly because stoppages always seemed to occur at critical moments. The Gardner was a manually operated weapon with five barrels mounted side by side, served in turn by a crank-operated sliding feed block. During Admiralty trials it had fired nearly 17,000 rounds with only 24 stoppages and at one stage had achieved a rate of 812 rounds per minute. The gun, therefore, was apparently tried and tested, but now the proof of the pudding was to be in the eating. It opened fire, cutting down those who crossed its path, them jammed after firing thirty rounds, with the dervishes only 200 yards distant and closing fast. What happened next is described by Lord Charles Beresford, who commanded the seamen.

'The captain of the gun, Will Rhoods, chief boatswain's mate, and myself, unscrewed the plate to clear the barrel, or take the lock [bolt] of the jammed barrel out, when the enemy were upon us. Rhoods was killed with a spear. Walter Miller, armourer, I also saw killed with a spear at the same moment on my left. I was knocked down in the rear of the gun, but uninjured, except for a small spear scratch on my left hand. The crowd and crush of the enemy were very great at this point and, as I struggled up, I was carried against the face of the square, which was literally pressed by sheer weight of numbers about twelve paces from the position of the gun. The crush was so great that at the moment few on either side were killed, but fortunately this flank of the square had been forced up a very steep little mound, which enabled the rear rank to open a tremendous fire over the heads of the front rank men; this relieved the pressure and enabled the front rank to bayonet or shoot those of the enemy nearest them.'

While the Gardner was being overrun, another drama was being enacted only yards away. Stewart's Second-in-Command was a Colonel Fred Burnaby, an archetypal Victorian hero figure who combined the virtues of fire-eating soldier, adventurer, traveller, sportsman and balloonist. It was said that Burnaby had a death wish, and this was apparently confirmed when, sword drawn, he shouldered his horse out of the ranks towards an emir leading the dervish charge. Before the two could close the emir was brought down by rifle fire, but Burnaby immediately found himself duelling with a spearman. Suddenly a second dervish, pursuing a skirmisher, turned and ran his spear into the colonel's shoulder. The man was promptly bayonetted by a soldier who ran out from the square, but Burnaby's attention had been fatally distracted and his first assailant stabbed him twice in the neck. His jugular severed, he reeled from his horse but was quickly on his feet and slashed at those around him until he collapsed and died.

The weight of the attack struck the Heavy Camel Regiment, holding half the left face and the rear of the square. Led by an elderly mounted emir, a number of dervishes broke through the vulnerable angle between the two faces and swarmed into the interior of the square. The emir planted his banner, inscribed with texts from the Koran, and was immediately shot dead, falling upon it. His men, balked by the lines of tied-down camels, swung left. The rear ranks of the Heavies and the Mounted Infantry faced about and opened fire; in so doing they undoubtedly killed or wounded several of their comrades beyond, but the situation was desperate and had to be brought under control very quickly. It was probably a round so aimed that killed Stewart's horse under him. As the general fell, three dervishes rushed at him; Colonel Sir Charles Wilson, who assumed Burnaby's duties, shot one dead with his revolver, and the other two were dispatched by Mounted Infantry officers. The rest of the intruders were hunted down with the bayonet; none survived.

Writing some years after the event, Private Harry Etherington of the Royal Sussex ventured the opinion that the dervishes had achieved the unique distinction of breaking into a British square because the Heavies were more used to the sabre than the bayonet. Most infantrymen would have agreed with him, although the reasons were more complex than that and, in any event, it was with rifle and bayonet that the cavalrymen closed the gap in desperate hand-to-hand fighting, the heaviest loss falling on the Royal Dragoons and Scots Greys. However, the pressure remained immense and the corner of the square, with the adjacent faces, was forced back towards the rear of the front and right faces. Fortunately, the camels formed a buttress and, as the Guards and Royal Marines were on slightly higher ground, their rear ranks were able to face about and direct aimed fire over the heads of the embattled troopers into the enemy mass behind. Some of the dervishes, unable to come to grips near the broken corner, had run further along the rear face only to be repulsed by the 4th and 5th Dragoon Guards. Almost immediately, the dervishes directed a cavalry charge against the right-rear corner of the square, but this was beaten off by the heavy, sustained fire of the Dragoon Guards and the Royal Sussex. Suddenly, it was all over. From start to finish, the hand-to-hand phase of the engagement had taken a mere five minutes, although its horrific memory would last a lifetime. The dervishes simply turned and walked slowly away, pausing now and then to yell insults. The square responded with a cheer, followed by several volleys and a few rounds of case-shot to speed them on their way. Beresford, almost half of whose men had been killed or wounded in defence of the Gardner, went out and cleared the stoppage, exacting what revenge he could before the enemy disappeared.

Stewart moved the square some distance to sort itself out, then began clearing the battlefield. Wilson wrote that the place where the square had been broken was 'too horrible for description'. Indeed, the victory had not been cheaply won; the column's losses amounted to nine officers and 65 other ranks killed, plus nine officers and 85 other ranks wounded. The enemy's dead, amounting to 1,100, lay everywhere; it was possible to identify the emirs by their *jibbahs* which, while patched to denote poverty, were of finer cotton than those of their followers. Prisoners later confirmed that the number of their wounded had been equally heavy. After burning the enemy's discarded weapons, Stewart occupied Abu Klea wells without further opposition. The baggage had not yet come up from the zareba so the force had to bivouac in the open. Few slept, as the night was bitterly cold, and no doubt for some shock played its part too.

On the morning of the 18th a stone fort was built for the wounded, who were to be left under the guard of 100 men of the Royal Sussex. Stewart had decided to strike straight for the Nile, now only 23 miles away. That afternoon, after the baggage arrived, the column set off again. A moonless night march with difficult going followed and for a while direction was lost in a dense wood of spiky mimosa. Halts were frequent and during these the exhausted men fell so deeply asleep that they had to be kicked awake. A few slept in the saddle and their mounts wandered off; they were never seen again. Doubts began to arise as to the loyalty of the guide, a known thief named Ali Loda, but at 01.00 more open going was reached and the pace increased. By dawn on the 19th the column had reached a point some five miles south of Metammeh and the same distance from the Nile to the west, having taken eighteen hours to cover the fourteen miles from Abu Klea. At 07.30 the 19th Hussar squadron, scouting ahead, crossed a low gravel ridge and saw the Nile flowing through its narrow green belt of palms and agricultural land; and, between the ridge and the river, an even larger dervish force than that which had been defeated at Abu Klea.

The weary column was hardly in a condition to fight a second major engagement, but its survival depended upon it. Besides, everyone had had more than enough of the Bayuda Desert, its heat, dust, flies and thirst, and of endless, jolting marches into the unknown, ahead lay the Nile, a desirable, tangible objective towards which the men would willingly fight their way, although many doubted that they would ever reach it. Ordering the construction of a zareba, and a redoubt on a nearby knoll, Stewart ordered his staff to pass on his intentions: 'We shall first have breakfast, and then go out to fight.'

While the work was going on, the dervishes had moved forward to the gravel ridge and pushed out riflemen to snipe at the zareba. Two journalists, Cameron of *The Standard* and St Leger Herbert of *The Morning Post*, members of the small press corps who had been allowed to accompany the column, sharing all its hardships and dangers, were killed by this fire. Shortly afterwards, Stewart was himself struck in the groin by a bullet and the wound was to prove mortal.

Wilson, assuming command, continued with Stewart's plan. Half the Heavy Camel Regiment, the 19th Hussars, the Naval Detachment and the artillery were to be left behind for the defence of the zareba and the redoubt. The screw-guns and the Gardner were to provide covering fire while the rest of the column, formed in square as at Abu Klea, advanced towards the ridge. The square itself, now reduced to a mere 900 men, moved off from the zareba during the afternoon, its slow advance towards the ridge being made under fire with frequent halts to pick up the wounded. Only puffs of white smoke revealed the positions of the enemy riflemen, but wherever a concentration of these appeared the screw-guns, firing from the redoubt, began bursting shrapnel above it. Likewise, the Gardner was now earning its keep, hammering away to good effect against dervish cavalry attempting to approach the zareba from the left.

Nevertheless, those in the square continued to be galled by the fire of the invisible snipers. It was with a sense almost of relief that they observed the main body of the enemy suddenly surge forward off the ridge towards them, behind its banners and mounted emirs. Volley-firing started at once but caused few casualties. Wilson told his bugler to sound Cease Firing and, to his surprise, the order was obeyed. The square waited in absolute silence, the only movement being a regular lowering of sights as the dervishes came on at a steady run. Not until they had closed to within 300 yards was Commence Firing sounded. At once the volleys blasted out, followed by rapid independent fire. The men had learned much at Abu Klea and they shot deliberately, aiming low and to kill. Wilson describes the result: 'All the leaders and their fluttering banners went down, and no one got within fifty yards of the square. It only lasted a few minutes; the whole of the front ranks were swept away and then we saw a wild backward movement, followed by the rapid disappearance of the Arabs in front of and all round us. We had won, and gave three ringing cheers.' The engagement, which took its name from the nearby village of Abu Kru, had cost the column one officer and 22 other ranks killed, and eight officers and 90 other ranks wounded. The dervishes, streaming away in the direction of Metemmeh, left behind several hundred dead.

The column closed up and reached the Nile where it thirstily drank its reward. It had already achieved the apparently impossible, but now Wilson was faced with a set of very serious problems. His little force, deadly tired and reduced to about 1,000 effectives, was absurdly exposed. The enemy was still poised on his flank in overwhelming strength at Metemmeh, a well-built town with defensive walls; a probe in that direction was met with cannon fire, indicating that while the dervishes might have reservations about meeting the Desert Column again in the open, any attempt to storm the defences would result in heavy loss. Furthermore, there were large numbers of wounded to care for and supplies would remain short until more were brought forward.

The first task, therefore, was to consolidate the column's own position at Gubat. A fort was constructed, consisting of stone breastworks fronted with sand and gravel banking to absorb the enemy's artillery fire should he choose to attack, and beyond this was a thorn hedge to break the assault of his infantry, sited at optimum killing range. A detachment was ordered to escort a convoy of supply camels back to Gakdul; it did not augur well for the future that on the first night alone 23 of the overworked animals dropped dead in the their tracks. On the 21st, smoke approaching from up-river marked the arrival of four of Gordon's steamers, none of which was larger than a modern tugboat. The news they brought was that Khartoum, though hard-pressed, was still holding out; on the other hand, 3,000 more dervishes had been dispatched north with strict orders to avenge the defeat at Abu Klea, and they were within two days' march of Gubat. In the event, no attack materialized, for the enemy reinforcements merely joined their comrades in Metemmeh. Such pressure as they brought to bear was psychological, involving the incessant beating of drums during the night.

The delay at Gubat was regrettable but unavoidable, and Wilson cannot be criticized for taking every possible measure for the security of his troops, without whom nothing further could have been accomplished. He appreciated that, while the Desert Column had succeeded in drawing off many of Khartoum's besiegers, he could only provide Gordon with a token reinforcement, which he would lead personally. On the 24th he set off with two of the steamers, determined to break through. Aboard were a handful of seamen and a score of Royal Sussex, the latter dressed in scarlet tunics borrowed from the Guards because Gordon had once said that the sight of a few red coats would convince the Mahdi that Great Britain meant business. Wolseley, kept informed of these developments, despatched Colonel Redvers Buller, his Chief of Staff, along the desert track to take command at Gubat; by the time Buller arrived, however, the issue would have been long decided.

The truth was that for some time the fate of Khartoum had rested with the Mahdi. His reasons for not launching a decisive assault have aroused much speculation, especially regarding his attitude to Gordon. It would not seem well for one holy man, Mohammed Ahmed, to kill another, Charles Gordon, for even if the latter were not a true believer he was still a man of unquestioned piety whose acts of goodness were still spoken of throughout the Sudan. The Mahdi offered Gordon what he considered to be honourable terms, in which Gordon was to be allowed to depart without even the payment of a ransom, but his offer was ignored. Now, it was better that Khartoum should be starved into surrender, since the end could not be long delayed.

This attitude changed with the tidings of Abu Klea and Abu Kru. Undoubtedly, the disciplined firepower and ferocity of the Desert Column was described in detail, and doubtless its strength was exaggerated. When the Mahdi learned that some 2,000 of his *Ansar* lay dead, including numerous faithful emirs, that many would never recover from their wounds, and that the British had reached the Nile and were less than 100 miles away, he decided to risk no further blows to his prestige. First, those still at Metemmeh were to be reinforced so that the British could be contained or, better still, destroyed. Secondly, Khartoum was to be stormed at once, although Gordon's life was to be spared. The falling Nile had exposed Khartoum's defences and at 03.30 on 26 January the dervishes swarmed over them. The garrison, weakened by starvation, offered only patchy resistance and were massacred. The whole town was then given over to an orgy of slaughter, rape and destruction. Accounts differ as to how Gordon met his end, but all agree that he died with courage. The Mahdi was furious that his orders had been disobeyed; it is said that when Gordon's head was brought to him he was unable to meet the gaze of the pale blue eyes, still open but hooded in death.

None of this was known to Wilson and his party, still pushing upstream against the current. As they approached Khartoum on the 27th they came under rifle and artillery fire. That was only to be expected and the little steamers, protected by timber baulks and sandbags, returned the fire with their own armament, as they had done many times in the past.

As Khartoum itself came into view it was apparent that something was wrong; the red flag of Egypt, with its sickle moon and star, was no longer flying above the Governor-General's palace. When fire was opened from the town's own fortifications Wilson's suspicions were confirmed; Khartoum had fallen. There was nothing more he could do save reverse course and fight his way downstream.

If, in the terms of epic cinema, the entire concept of the Desert Column might be considered overdrawn, the subsequent adventures of Wilson and his party belong to the pages of the *Boys' Own Paper*. The two steamers fought their way to apparent safety but both were wrecked near the Shabluka cataract. The troops got ashore, taking with them such weapons, ammunition and food as they could. As their strength amounted to less than a full platoon it would have been madness for them to have attempted to march further through country swarming with hostile dervishes, so they constructed a tiny fort. An officer named Stuart-Wortley rowed the rest of the way to Gubat to obtain help, assisted by the current and travelling by night. Beresford set out with some of his seamen aboard one of the remaining steamers, running a gauntlet of dervish fire which caused serious machinery damage. This took a day to repair but eventually he broke through to rescue Wilson and his troops.

The fall of Khartoum and the death of Gordon left the expedition without a purpose. Wolseley toyed with the idea of securing Berber with a pincer movement by the River and Desert Columns. The former, commanded by Major-General Earle, inflicted a defeat on the dervishes at Kirbekan on 10 February, but Earle was killed during the closing minutes of the battle. The first step for the Desert Column, which had been reinforced with three more screw-guns and a handful of seamen, all that Wolseley could spare, would have been the capture of Metammeh. However, Buller had arrived to assume command from Wilson and he could not steel himself to mount an attack. His unquestionable courage had won him the Victoria Cross during the Zulu War, he was popular with the troops and was an efficient Chief of Staff, but was uneasy when it came to exercising independent command. He later commented that he would dearly have liked to have cleared Metemmeh of the dervishes, and would always regret not having done so, but on balance had decided to withdraw because of his tenuous line of communications. He had a point, for the supply camels were dying at a rate at which they could not be replaced and, sooner rather than later, the isolated Desert Column would find itself in serious difficulties. Yet, this consideration must have been in his mind when he reached Gubat, so why did he wait for more than a week before starting his withdrawal?

The first step was to pull back as far as Abu Klea. The enemy followed, occupying a nearby hill, but did not attack. Next morning, the 19th Hussars began demonstrating against their rear, exaggerating their own numbers by appearing at different points, and under this threat the dervishes were easily driven off. That night, leaving his camp fires burning and some buglers to sound routine calls until the rearguard pulled out, Buller broke contact and headed for Gakdul. The withdrawal of the Desert Column became progressively easier as it reached the dumps which had been established along the way, the men eating their fill and burning what remained since it could not be transported.

The retreat of the Desert Column meant that the River Column would have to be withdrawn too. Descending the cataracts was infinitely more dangerous than ascending them and lives were lost, including a number of the Canadian *voyageurs* without whom, it was generally agreed, the task would have been impossible. As Wolseley's troops withdrew, the intentions of Gladstone's government became clear: beyond the defence of the Egyptian frontier and Suakin on the Red Sea, there would be no further direct British involvement in the Sudan.

At home, the news that Gordon was dead was received with shock and anger. No one blamed the troops who, despite being asked to achieve an unattainable objective, had arrived just one day late. The obvious argument was that, had they been dispatched earlier, they would have arrived in time, and for that the government must be blamed. Queen Victoria expressed her displeasure in an open telegram to Gladstone and was supported by half the electorate.

To his generation, Charles Gordon was the personification of a Christian gentleman who went willingly to his martyr's death; it is also true that he interpreted his orders in a narrow and personal way, and that he won and lost two battles simultaneously, one against Gladstone and the other against the Mahdi. Gladstone has been judged more harshly by popular history. Apart from social historians, few can remember the beneficial reforms introduced during his periods in office; rather more recall him as a worthy but dull man who addressed his sovereign as though she were a political meeting; most, unfairly, think of him only as the prime minister who left Gordon in the lurch. Mohammed Ahmed, the Mahdi, died of smallpox only five months after he had captured Khartoum and was succeeded by the Khalifa Abdullah. Wolseley, despite the failure of the expedition, was created a viscount, promoted field marshal and became the British Army's Commander-in-Chief in 1895. Kitchener, his senior intelligence officer, regarded the abandonment of Gordon as a national disgrace. By 1896 he was serving as Sirdar (Commander-in-Chief) of the Egyptian Army and, with British support, commenced the reconquest of the Sudan. This second intervention by the United Kingdom was not for altruistic reasons, although the campaign was presented as a crusade against barbarism, but because a serious Italian defeat in Abyssinia had damaged European prestige, and above all, because active French interest in the southern Sudan and the upper reaches of the Nile was not considered acceptable in London.

Having destroyed the Khalifa's army at Omdurman and hoisted the British and Egyptian flags over the ruins of Gordon's palace in Khartoum, he was to bring the Second Boer War to a successful conclusion and served as Secretary of State for War during the First World War until drowned in HMS *Hampshire* in 1916. During the opening phases of the Second Boer War, Buller, by then General Sir Redvers, was to repeat the hesitation he had shown at Metemmeh, with disastrous consequences, and he was replaced by Wolseley's old rival, Field Marshal Lord Roberts.

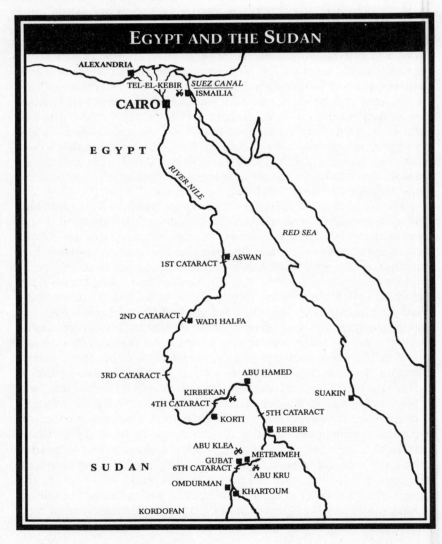

THE ARRAS COUNTER-ATTACK
21 May 1940

The plan was the brainchild of the then Major-General Erich von Manstein, although Hitler was to claim it as his own. During October 1939 Manstein was serving as Chief of Staff to Colonel-General Gerd von Runstedt's Army Group 'A' on the Western Front. Like the majority of senior German officers, he was not looking forward to the forthcoming confrontation with the Western Allies, however quiescent they might be for the moment. It was true that the combination of the Luftwaffe and the panzer divisions had overrun Poland without difficulty the previous month, but the Polish Army was technically a generation behind those of western Europe and in any event had been strategically outflanked by German-held territory even before the war began. Fighting the French Army and the British Expeditionary Force presented an altogether different prospect, for not only could France field 3,000 tanks to oppose Germany's 2,500, but some 1,300 of these were in the vital medium and heavy class whereas approximately 1,500 of the German vehicles were light tanks armed only with machine-guns. For the moment, the BEF did not possess a large tank element, but in due course their numbers were to be augmented by an armoured division which was fitting out in England. Furthermore, as the formidable defences of the Maginot Line inhibited an offensive along the Franco–German frontier, France could only be attacked from the north-east by crossing Dutch and Belgian territory and, while Holland and Belgium were still anxious to preserve their neutrality, there could be no doubt that in the event of an invasion their armies would fight, which would further tilt the scales against the Wehrmacht. To Manstein's mind, therefore, the so-called Phoney War must be used to create an operation that would guarantee a decisive victory in the shortest possible time.

Von Manstein had begun his military career in the 3rd Foot Guards and, like every German officer of his generation and rank, his thought processes automatically turned to the concept of the Annihilation Battle perfected by the elder von Moltke, in which the wings of the enemy army were enveloped and driven in on their centre until the whole became a disorganized mass which could be destroyed where it stood, just as the Roman army had been at Cannae in 216 BC. That had been the thinking behind the Schlieffen Plan which, in 1914, required the German right wing to wheel through Belgium, pushing back the French left against its centre and right to create a pocket from which no escape was possible.

The plan had failed narrowly, and one of the reasons was that it demanded too much of the marching ability of the heavily-laden infantry on the right wing, who were physically unable to cover the great distances involved within the permitted time-scale, to say nothing of having to fight battles along the way. Nevertheless, by 1940 the advent of mechanization had made the Schlieffen Plan a practical proposition and its dangers were clearly apparent to the Allied commanders who, in the event of a German invasion of the Low Countries, would enter Belgium and wheel into line with the Belgian Army, simultaneously prolonging the front northwards to effect a junction with the Dutch Army. In fact, while the German intention was indeed to repeat the opening phases of the Schlieffen Plan, this time under the code-name of 'Plan Yellow', the objectives were limited and the best that could be expected was the capture of the Belgian coastline and an advance to the approximate line from which the German Army had withdrawn in 1918.

This, Manstein believed, was not to Germany's advantage, for under Hitler the Army had been re-armed in breadth but not in depth and was therefore better suited to short campaigns rather than the sort of attritional struggle which had taken place during the First World War. On the other hand, he saw that 'Plan Yellow' could be used to entice the best of the Allied armies northwards, where they could be isolated by a thrust through the centre, then destroyed in detail, leaving the remnant of the French armies to the south to be dealt with at leisure. The thrust, code-named 'Sichelschnitt' (Sickle Cut), was to be delivered through the Ardennes, which the Allies mistakenly believed to be tank-proof, and would cut a swathe across northern France to the Channel coast. With the exception of one panzer division which, in conjunction with the Luftwaffe's parachute and air-landing divisions, would be used to isolate Holland during the early stages of the offensive, the drive would be spearheaded by the armour, concentrated and fighting in panzer corps; behind would come the marching infantry divisions, lining the flanks of the 40-mile-wide corridor as they came up. At the higher levels the invasion of the Low Countries, referred to by Manstein as the Matador's Cloak since it was intended to draw the Allies northwards, would be executed by von Bock's Army Group 'B'; Sichelschnitt was the responsibility of von Rundstedt's Army Group 'A'; farther south, diversionary attacks were to be mounted against the Maginot Line by von Leeb's Army Group 'C'.

After obtaining von Rundstedt's approval, Manstein forwarded his plan to Army General Headquarters (OKH) on 31 October. Having received no response, he submitted it again, three times in November and twice in December. In January 1940 his seventh submission was accompanied by a personal note from Rundstedt requesting that the plan be shown to Hitler. On the 27th Manstein was appointed commander of a corps based on Stettin, far removed from the concerns of the Western Front; obviously, OKH regarded him as an importunate pest.

The trouble was that Field Marshal Walther von Brauchitsch, the Army's Commander-in-Chief, disliked having to deal with Hitler and was unwilling to raise a fresh issue with him, although he agreed with some aspects of the idea. Furthermore, both he and General Franz Halder, his Chief of Staff, were instinctively conservative and only too aware that no precedents existed for the type of operation that Manstein was proposing. What concerned them most was the serious risk that if the Allies cut the corridor, up to 70 per cent of Germany's armoured troops would be isolated in north-western France; beyond that, the implications were too frightening even to consider.

'Sichelschnitt' however, was not dead. When Hitler's adjutant, Colonel Schmundt, visited Army Group 'A' Headquarters he was shown the plan by Manstein's supporters. Recalling that Hitler had once expressed interest in the Somme estuary as a strategic objective, Schmundt returned to Berlin and informed the Führer of Manstein's ideas. The originality of the concept attracted Hitler, who was confident that if none of his own senior commanders had recognized the potential of the thrust Manstein was proposing, then neither would those of the enemy. Manstein was ordered to present himself on 17 February, ostensibly to attend a lunch for newly promoted corps commanders, after which he was taken into the Führer's study to discuss the plan. Beyond commenting that Hitler was quick to grasp his points and was in complete agreement with him, Manstein did not record the details of the conversation, but he would almost certainly have pointed out that the Allies, initially preoccupied with Army Group 'B's invasion of the Low Countries, then knocked off balance by Army Group 'A's breakthrough, would lack either the immediate resources or the time to sever the 'Sichelschnitt' corridor before the trap had closed irrevocably on their northern armies. On 20 February a new set of operational orders for the campaign in the west, incorporating Manstein's plan, was issued on the personal instructions of the Führer.

Here Manstein leaves the story. When the German offensive opened on 10 May the battle developed exactly as he had predicted. The BEF and the best French armies hurried north into Belgium to confront Army Group 'B' while Army Group 'A's three panzer corps closed up to the Meuse, fought their way across with concentrated Luftwaffe support and commenced their drive across northern France, encountering only light resistance once they had achieved their breakthrough. By the night of 20 May their position was as follows: Guderian's XIX Panzer Corps (1st, 2nd and 10th Panzer Divisions) had reached the sea and secured several useful bridgeheads over the Somme on its left flank; Rheinhardt's XLI Panzer Corps (6th and 8th Panzer Divisions) was echeloned to its right rear; in Hoth's XV Panzer Corps, echeloned to the right rear of Rheinhardt's troops, 7th Panzer Division was south-east of Arras with the SS Motorized Division *Totenkopf* coming into line on its left, while 5th Panzer Division was closing in on Arras from the east. The Allied armies in the north were inside a trap and all that remained was for the German armour to wheel right up the Channel coast and their destruction would be complete. German fears for the flanks of the corridor had begun to fade when, on 17 June, Major-General Charles de Gaulle's newly raised 4th *Division Cuirassée* had counter-attacked Guderian near Laon and been driven off.

For the first few days the Allies had been unable to interpret the battle correctly. Some commanders believed that the German armour was heading for Paris, others that it was about to wheel south behind the Maginot Line. By the time the truth dawned it was almost too late for any sort of concerted response. Nevertheless, General Maxime Weygand, who replaced the discredited Maurice Gamelin as Commander-in-Chief on 20 May, quickly appreciated that the only measures likely to produce decisive results were converging counter-attacks into the northern and southern flanks of the corridor. It proved impossible to assemble sufficient troops in the south, but in the north a scratch force was hastily brought together under Major-General H. E. Franklyn and given the task of blocking the roads east of Arras.

The major element of this was Brigadier Douglas Pratt's 1 Army Tank Brigade, the only armoured formation serving with the BEF. The function of the brigade, which consisted of the 4th and 7th Royal Tank Regiments, was to provide support for infantry operations and its principal item of equipment was the odd-looking two-man Infantry Tank Mk I, otherwise known as the Matilda I; this had a maximum speed of 8mph and was armed with either a .303in or .50in Vickers machine-gun. 7th RTR was also partially equipped with the Infantry Tank Mk II (Matilda II), which had a four-man crew, was armed with a 2pdr gun mounted co-axially with a .303in Vickers machine-gun, and had a maximum speed of 15mph. Because of their role, both designs carried heavy frontal armour for their day, 60mm on the Matilda I and 78mm on the Matilda II. In addition, regimental and squadron headquarters were equipped with the Vickers Light Tank Mk VIB, which was fast and armed with machine-guns though dangerously thin-skinned. It can thus be seen that neither the training nor the equipment of the brigade was suited to the task it was required to perform.

During the early days of the German offensive the brigade had conformed to the northward movement of the BEF and leaguered in the Forest of Soignies, between Brussels and the battlefield of Waterloo. On the night of 15/16 May it was ordered south and, because no railway flats were available, was forced to make a painfully slow 130-mile road march over rough pavé roads crowded with refugees. Although the column was attacked regularly by the Luftwaffe the only casualty was a Matilda I blown on to its side by a bomb. However, it was not until after dusk on 20 May that the brigade began reaching its new concentration area behind Vimy Ridge, to the north of Arras. Here the counter-attack force, including 1 Army Tank Brigade, 6th and 8th Battalions Durham Light Infantry, two motor-cycle machine-gun companies and two scout platoons from 4th Royal Northumberland Fusiliers, plus anti-tank gunners and a field artillery battery, was to assemble. The advance was to be made in two parallel columns consisting of:

Left Column	Right Column
4th RTR	7th RTR
6th DLI	8th DLI
'Y' Coy, 4th RNF	'Z' Coy, 4th RNF
Scout Pln, 4th RNF	Scout Pln, 4th RNF
368 Field Battery, RA	
206 Anti-tank Battery, RA	260 Anti-tank Battery, RA
One Pln 151 Bde A/Tk Coy	One Pln 151 Bde A/Tk Coy

The attack would descend Vimy Ridge, pass to the west of Arras, then wheel left across the southern approaches to the town to form a front facing east. Altogether, from Vimy Ridge to the objective, the Left Column would cover eighteen miles and the Right Column 21 miles. The right flank of the advance was to be covered by elements of the French 3ème *Division Légère Méchanique* which, a week earlier, had fought a successful but costly tank battle again Army Group 'B's XVI Panzer Corps near Namur.

If, on paper, the counter-attack force seems woefully inadequate for the ambitious objective which had been set, on the morning of 21 May it appeared highly improbable to those involved that anything at all could be accomplished, so great was the haste and confusion in which the final preparations were made. In 1 Army Tank Brigade the regimental commanders returned from their briefing at brigade headquarters at noon with just sufficient time to issue sketchy orders to their officers. There were very few maps and it was impossible to effect any detailed planning with the infantry, who were still marching towards the forming-up area. It was, however, decided that the 7th RTR's Matilda IIs would be divided equally between the two regiments and used as a support wave behind the Matilda Is.

Within the regiments the most serious deficiency was the lack of radio communications. Radio silence had been imposed while the brigade was in Belgium and maintained during the march south right up to zero hour. When the sets were switched on, therefore, most of them had drifted off frequency and in the time available it was impossible to re-tune. This meant that communications within squadrons were restricted to hand or flag signals, although the light tanks, which had

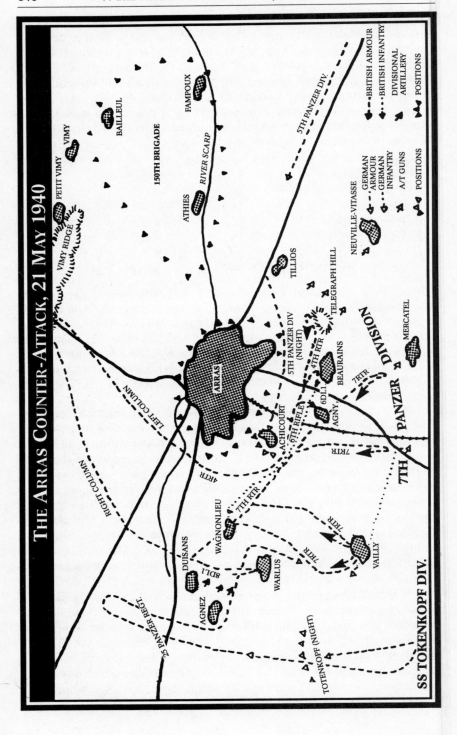

THE ARRAS COUNTER-ATTACK, 21 MAY 1940

been allowed to use their radios while patrolling to the east, could provide the skeleton of a command net. Weary stragglers continued to come in throughout the morning and were told to replenish their fuel and prepare for action immediately. At 13.00, the infantry still not having arrived, it was decided to send the tanks on alone and the brigade's dozen or so light tanks, 58 Matilda Is and sixteen Matilda IIs began rolling down the forward slopes of Vimy Ridge. Their crews were regulars or recalled reservists and, while some of the senior officers were veterans of the First World War, very few of their men had been in action before, save for a handful who had served with the armoured car and light tank companies on the North-West Frontier of India.

Their principal opponents would be the 7th Panzer Division commanded by Major-General Erwin Rommel, who during the present campaign had exhibited the same drive and energy that had won him Imperial Germany's highest award, the *Pour le Merite*, at Caporetto during the First World War. Nominally his tank strength amounted to 36 PzKw IVs, armed with a short 75mm howitzer, and 106 PzKw 38(t)s armed with a 37mm gun, the latter being a Czech-built design which served as a substitute for the PzKw III in some divisions. However, at one period during XV Panzer Corps' advance Hoth, the corps commander, had temporarily placed the leading armoured regiment of 5th Panzer Division under Rommel's command and it seems that as a number of unauthorized PzKw IIIs were present with 7th Panzer at Arras not all of this had been returned to its rightful owner. This would certainly be in keeping with what we know of Rommel as an awkward subordinate and a difficult neighbour.

On 21 May his division had a comparatively short run to make in conformity with the general northward wheel of German armour against the Allied armies trapped within the pocket, its specific task being to isolate Arras from the west. Its axis of advance would, therefore, be the reverse of 1 Army Tank Brigade's and it was inevitable that at some point the two would come into contact. The morning had been spent performing essential maintenance and allowing as many as possible of the division's numerous stragglers to catch up. At about 14.00 (British time) Rommel ordered 25th Panzer Regiment, the divisional spearhead, to advance, taking as its objective the village of Acq to the north-west of Arras. His intention was to follow his normal custom of travelling among the tanks with his command group but shortly after moving off he turned back to chase up his two motorized rifle regiments, which should have been following on either side of the divisional centre-line. To his horror he found that both regiments were heavily engaged with an apparently large force of British tanks, whose fire was causing 'chaos and confusion' among the columns jammed in the villages and along the roads between. Neither regiment was holding its own and, as the fire of the division's anti-tank guns seemed unable to halt the enemy advance, both were on the point of breaking. Finding himself in 'an extremely tight spot', he drove on to find his divisional artillery units, which offered the last chance of bringing the British drive to a standstill.

4th RTR, leading the left column of the counter-attack force, drew blood first, driving into the flank of the 6th Rifle Regiment. 'Earth was being thrown up all round and strange thudding noises were heard and felt,' recalled Sergeant H. D. Reid, commanding a Matilda I. 'I distinctly remember Squadron Sergeant-Major Armit, just ahead of me, getting repeated hits on his tank turret. Everyone was firing away briskly and I claimed a motor-cycle and sidecar machine-gun outfit, which divided itself round a tree, and a lorry. I could not get at an anti-tank gun concealed in front of a railway bridge but decided to polish off two lorries parked nearby. Next thing, a flash and a cloud of smoke – even inside the tank I felt the blast. This had been an ammunition lorry and its demise also put paid to the gun.'

The Matildas continued their career of destruction, wrecking lorries, half-tracks and troop carriers in a hail of machine-gun fire. Several of the enemy's tank stragglers which attempted to join in the fighting were also destroyed. The German riflemen, taken completely by surprise and sustaining heavier casualties than at any time since the campaign began, were further shocked to find that their sole immediate defence, the 37mm anti-tank gun, was incapable of penetrating the thick armour of the British tanks. Most of the anti-tank guns were overrun, their trails crushed and the crews shot down. Even when apparently ablaze the Matildas ground inexorably on, although this was an illusion caused by fires started in their external stowage bins, which were unarmoured. Not surprisingly, the Germans broke, heading south in a jumble of vehicles and frightened men to cause yet greater confusion when they met 7th Rifle Regiment, itself now under pressure from 7th RTR.

4th RTR's advance took it past the villages of Achicourt, Agny and Beaurains. As it neared Telegraph Hill, however, Rommel's counter-measures began to come into effect. His entire divisional field and anti-aircraft artillery was brought into action over open sights with Rommel personally directing the fire of many of the weapons, and Stuka dive-bomber squadrons had begun operating over the battlefield. Within a comparatively short period 4th RTR lost more than twenty tanks and its commanding officer, Lieutenant-Colonel J. G. Fitzmaurice, was killed when the side of his Light Mk VIB was blown in.

Second-Lieutenant Peter Vaux, the regiment's reconnaissance officer, arrived on the scene shortly after: 'Up to that moment the battle had been great fun – we had enjoyed it, but when we reached this line of field guns we could go no further. I was sent off to contact some tanks to tell them to pull back to Achicourt. Some small anti-tank guns opened fire on my light tank and a shot went in through the left of the turret, just behind my gunner's head, and out through the right of the turret, just behind my head. I suppose we both turned a bit pale. Then, without a word, the gunner bent down, brought out his small pack, opened it and took out a very smelly pair of socks. He handed one to me; the other he stuffed into the hole on his side and I stuffed mine into the hole on my side – somehow or other we felt safer like that!'

While the Regiment's withdrawal was in progress a handful of German tanks, rejoined stragglers from 25th Panzer Regiment, attempted to intervene in a series of piecemeal local counter-attacks, but all were destroyed. During the evening 4th RTR's remaining tanks, six Matilda Is, one Matilda II and two Lights, rallied under Major J. S. Fernie. A German counter-attack was expected and in anticipation of this the machine-gun ammunition was shared out; it amounted to no more than 50 rounds per tank, so heavy had been the expenditure during the day. At about 21.30 six tanks were heard approaching through the gathering darkness, and the adjutant, Captain Robert Cracroft, thinking they were stray Matilda IIs making for the rally point, stepped out to flag them down with his map case. Obediently, they halted, and it was then that he noticed the black crosses stencilled on their hulls. Their dignity outraged by such impertinence, the astonished Germans stared back for a few seconds. 'Then', Reid remembered, 'a revolver shot rang out, then a burst of machine-gun, then a bigger gun. To our left a lorry went on fire and in the light of that we saw the doubled-up figure of the adjutant scurrying towards his light tank, he in a very white-looking trenchcoat. Next minute all hell was let loose, tracers everywhere, especially the rapid fire green tracer of the German motor-cycle outfits.'

When the duel, fought at 250 yards' range, was over, the Germans had vanished into the darkness, leaving behind two tanks and some casualties from their motor-cycle unit. The Matildas had now expended the last of their ammunition and as there was no further point in their remaining where they were, Cracroft, unable to find Fernie, led them on a difficult cross-country march back to Vimy. In fact Fernie and Vaux had become separated from the other tanks during the confusion of the skirmish and after numerous adventures, including capture, escape and swimming the Somme, rejoined the regiment in England.

7th RTR, leading the Right Column, had its first encounter with the enemy at Duisans. Here, during the morning, an armoured car patrol of the 12th Lancers had shot up a howitzer battery belonging to 8th Panzer Division as it hurried west; the survivors were flushed out by 'B' Squadron and the Durhams and handed over to the French for escort to the rear.

This incident, while small, altered the course of the battle. Lieutenant-Colonel H.M. Heyland, commanding 7th RTR, was conscious that if the regiment were to keep pace with 4th RTR on its inner flank it must make up the lost time, and decided to cut the corner by avoiding Warlus. Had 7th RTR continued through the village it would have come into contact with 25th Panzer Regiment, which had just moved off on its parallel but opposite course; indeed, as the Matildas approached Dainville, some commanders observed the Germans in the distance but because of the problems with the radio net their contact reports went unheard. If a clash had taken place, every German tank on the field was vulnerable to the 2pdr gun of the Matilda II, while the PzKw 38(t) was far from proof against the heavy machine-guns carried by some Matilda Is; for their part, the Germans would have been unable to penetrate the armour of either British tank. Again, it is probable that the French 3ème DLM, which still possessed some 60 tanks of its own, would have been drawn into the fight. 25th Panzer Regiment, therefore, would have faced the alternatives of either being destroyed in attritional fighting, or using the greater speed of its tanks to break contact and withdraw. In either case, the consequences would have been extremely serious for Rommel and indeed the whole of XV Panzer Corps; as it was, both sides went on their way.

Reaching Dainville, 7th RTR fanned out to the south-east and was quickly in contact with the 7th Rifle Regiment, which was no more able to halt the advance of the Matildas than had been its comrades to the north. The sudden appearance of dazed and demoralized survivors from both rifle regiments caused a panic in the neighbouring SS Division *Totenkopf*, which had barely been touched by the fighting, and several units bolted.

At about 15.00, however, the tanks came under fire from Rommel's artillery stop-line, which included 88mm anti-aircraft guns firing in the anti-tank role from a position near Mercatel. Several Matilda Is were knocked out and the advance slowed down. Heyland and his adjutant were killed, but by 16.50 Achicourt and Beaumetz had been taken and the Matilda IIs went into the lead under Major John King. Accompanied by Sergeant B. Doyle, King smashed through the stop-line, causing havoc. First, the two tanks overran an anti-tank battery, then met and destroyed four enemy tanks, evidently PzKw 38(t)s as the 2pdr shot 'went right through them', leaving two of them burning fiercely. One of King's forward stowage bins had been set on fire during these encounters, forcing him to open up to avoid suffocation. While ramming its way through a barricade of farm carts the tank was hit by a large-calibre shell which jammed the turret; the shock wave, transmitted through the armour, broke the left arm of the gunner, Corporal Holland. Next, a second anti-tank battery was overrun, Doyle crushing one of the guns under his tracks. King then spotted an 88mm gun and, manoeuvring in dead ground until his jammed turret would bear, distracted its crew with fire from his coaxial machine-gun while Doyle administered the *coup de grâce*. Shortly after, King's crew were forced to bail out because of an internal fire and Doyle was knocked out by a direct hit from a field gun, having almost penetrated the enemy's last line of defence. By 18.00 it was apparent that the attack had shot its bolt. In anticipation of a German counter-stroke the Durhams and Fusiliers prepared the captured villages for defence. 7th RTR was pulled back to provide close support for them but later orders directed the regiment to Petit Vimy, which it reached at 23.00.

Although under fire himself, Rommel had continued to direct his guns and, even as the pressure eased, his ADC was shot dead beside him. It is some measure of his personal involvement in the fighting that he had allowed 25th Panzer Regiment to remain passively on its objective throughout the afternoon. It was not, in fact, until 19.00 that Colonel Rothenburg, the regiment's commander, received orders to attack the rear of 1 Army Tank Brigade. This proved to be a great deal easier said than done as the Allies had allowed for the contingency and deployed the 2pdrs of 260 Anti-tank Battery in a screen facing west. In attempting to comply with his instructions, Rothenburg ran into the screen and was also counter-attacked by part of 3ème DLM. Rommel recorded that: 'In severe tank v tank fighting the (Panzer) regiment broke through the enemy lines, destroying seven heavy tanks and six anti-tank guns. The regiment itself lost three PzKw IVs, six PzKw IIIs and a few light tanks.' This places the most favourable construction on the result and almost certainly minimizes the German loss. It seems more probable that Rothenburg was pushed southwards, where he was able to slide past the flank of the screen; whatever the truth, 25th Panzer Regiment played no further part in the battle and at 23.00 was ordered into leaguer south of Dainville.

Nevertheless, Rommel was determined to salvage something from the day and drove his rallied 6th and 7th Rifle Regiments very hard. By midnight the leading elements of the Sixth had reached the Scarpe south-east of Acq, having overrun the Fusiliers' 'Y' Company as it covered the withdrawal of 6th DLI. On the left flank the Seventh RTR met determined resistance from two companies of 8th DLI at Warlus. Constant shelling and mortar fire set the village ablaze and against this background a ferocious struggle developed. As casualties mounted and ammunition stocks began to run low, it began to look as though the defence would not last out the night, but at midnight six French tanks and two troop carriers broke through the attackers and, with their assistance, the garrison fought its way out and reached Petit Vimy.

The apparent failure of the Arras Counter-Attack was deeply depressing to Allied commanders, who saw no escape for their trapped northern armies other than an evacuation by sea. Those who had taken part in the fighting, particularly 1 Army Tank Brigade, believed that they could have achieved a great deal more if only they had had half the artillery and air support available to the enemy. This was almost certainly true, although in the longer term it would not have made much difference. Yet, had they known it, the battle was to have far-reaching consequences.

As the fires on the battlefield died down during the night of 21/22 May, Rommel was drafting his report on the day's events, which had cost him up to forty tanks, most of his anti-tank guns, a great deal of his transport and about 600 casualties. The report itself was the work of an able and extremely ambitious general who had been caught wrong-footed and it therefore put the situation in its most favourable light, simultaneously emphasizing the severe nature of the problems he had overcome, which included a groundless suggestion that the commander of the neighbouring 5th Panzer Division was partly responsible for his troubles. Most revealing of all was the statement that he had been counter-attacked by 'hundreds' of enemy tanks.

The report was quickly transmitted through Hoth at XV Panzer Corps to Runstedt at Army Group 'A', thence to Brauchitsch and Halder at OKH and finally to Hitler's Supreme Headquarters (OKW). Suddenly it seemed as though all the reservations concerning Manstein's plan had been justified. If the Allies had indeed concentrated 'hundreds' of tanks, i.e., the equivalent of several divisions, at Arras, then their intention was obviously to sever the corridor and isolate the German armour to the west. It was not a risk which could be taken and, during 22 May, Army Group 'A's offensive drive was halted and Reinhardt's XLI Panzer Corps was even directed to retrace its steps towards the major crisis apparently developing in the area of Arras. That same day the Royal Navy lifted garrisons into the ports of Boulogne and Calais, so that when the drive was resumed on the 23rd time and resources had to be diverted to the reduction of these. Nevertheless, by that evening elements of 1st Panzer Division had reached the River Aa, south of Gravelines, and secured bridgeheads beyond, and it is reasonable to assume that if the German armour had been given its head on 22 May it would have reached Dunkirk within forty-eight hours. As it was, the time gained for the Allies by the Arras Counter-Attack had enabled them to establish a defensive perimeter around the evacuation area.

There were, of course, other influences at work. On 24 May Hitler again halted the forward movement of his armoured divisions, to the rage and incredulity of many senior officers from Brauchitsch downwards. The order was probably issued in response to the urgings of Rundstedt, whose pragmatic view was that since the war in the north had already been won, the armoured divisions must be re-deployed as quickly as possible against the remaining enemy to the south; furthermore, as the tank strength of some divisions had been reduced to 50 per cent, time was urgently needed for them to reorganize, to allow their stragglers to catch up, and to unscramble their logistic elements, which trailed back all the way to Germany. The reduction of the Dunkirk pocket was left to the Luftwaffe and the infantry divisions; by 4 June, when the evacuation ended, 336,000 Allied troops, one-third of them French or Belgian, had been lifted off the beaches, although at the cost of all their heavy equipment.

The 4th and 7th Royal Tank Regiments, whose action at Arras made so great a contribution to the success of the Dunkirk evacuation, went on to distinguish themselves further in North Africa, and it was there that Rommel finally avenged the mauling they had given his division. On 20 June 1942 both regiments, which still contained many veterans of Arras in their ranks, fought to the last tank and beyond when the Afrika Korps stormed Tobruk; the survivors spent the rest of the war in captivity. The story had a strange sequel. Peter Vaux, now a captain serving as 7th Armoured Division's Intelligence Officer, had under his command a radio intercept unit. On 20 June, knowing that so many of his old friends were with 4th and 7th RTR in Tobruk, he was deeply saddened by the stream of German signals recording success. The following day the surrender formalities were concluded, but on 23 June the intercept sets picked up two remarkable messages. First: 'Three English tanks continue to attack from the east along the beach towards the town.' Then, an hour later: 'All the English tanks are now burning: the battle is ended.' Later that year, when Tobruk was recaptured, Vaux examined the site of the action. 'Astride the coast road on the east of the town, pointing west and with their backs to the east and safety, there were indeed three Valentines. Their numbers and names had been burnt off by fire and in their turrets were bones.' Speculation would be idle. Yet the men of Arras had a closer comradeship than most and took great pride in their achievements both in France and the Western Desert; herein, perhaps, lies the germ of understanding.

THE TAKING OF LONGSTOP
December 1942 – April 1943

In total warfare certain places quickly acquire an evil reputation because their strategic value is of such importance that both sides are prepared to invest to the limit in their retention or acquisition. Among the more obvious of these killing grounds to spring to mind are the Ypres Salient, Verdun, Stalingrad and Monte Cassino, but there were many others where, while the casualties might not have been on so vast a scale, the fighting was equally stubborn and bitter. One such was Longstop Hill in Tunisia.

Longstop is a detached feature lying at the south-eastern entrance to the Medjerda valley, along which lies the route from Medjez-el-Bab to Tebourba and on to the coastal plain around Tunis. The form of the hill is an elongated hog's back with two peaks divided by a steep ravine; the western and higher peak is named Djebel el Ahmera and the eastern peak is Djebel el Rhar. The surface of both rolls gently with frequent spurs, re-entrants and unexpected hollows which make them eminently suitable for defence. To the north a shallow saddle connects the hill with the main mountain massif. Below the southern slopes the main road and a railway run through a narrow gap between the foot of the hill and the winding River Medjerda; within the gap the only buildings of note consist of a small railway station known as the Halte d'el Heri.

At first glance Longstop, with a height of only 900 feet, is not only dwarfed by the 2,000-foot peaks to the north but is also unimpressive in itself. From the summit, however, it clearly dominates the entrance to the valley and provides uninterrupted views along its length, enabling artillery fire to be concentrated quickly at any point. The possession of the hill, therefore, is a prerequisite to any contemplated advance down the Medjerda in the direction of Tunis. It was in fact the British who gave Longstop its name, taken from the lay-back position near the boundary of the cricket field: containing as it did a hint of *ne plus ultra*, thus far and no further, it is more than possible that unconscious prescience played a part in the decision.

When the Allied First Army had landed in North Africa in November 1942 it had attempted to seize Tunisia by *coup de main*. The attempt had failed for a variety of reasons but mainly because the Germans had rushed reinforcements, including Tiger tanks, into Tunisia, and because they were operating much closer to their own bases. At about this time both sides realized the importance of Longstop Hill, but again the Germans were quick to react and installed a garrison consisting of one battalion of the 69th Panzergrenadier Regiment.

By the third week of December Lieutenant-General Sir Kenneth Anderson, commanding First Army, felt strong enough to try for Tunis again, using Lieutenant-General C. W. Allfrey's V Corps. Allfrey's plan involved the 78th Division (Major-General V. Evelegh) securing several features, including Longstop, on the left flank of the advance, following which the 6th Armoured Division (Major-General C. F. Keightley) would sweep down the Medjerda valley and through Massicault on to the coastal plain. The troops detailed to capture Longstop were Brigadier R. A. V. Copland-Griffiths' 1 Guards Brigade, who were to be relieved on completion of the task by an American battalion, the 1/18th Infantry, whose parent formation was the US 1st Infantry Division, otherwise known as 'The Big Red One' because of its divisional sign. It was an interesting combination in which both partners considered themselves an élite. The Guards, with their traditions, toughness and discipline, felt under no obligation to prove anything to anyone; as a whole or in part the 1st Infantry Division, with a history dating back to the Civil War, regarded itself a being a cut above the rest of the US Army, by whom it was regarded in turn as being a mite too sure of itself.

The planning of the attack underestimated both the physical difficulties of securing Longstop and the store set by the enemy on retaining the feature. The artillery support programme, for example, consisted of two field batteries and a small number of medium guns firing concentrations for just fifteen minutes. Again, because it was believed that the hill was held in company strength, only one infantry battalion, 2nd Coldstream Guards under Lieutenant-Colonel Stewart-Brown, was to be used in the assault. Like the majority of British infantry battalions at the time, this consisted of four rifle companies, a support company with medium machine-guns, mortars and anti-tank guns, and a head-quarters company. Only the rifle companies would be engaged in the assault and Stewart-Brown decided to use one against the Halte d'el Heri, a second against the saddle connecting Longstop with the main massif, a third against the summit, and keep the fourth in reserve. It can therefore be seen that even while the arithmetic might have been correct if the enemy's strength had been accurately assessed, a comparatively small number of troops were being dispersed over a very wide area of ground. The best feature of the plan, in fact, was that the attack would be made at night.

Earlier in the month the winter rains had turned the clay subsoil of the lower ground into a clinging quagmire. However, several days of fine weather had dried the surface and when the Coldstream crossed their startline during the evening of 22 December they did so in bright moonlight. On the right the Guardsmen fought their way into the Halte d'el Heri at some cost but were then forced to abandon it when the panzergrenadiers counter-attacked. On the hill itself the Germans, alerted by the short bombardment, sent up flares which revealed the ranks toiling up the lower slopes. At once, machine-gun tracers began slashing across the hillside, often from unexpected places. The strength of the opposition startled the Coldstreams but they kept moving, hot and winded by a hard climb which repeatedly took them up the shoulder of a spur, then down into the hollow at the head of a re-entrant, then up the next spur, always climbing a little higher. The company commander went down, mortally wounded, and his second-in-command took over, although much of the fighting had already resolved itself into junior leaders' battles in which platoons and sections employed fire and movement to subdue each German post in turn with automatic fire, grenades or rifle and bayonet. After two hours of fighting and scrambling the Coldstreams reached the summit and were able to recover their breath. They had taken a number of prisoners, mostly wounded, the saddle to the north had also been captured, and Stewart-Brown felt confident enough to send down guides to bring up the Americans. At this point it began to rain heavily.

At about 03.00 on 23 December the 1/18th began reaching the summit from an unexpected direction, having missed the guides in the dark. This was the first campaign of the Second World War in which British and American troops had fought together and while they shared a common language some words in the military vocabulary differed somewhat in their interpretation, adding to the problems of the relief. The battalion commander was very much a product of The Big Red One and inclined to dispute his orders, an attitude of which senior American officers were becoming so tired that, in due course, the division's commander and his deputy were both relieved. With the fight for the Halte d'el Heri still raging in the valley below and the summit still under sporadic fire, he was indignant at being asked to take over an active sector in the middle of a battle when he had been assured that his men had been assigned a defensive role, and he refused to do so. Stewart-Brown explained that, having taken Longstop, the 2nd Coldstream were needed urgently elsewhere, but it made no difference. It seems probable that some reference was made to 6th Armoured Division's impending advance, which the American interpreted as a promise of tank support. This was not in Stewart-Brown's power to bestow, nor does it seem likely that he would have phrased the reference in so improbable a manner. Be that as it may, the commander of 1/18th realized that he had painted himself into something of a corner and, rather than create a major incident when he had been placed under British orders, he accepted the suggestion and, with an ill grace, began directing his companies to their positions. The Coldstreams, however, were also at fault. They had indeed captured the high ground, but only Djebel el Ahmera was in their physical possession. Beyond the ravine lay the lower Djebel el Rhar, which was still in German hands, and the full implications of this were concealed by the rain-laden darkness. Thus, as the Guards filed off the hill, both they and the Americans were under the mistaken impression that all the vital ground on the Longstop massif had been secured.

The Coldstreams had completed the long march back to their base camp and were enjoying what they felt was a hard-earned breakfast when Stewart-Brown received an urgent message from Brigadier Copland-Griffiths. The Americans, it seemed, had been driven off Longstop and, as no one else in the brigade was available to do the job, 2nd Coldstream Guards would have to retrace their steps and recapture the feature. The message was not altogether accurate. The Americans had launched a further attack on the Halte d'el Heri but had been beaten back. The Germans had then gone over to the offensive, mounting a two-pronged assault up the flanks of Djebel el Ahmera which forced 1/18th off the summit and partway down the slopes. In due course this had been halted by 78th Division's artillery and, while a counter-attack failed to recover the lost ground, some American machine-gun teams managed to hold their positions on the upper slopes. As they shrugged into their packs for the march back the Guardsmen's language was unprintable; it would have been even more colourful had they understood the context in which their second assault would be set. Because the renewed onset of bad weather had again reduced tracks to mud wallows and virtually eliminated the possibility of air support, General Dwight D. Eisenhower, the Allied Commander-in-Chief North Africa, had cancelled the drive on Tunis, although Lieutenant-General Allfrey, commanding V Corps, decided that Longstop would be retained in view of its importance to any subsequent advance down the Medjerda valley.

Slogging through the pouring rain, the Coldstreams reached Longstop late in the afternoon to find the chagrined 1/18th occupying Djebel el Ahmera's lower re-entrants. At dawn on 24 December the long fighting climb to the summit began. By 17.00 the Guardsmen had again taken the high ground, leaving behind a trail of casualties which included Stewart-Brown and his adjutant, both wounded. Using the last of the light in an attempt to rectify the earlier mistake Major Hill, who had taken over the battalion, carried the attack across the ravine and up the slopes of Djebel el Rhar. The ravine, however, proved to be a more formidable obstacle than any ditch devised by a fortress engineer and the assault was stopped dead by the enemy's crossfire. Once again the Coldstreams consolidated their hold on the summit of Ahmera while the 1/18th dug in on the lower western slopes.

Even in the era of total war Christian armies tended to live and let live at Christmas, but for Colonel Rudolph Lang, the German sector commander, the need to break the Allied grip on Longstop held a higher priority. On 25 December he launched a counter-attack in regimental strength around the north-western slopes of the massif, led by tanks which broke through a French unit lacking the means to defend itself. The intention was to recapture Ahmera from the rear, but as the assault swung up the lower slopes it ran into the positions of the 1/18th, now fighting with grim determination to recover its prestige, and was brought to a temporary halt. Nevertheless, it was apparent that, sooner or later, unless the remnant of the Coldstreams was withdrawn from the summit they would be isolated and, lacking further resources to commit to the battle, Allfrey sanctioned the abandonment of the hill. Copland-Griffiths brought up two companies of 3rd Grenadier Guards and deployed them across the base of the hill to cover the Coldstreams as they came down through the narrowing corridor being held open by 1/18th. In the three days of their first action of the campaign the Coldstreams had sustained 178 casualties, including their commanding officer, adjutant and three company commanders. Haggard, hungry and soaked to the skin, they were too tired even to exchange the usual banter with their ancient rivals as they filed away to the rear. However, of the 1/18th, who were so closely engaged that they were unable to break contact and leave the hill until after last light, they recorded in their history, 'The Americans fought with stubborn courage to the very end.' The 1/18th, also fighting their maiden action, had lost a total of 356 men, killed, wounded and missing. As was to happen elsewhere in Tunisia, in the heat of battle an inauspicious beginning between allies was replaced by mutual respect.

The Germans had also suffered severely during the three-day battle and to them Longstop became known as Christmas Mountain. The Allies decided that a further advance down the Medjerda valley could not be made until the ground dried out after the winter rains, which meant April at the earliest. During the intervening period German artillery observers on Longstop made life unpleasant for those in Medjez-el-Bab and many other places within range of their guns, and in return the hill was hammered by the Allied artillery. Longstop and its approaches were turned into a fortress covered by interlocking fields of fire, not only from positions which had been tunnelled through from the reverse slopes of spurs on the hill itself, but also from neighbouring features to the north, notably Djebel Tanngoucha. Anyone attacking the feature now faced a far more formidable task than had been the case in December.

By April the war in Tunisia was going well for the Allies. Despite temporary respites won by local counter-offensives, the Axis forces were confined to the north-eastern corner of the country, contained in the south by Montgomery's Eighth Army, which had just completed its advance across North Africa from El Alamein, and in the west by Anderson's First Army. Few doubted that the enemy would continue to fight until the last possible moment and as part of the offensive intended to administer the *coup de grâce* a drive was again planned down the Medjerda valley, this time using the 6th and 7th Armoured Divisions. Once again, Longstop would have to be taken and, once again, the task would fall to Major-General Evelegh's 78th Division in V Corps. First, however, it was necessary for Evelegh's brigades to clear the high ground to the north-west of Longstop, and this occupied the middle weeks of April.

The campaign as a whole had already seriously eroded the strength of infantry battalions and this series of engagements, known collectively to its participants as The Battle of the Peaks, reduced their numbers to dangerously low levels. Casualties among junior leaders had been particularly high, confirming that nothing could be taken for granted against a determined and professional opponent. As far as possible, all the tell-tale signs which would attract a sniper's bullet or a mortar strike had already been eliminated. Officers replaced the brass insignia on their shoulder-straps with embroidered cloth slipovers, discarded their useless revolvers in favour of rifles or Sten guns, kept their binoculars concealed inside their battledress or shirt, memorized their maps before consigning them to the appropriate trouser pocket and, as far as possible, avoided pointing. Nevertheless, there were some things which could not be concealed from a sharp-eyed enemy and among them were the antennae of the signallers' manpack radio sets; once a signaller had been spotted, an alert sniper had only to wait until an officer needed to use the set for him to pick off both of them.

Well aware that its infantry had become a precious commodity, First Army employed every means in its power to reduce casualties. First, the artillery had become adept at controlling the fire of large numbers of guns, simultaneously hitting defended areas with heavy concentrations and dropping rolling barrages ahead of the assaulting infantry to walk them on to their objective. It was understood, of course, that not all of the enemy, who were invariably well dug in, would be eliminated, and to further assist the infantry two tank brigades, each of three regiments, were now active along the front. The tank brigade was quite unlike the armoured brigade in that its specific function was to provide immediate support for infantry operations and its regiments rarely fought together. In theory, one regiment was allocated to an infantry brigade, one squadron to an infantry battalion and one troop to an infantry company, although circumstances and terrain often dictated different ratios. Tanks and infantry were used to working together and had established proven methods of close co-operation. The tanks, for example, were responsible for destroying bunkers and machine-gun posts which were holding up the infantry advance and for beating off counter-attacks by the enemy's armour; for their part, the infantry would knock out anti-tank guns which were troubling the tanks. In joint operations of this kind it was usual for the artillery's forward observation officer (FOO) to control the fire of his guns from one of the tanks because of the better radio communications available.

The tank brigades were equipped with the Infantry Tank Mk IV, better known as the Churchill, manned by a crew consisting of commander, loader/operator, gunner, hull gunner and driver. The versions which served in Tunisia were, like every British tank of the period, under-gunned. The Mk I, usually retained in squadron head-quarters, was armed with a 2pdr gun firing armour-piercing shot, a co-axial machine-gun in the turret and a 3in howitzer firing a high-explosive shell in the front plate. The Mk III, which provided the bulk of the brigades' strength, was armed with a 6pdr gun firing AP shot, and a co-axial machine-gun plus a second machine-gun in the front plate. The armour had a maximum thickness of 102mm and, while old-fashioned in its arrangement, could absorb tremendous punishment. Driven by a Bedford 350hp engine, the 39-ton Churchill could achieve 15½mph on roads and 8mph across country. To equate speed with mobility, however, would be a mistake, for when the design was first conceived in September 1939 senior officers had believed that the fighting on the Western Front would follow the pattern of the 1918 battles and had specified their primary requirements as being a wide trench-crossing capacity and the ability to cross badly shell-torn ground. The designers had done their work so well that during the Tunisian winter only the Churchills had been able to plough through the worst of the mud unhindered, and in more recent operations they had demonstrated an ability to climb hills unmatched by any other tank in the field, an ability which had not yet been pushed to its limits.

Within the overall context of the Allied offensive, code-named 'Vulcan', Evelegh's plan for the capture of Longstop therefore envisaged an all-arms battle very different from those of the previous December. Given the comparatively narrow sector of front to be assaulted, the artillery support allocated to the operation was tremendous, being drawn from several divisions and corps of both the First and Eighth Armies, including 17, 23, 132, 138 and 166 Field Regiments, 4, 5, 58 and 74 Medium Regiments and several Heavy batteries. Centrally controlled and extremely flexible, the artillery programme would include concentrations and counter-battery fire and, during the assault on Longstop itself, the infantry would advance behind a creeping barrage which lifted 100 yards every five minutes; the latter would include a proportion of smoke shells intended to blind the defenders, while more smoke would be fired against Tanngoucha and other features on the left as a defence against flanking fire. During the daylight phases of the operation continuous air cover would be provided by the Spitfires and Hurricanes of No. 242 Group RAF.

Evelegh's division was to attack on a two-brigade frontage. On the left, Brigadier N. Russell's 38 (Irish) Brigade (6th Royal Inniskilling Fusiliers, 1st Royal Irish Fusiliers and 2nd London Irish Rifles) was to secure the mountain villages of Heidous and Djebel el Tanngoucha, from both of which fire could be directed into the flank of the assault on Longstop itself. This would be delivered by Brigadier B. Howlett's 36 Brigade (5th Royal East Kent Regiment (The Buffs), 6th Queen's Own Royal West Kent Regiment and 8th Argyll and Sutherland Highlanders, reinforced with 1st East Surrey Regiment and supported by the Churchill tanks of the North Irish Horse) and would involve two phases, both of which, it was hoped, would be completed during the hours of darkness. During the first phase the West Kents, on the right, would capture the village of Chaibine and the ridge immediately to the north of it, which provided a natural start-line for the attack on Longstop; on the left the Buffs were first to capture an outlying hill, Djebel Bechtab, then go on to secure Points 196 and 303 on Djebel el Ferdjane, covering the saddle from the west. In the second phase the Argylls were to storm the crest of Ahmera. Finally, in daylight, the East Surreys were to exploit along the main road east of the Longstop massif with Churchill support, over-running the Halte d'el Heri in the process. Plans would then be made for the capture of Djebel el Rhar.

To most Tunisians, their lives hopelessly disrupted by the war, it was a matter of supreme indifference which crowd of foreigners triumphed.

Business, on the other hand, was business, and information was sold to both sides with a fine lack of partiality. Thus, while Colonel-General Hans-Jurgen von Arnim, now commanding the Axis forces in Africa, was warned of the preparations for Operation 'Vulcan' and that these centred on opening the Medjerda valley, so too was Sir Kenneth Anderson warned that the enemy intended mounting a spoiling attack. When this materialized, as it did on 21 April, it was delivered *south* of the river against sectors held by the British 1st and 4th Divisions. For a while it threatened to break into the gun lines of the artillery assembled for the attack on Longstop, but it was beaten off by the combined fire of 48th RTR's Churchills, recently arrived 17pdr anti-tank guns, and 25-pounders firing over open sights for the last time in the North African campaign. German losses amounted to some 33 tanks and more than 300 personnel casualties; First Army's plans were not affected in any way.

During the night of 21 April the Buffs, West Kents and Argylls began moving into gullies around the abandoned hamlet of Chassart Teffaha, lying in no man's land some two miles south-west of Longstop. There they lay up during the following day while their officers attempted to examine the ground ahead. In this they were frustrated because the one good observation point was known to the enemy and shelled regularly, and the details of Longstop itself were obscured by a heat haze. At 22.45 the Buffs and the West Kents, heartened by the scale of the bombardment, emerged from their gullies to the north and south of Chassart Teffaha and crossed their start-lines. Despite attracting immediate machine-gun and mortar fire the Buffs, under Lieutenant-Colonel McKechnie, advanced steadily with their 'A' and 'B' Companies in the lead and by 02.30 had taken Djebel Bechtab. Leaving 'A' Company to mop up, McKechnie sent on 'B' and 'D' Companies which, by 05.30, had seized Points 196 and 303 without undue difficulty.

This, however, was the only part of the original plan that succeeded completely. On the right the West Kents, under Lieutenant-Colonel Heygate, had come under fire before they reached Chaibine, which was found to be wired in and strongly held. 'C' Company fought its way into the houses, many of which contained booby-traps, but was pinned down beyond, while 'D' Company, after reaching its objective, was pushed back by a counter-attack. As the struggle for Chaibine continued the hours ticked steadily away until it became clear that the second phase of the attack could not be delivered under cover of darkness. At first light, however, it became possible for some Churchills of the North Irish Horse to intervene and, at last, the start-line for the assault on Djebel Ahmera was secured.

Well aware that his plan would have to be altered, Brigadier Howlett had come forward during the final phases of the fighting to assess the situation. On the one hand the advantages of darkness had been lost and

38 Brigade was still engaged in bitter fighting for possession of the hills on the left flank. On the other, daylight permitted full use to be made of Lieutenant-Colonel Dawnay's North Irish Horse, whose tanks would be able to follow the advancing rifle companies and provide them with direct gunfire support. He decided, therefore, that after appropriate adjustments had been made to the artillery programme, 8th Argylls, followed by 1st East Surreys, would commence their attack at 11.30 with the direct support of 'B' and 'C' Squadrons NIH, while the remaining Churchill squadron went up to reinforce the Buffs to the north.

He had selected the Argylls to make the critical attack on Ahmera because he believed that their natural Highland aggression would carry them through. Like many Territorial battalions, the Eighth had been raised in 1860 when war with Napoleon III seemed probable. At first it had been known as the Argyll Rifle Volunteers but underwent several changes of title before its identity was finally confirmed under the Haldane Reforms of 1908. The battalion served with distinction throughout the First World War and, on being mobilized again in 1939, had joined the 51st (Highland) Division and been heavily involved in attempts to stem the German *Blitzkrieg* advance across France the following year. On that occasion its 'C' and 'D' Companies sustained such severe losses that, for practical purposes, they ceased to exist, and when they were re-formed it was as 'X' and 'Y' Companies, the new arrivals being stiffened by older hands from other companies. During the campaign in Tunisia the battalion had been employed on a wide variety of tasks, often serving away from its parent brigade, and was highly regarded for its efficiency. It was, nevertheless, as tired as any infantry unit that had been involved in the recent weeks' fighting, and its ranks were so seriously depleted that the original 'A' Company had been replaced by 'R' (Reinforcement) Company, which had travelled out from Scotland to join the battalion in December. The average strength of the rifle companies, in fact, was between 50 and 60 men, producing an assault force some 200 strong. If the grim old ghost of Sir Colin Campbell was present, he might not at first have recognized in the drab battledress the descendants of his beloved 93rd, who had fought at Balaclava in all their glory of feathered bonnets and scarlet tunics, but if he had looked under the helmet rims he would have seen that they were of just the same stock, softly-spoken but terrible in their wrath, and here and there he might have heard a word or two of Gaelic, exchanged between neighbours or old friends.

In command of 8th Argylls was Lieutenant-Colonel Colin McNabb, originally a Seaforth Highlander who, between the wars, had been seconded for three years to the King's African Rifles. There was no doubt among the Argylls that McNabb was destined for higher command; he had actually served for a period as First Army's Brigadier General Staff, but rather than accept the easy route upward he had chosen to revert to his substantive rank in order to obtain command of an active unit before taking the next step. While the Buffs and West Kents were fighting to secure their objectives he had brought the battalion forward until by 02.00 it was lying in a cornfield a mile west of the Longstop massif. At first light, which appeared at about 03.30, he began moving the companies into a ravine to the north. Suddenly, fire was opened from a knoll dominating the gully. Major Jack Anderson's 'Y' Company, being nearest, attacked at once and took the feature, bringing in 25 prisoners. During this exchange the mules carrying the Support Company's heavy weapons took fright and bolted, as did their Arab muleteers. Most of the loads were shed and after dawn they were collected, to be man-packed for the rest of the operation.

The Argylls remained in this position while Brigader Howlett re-planned the battle and at 10.30 McNabb received orders to bring his battalion forward and commence the attack. By 11.30 the Argylls had married up with their tank support and, having passed through the West Kents, were approaching the base of the hill. McNabb had decided to attack on a two-company frontage, led by 'R' on the right and 'Y' on the left, followed respectively by 'X' and 'B', with the battalion headquarters group located in the middle, rather like the central dot on a five dice. This was a textbook deployment which would have permitted him to control all his companies with ease, but a number of the older hands were uneasy about it, for the Germans had also read the textbook and would instantly recognize the group for what it was. There was, too, some concern about the size of the group, which contained most of the battalion's key personnel, men who could not be easily replaced if they were hit. In retrospect, many thought that it would have been wiser to employ a smaller command group and attach it loosely to one of the companies, for in the skilled killing match between professionals which the Tunisian campaign had become it was rash to tempt Providence too often.

With the creeping barrage thundering ahead, the Argylls closed in on the lower slopes, traversing a broad belt of corn about three feet tall. Like the veteran infantry they were, the rifle companies were well spread out with large intervals between men to reduce casualties. The mud of the December battles had given way to dust and in the shallow topsoil the flowers of early summer were bright. Sufficiently far behind to avoid drawing fire on the trudging infantry, now grim-faced and silent, the Churchills were moving forward slowly, their commanders searching for opportunity targets among the known positions of the German sangars.

The Argylls were halfway across the cornfield when the enemy's artillery and mortar fire began to burst among them. The smoke-screen was never thick enough to hide them completely and as the companies began to climb they were raked by machine-gun fire from Longstop itself and from Tanngoucha on the left flank. At this point the worst fears of many were realized when the Germans made the command group the focus of their attention, all but wiping it out before it had even reached the foot of the hill. Among those who died were McNabb himself; his adjutant, Lieutenant Robert McLeish; the battalion communications officer, Captain Barry Erskine; the intelligence sergeant; Orderly Room Sergeant Macmillan; Pipe Major Wilson, whose Pipes and Drums acted as stretcher-bearers in action; and many others.

Few in the rifle companies were aware of the full extent of the tragedy for no sooner were they on the hill than they became involved in the same sort of section leader's battle that the Coldstream Guards had fought the previous December, in which machine-gun posts and weapon pits had to be taken in succession. This was hard, gruelling work carried out under a broiling midday sun which added cases of heatstroke to the constant battle casualties that were shredding the ranks.

The Argylls, however, were not alone. Behind them the North Irish Horse had set their tanks at the apparently impossible slopes and now, engines roaring, multiple coil-spring suspensions squealing in protest and steel tracks scrabbling to grip the naked rock, the Churchills were clawing their way steadily upwards. There was between infantry and their supporting armour a strong empathy stemming from a recognition by each that they would hate the other's job. Too often the Argylls had seen the flames of ammunition fires flaring fiercely through the open turret hatches of knocked-out tanks for them to want any part of the tank man's war. For their part the tank crews, hearing the flat tonk of bullets and the rattle of shell splinters against their armour, observed the infantry through their episcopes and marvelled that, protected by nothing thicker than a battledress, the latter could display such iron determination. There was, therefore, an equal determination among the North Irish Horse that everything in their power would be done to see the Argylls through their ordeal. As a tank closed up to them it became possible for the infantry to indicate the enemy's sangars, using either a flare pistol or a burst of tracer fired from a Bren. The tank's main armament would bang once or twice, the ground would heave a little as the tracers flashed into the enemy fire slit then, while the Argylls closed in with Tommy-gun, bayonet and grenade, the vehicle's co-axial and bow machine-guns would keep the position under continuous fire.

In this way the advance kept pace with the barrage until the first of the designated objective lines had been reached. Approximately half of those who had begun the attack reached this point, but the internal structure of the companies had gone and the battalion had simply become a body of men. Of the four company commanders only Major Jack Anderson, described by those who knew him as 'a quiet and reserved person of very high quality', was still on his feet and, now aware that Colonel McNabb had been killed, he set about reorganizing the assault force. The men, he noted, were all in good heart and had faced the enemy's fire without flinching, and he knew that, when the moment came, they would continue the attack in the same way. Almost immediately, an incident occurred which left him without the slightest doubt that the battalion would capture Djebel Ahmera.

For the moment, the troops were resting, wiping the sweat from the helmet bands and smoking, temporarily relaxed and starting to joke among themselves. A group of prisoners was sitting nearby, sullen but by no means completely cowed. Perhaps the thoughts of one of them were of the shame of losing Christmas Mountain, which had been held for so long and for which so many of his comrades had died; or perhaps the very proximity of his detested enemy inflamed him with hatred; or perhaps the intensity of the barrage had unhinged his mind; we shall never know. What we do know is that the man snatched up a discarded Schmeisser machine pistol and killed several Argylls with it. He was himself killed very quickly, as were many of his fellow prisoners.

Thus, when the second phase of the assault began minutes later the Argylls had been roused to a state of berserk fury which bode ill for the remaining defenders of Ahmera. When calm had returned after the battle Anderson commented simply to the battalion's Second-in-Command, Major Hamish Taylor, 'We just had a hate at the Germans, the hill, and everything'. At the time he saw his enemy through as red a mist as any of his men, personally leading attacks on three machine-gun posts at which he arrived first to treat the occupants to a full magazine from his Tommy-gun. Elsewhere across the face of the hill the line of Argylls was moving steadily upward, overrunning one sangar after another. 'Generally speaking', wrote Anderson, 'the Boche stayed put and fired until we were right upon their positions. They then packed in and tried to surrender, but the Jocks were very angry and in most cases they died pretty rapidly.'

At length Anderson reached the last crest before the summit. He had received a leg wound which he described as a 'scrape', but had managed to keep moving. Only one officer and a handful of men had kept up with him, the battalion's radio rear links to the artillery and brigade had gone, and the going was now so steep that not even the Churchills could tackle it. At length others arrived, all exhausted by the exertion, heat and fighting, until a total of four officers and thirty men had been collected. Anderson was worried that, since so few Argylls were left, the enemy would begin filtering back into the captured positions, and he sent back one officer with a message for the East Surreys to hurry forward and occupy them: this battalion had, in fact, been pinned down by machine-gun fire from positions to the north which were eventually neutralized by one of the Buffs' supporting Churchills. Major A. D. Malcolm, commanding the Argylls' Support Company, also reached Anderson's little group to make arrangements for bringing up the battalion's medium machine-guns, mortars and ammunition, and he was able to take back a message for Brigadier Howlett.

While Anderson's men were recovering their breath the barrage had rolled ahead until its benefit was lost. It could not be helped and, as soon as they were ready, he led them in the final bayonet charge on the summit. Compared with what had gone before it was child's play. 'Shortly after starting I came upon a mortar position, and we all loosed off at a group of Germans in the dugouts. They promptly put up their hands and about twenty others flooded out from various holes and corners. I sent them back with a very belligerent private soldier. In the position we found four mortars complete with ammunition and also a great many stores. Later we captured a 75mm anti-tank gun complete with ammunition after a brush with the crew. Otherwise our final advance was uneventful and we set about reorganizing at the top.'

Despite their full acknowledgement of the support given by the artillery and the tanks of the North Irish Horse, the capture of Djebel Ahmera by 8th Argylls was a tremendous feat of arms. For his inspired leadership during the attack Major John Thompson McKellar Anderson was awarded the Victoria Cross; tragically, he was to be killed by shellfire in Italy some six months later. There were many other deeds of gallantry that day, only some of which were acknowledged by decorations. Typical of the spirit in which the battle for Ahmera was fought was the story of Corporal Harris of the Royal Corps of Signals, a survivor of the battalion headquarters group who had also taken part in the final assault. Harris was responsible for the rear link to brigade and he carried a large manpack radio linked by an umbilical cord to heavy batteries carried by another soldier. When the latter was killed the link was broken, but after the summit was taken Harris retraced his steps, recovered the batteries, climbed to the summit again and re-established contact, despite the weariness which would have overcome many a lesser man after a bitter five-hour struggle in intense heat.

Perhaps the greatest tribute to the Argylls' achievement came, unwittingly, from the enemy. Before setting off for the summit to take command, Major Taylor sent up every man he could muster to join Anderson, including recovered heatstroke cases, the lightly wounded and otherwise unemployed men from Support and Headquarters Companies, until by evening there were approximately 100 Argylls on the high ground. One of those sent up was still wearing the regiment's tartan shoulder patch, contrary to regulations, and a captured officer was observed staring at it. After a moment the man shrugged and turned away with the comment 'So – that explains it!' The kilt may not have been in evidence but he clearly understood the significance of tartan and it was, after all, his own army which, after its experiences during the First World War, had nicknamed Highland infantry in general 'The Ladies From Hell'.

In addition to those casualties already listed the Argylls' losses in the rifle companies amounted to one officer killed and six wounded, 25

NCOs and men killed, 66 wounded and sixteen missing, or approximately half of those who had taken part in the attack. Similar casualties had been inflicted on the Germans holding Ahmera and some 200 prisoners were taken.

During the evening the East Surreys and West Kents also dug in on the lower slopes of Ahmera, although the combined force, under the overall command of Lieutenant-Colonel Wilberforce of the East Surreys, numbered in total less than a single battalion. This was the time when a German counter-attack to recover the feature seemed probable and the Argylls, being closest to the enemy positions beyond the ravine on Djebel Rhar, felt distinctly vulnerable. The artillery, however, had made excellent provision for defensive fire tasks, one battery being laid all night to cover the battalion, plus one gun per battery in other units. Twice Major Taylor, believing he detected an enemy build-up beyond his front, called in DF tasks, and on each occasion was gratified when the shells began landing within seconds.

On the morning of 24 April 'A' Squadron NIH left its night leaguer and deployed on the southern slopes of Ahmera to support an attack by the East Surreys on an eastwards-jutting spur which dominated the Halte d'el Heri. This is referred to in Brigadier Howlett's report as Mosquito Ridge, but in other sources is named Mosque Ridge, presumably because it was surmounted by an Arab tomb named Sidi Ali ben Hassine. The attack commenced at noon but attracted such heavy fire from Djebel Rhar that the infantry were pinned down for a while, although they were able to take possession of the feature after it had been overrun by the tanks. One tank sustained mine damage at the base of the spur, close to the main road. During the afternoon Howlett ordered the West Kents, commanded by Major Lovell since Colonel Heygate had been wounded by shellfire during the consolidation phase the previous evening, to capture Rhar. The plan showed an alarming similarity to the Coldstreams' attempted exploitation of their advance in December and had almost certainly been anticipated by the enemy. When the battalion formed up on the reverse slopes of Ahmera it was clearly observed and immediately attracted a storm of shell and mortar fire which caused heavy casualties. Only 'C' Company managed to cross the ravine and although one section, led by Private Sullivan, eliminated a strongpoint, the intensity of the enemy's machine-gun fire was such that Howlett decided to put an end to what was becoming a slaughter and called off the attack. When the West Kents rallied, the total strength of their rifle companies amounted to only 80 men who were reorganized into two 40-strong companies.

On 25 April there was little activity on the Longstop massif, although the enemy continued to shell and mortar Djebel Ahmera. To the left it seemed that 38 Brigade was winning its battle for Heidous and Tanngoucha and towards evening it became apparent that the Germans were indeed retiring from these positions. After dark, however, the West Kents sent out patrols which confirmed that the enemy on Djebel Rhar was staying put. The patrols also brought back accurate information on the German positions, enabling Brigadier Howlett to plan the next phase of the operation. This would consist of a diversionary attack delivered by the Argylls and 'C' Squadron NIH in the form of a right hook commencing at Mosque Ridge. Once the enemy's attention was fixed in that direction, the main attack, consisting of a left hook mounted by the Buffs and the remainder of the North Irish Horse from Point 196, would commence.

The diversionary attack started at 08.30 on 26 April. The tanks led, clearing a spur on the north-eastern flank of Rhar, and the Argylls then worked their way forward, cleaning up several ravines which sheltered snipers and taking a dozen prisoners in the process. Encouraged by the sounds of battle, the Buffs began their attack at 09.00, its course being described by their historian: 'A Company moved on the right, D on the left, C following in reserve, and in advance went the tanks. The valley was negotiated without incident; but the moment the attackers started to breast the north-western slopes of Djebel Rhar a hurricane of shellfire came down on them. Without so much as a check, though, they pressed on as if on a peacetime manoeuvre, notwithstanding that whole platoons disappeared in the smoke of bursting shells. The spirit of the men was superb; and desperately weary though they now were, nothing stopped them as, following close upon the tanks, which were doing splendid work against machine-gun posts and anti-tank guns, they climbed relentlessly up to their objective.'

The story is taken up by the North Irish Horse *Battle Report*, which itself incorporates extracts from Brigadier Howlett's own report.

'A machine-gun post then threatened to hold up the attack but immediate action by 4 Troop silenced it and Sergeant O'Hare, climbing high on the southern side of Point 280, dealt with three more such posts. Major Russell, commanding B Squadron, ordered No 4 Troop to proceed to the west of Rhar to find a way up. At the head of the saddle between Ahmera and Rhar Lieutenant Pope encountered another machine-gun and mortar post and finally a 75mm gun badly sited to fire down the western re-entrant; after one round of 6pdr HE and a burst of Besa the crew surrendered. Sergeant O'Hare then tackled the ascent and on reaching the summit after a magnificent climb took over fifty prisoners. The forward companies of the Buffs now moved on to their objectives, receiving the surrender of an embarrassing number of prisoners. It is very unlikely that any of the Longstop garrison escaped. The final operations were an example of perfect co-operation between all arms, particularly between tanks and infantry.'

By 11.00 the battle for Longstop was over, the last attack having cost the Buffs nine killed and 83 wounded. More than 300 men of the

III/754th Grenadier Regiment had been captured, including all its senior officers. The battalion commander himself commented that 'Djebel Rhar is one of the strongest defensive positions that one could ever hope to occupy. I would have been prepared to hold it against a full-scale British infantry brigade attack. When it was apparent that tanks were being used over the high ground I knew all was over.' Other prisoners frankly admitted that until confronted with the evidence of their own eyes that morning they had simply not believed reports that tanks had played a part in the capture of Djebel Ahmera.

The cork had thus been removed from the Medjera bottleneck and in recognition of his brigade's achievement Brigadier Howlett was awarded the Distinguished Service Order; sadly, he too was to die in Italy, killed in the fighting along the Sangro. On 5 May the break-in phase of Operation 'Vulcan' commenced. Within 24 hours a corridor had been opened and through this two armoured and two infantry divisions drove hard down the valley. By coincidence the thousands of vehicles passed through the sector of front now held by 36 Brigade, covering everything with a coating of fine yellow dust. Axis resistance collapsed and a week later the war in Africa was over. The brigade had already moved into billets in the fashionable resort of La Marsa, near Carthage, a place of olive groves, white painted houses with bright window boxes and blue doors, and the sea sparkling beyond. For six months the men had never been more than a few miles from the front, often living in vile conditions, and they had never been given a chance of real relaxation or genuine undisturbed rest. Now, they were possessed by an unbelievable tiredness more mental than physical, induced by the constant demands on their internal resources.

9
ACROSS THE WAAL
The Fight for the Nijmegen Bridges
20 September 1944

On paper the plan was bold in its concept and breathtaking in its simplicity. What Field Marshal Montgomery intended, with the approval of General Dwight D. Eisenhower, the Allied Supreme Commander in Western Europe, was to end the war against Germany before 1944 was out, and to achieve this he proposed securing a crossing in force of the Lower Rhine in Holland, so outflanking both the formidable defences of the Siegfried Line, Germany's West Wall, and the heavily industrialized basin of the Ruhr, which he knew would be tenaciously defended. Once across the Rhine, the Allies would drive hard into the German heartland, securing victory before the Soviet Army, presently recovering its strength after a series of successful offensives in Poland and the Ukraine, could penetrate Central Europe. If successful, the plan would not only save many thousands of lives, but also curb the political ambitions of Joseph Stalin, who was anxious to secure for the Soviet Union as much of Europe as his troops could overrun.

The plan incorporated two phases, the first of which, code-named 'Market', involved dropping Lieutenant-General Sir Frederick Browning's I Airborne Corps to secure bridges along the route, the US 101st Airborne Division (Major General Maxwell D. Taylor) north of Eindhoven, the US 82nd Airborne Division (Major General James Gavin) between Grave and Nijmegen, and the British 1st Airborne Division (Major-General Roy Urquhart) at Arnhem. The second phase, code-named 'Garden', would consist of Lieutenant-General Brian Horrocks' British XXX Corps advancing along the corridor so formed from its position on the Dutch–Belgian border, relieving each of the airborne divisions in turn and maintaining its progress as far as the Zuider Zee, which would protect the Allied left while further preparations were made for the invasion of Germany; during the early stages of its advance Horrocks' Corps would be supported on the flanks by British VIII and XII Corps. Because its two phases were inextricably linked the operation as a whole has become generally known as 'Market Garden'.

Despite the apparent simplicity of the plan itself, however, its execution would prove to be an extremely complex matter, especially in terms of logistics and timing. Unfortunately, while some apsects of the planning were satisfactory others suffered from a complacency which may have stemmed partly from the brilliant success of the D-Day landings and partly from the more recent collapse of the German armies in France. Given that risk is an element inherent in any operation, insufficient allowance was made, *inter alia*, for weather conditions, the enemy's reaction and probable intentions, the suitability of the axis of advance, communications failures and other contingencies. In contrast, other aspects erred disastrously on the side of caution. For example, the RAF gloomily predicted that since the enemy's anti-aircraft defences in the Arnhem area had been strengthened recently, aircraft losses amounting to 40 per cent could be expected if 1st Airborne Division was dropped close to the town's road and rail bridges, as originally intended. Faced with the prospect of such heavy losses before the battle proper had begun, Urquhart was forced to accept alternative dropping zones on moorland seven miles west of Arnhem. This meant that surprise would be lost and also that, while the troops began their march into the town, the enemy would be given ample time to react. When the drops took place on 17 September this is exactly what happened. As they entered the town Urquhart's paratroopers found themselves facing a strong defensive front which the enemy was steadily reinforcing, not least with armour. Only one group, including Lieutenant-Colonel John Frost's 2nd Battalion Parachute Regiment, part of the divisional reconnaissance squadron, artillerymen, engineers, signallers, drivers and most of the personnel of HQ 1 Parachute Brigade, reached the northern end of the road bridge, which it held against incredible odds for several days. The remainder of the division was pushed back into the suburb of Oosterbeek where it was forced to establish a defensive perimeter.

It was in a hotel at Oosterbeek that Field Marshal Walter Model, commanding the German Army Group 'B', was having lunch when the drop began. He immediately drove to the headquarters of Lieutenant-General Wilhelm Bittrich's II SS Panzer Corps, which was refitting in the Arnhem area after the débâcle in Normandy. After the necessary steps had been taken to place a cordon between the paratroopers and their objective, he then carried on to his own headquarters, where his staff briefed him on the overall situation. Two American airborne divisions had landed in the Eindhoven–Nijmegen area and, led by an armoured spearhead, British XXX Corps had broken through the front to the south and was heading towards them.

Model had made his reputation on the Eastern Front where, time and again, he had shorn up the crumbling line with *ad hoc* units hastily assembled and flung into battle while he prepared a decisive counter-attack with his armour. Model was the ideal man to deal with a crisis of this magnitude and, from the manner in which the battle was developing, he was quick to divine Montgomery's intentions and plan his own response. As far as the local situation was concerned, once the bulk of 1st Airborne Division had been penned inside Oosterbeek it presented no immediate danger. Indeed, since the British possessed nothing heavier than a handful of pack howitzers, it would be wasteful and foolish to direct the entire resources of II SS Panzer Corps' two armoured divisions against them. Instead, one division, 9th SS Panzer, would remain in Arnhem to contain and in due course overrun the British presence, and it would be reinforced by *ad hoc* units drawn from every available source in Holland, including rear area personnel, railway troops, Luftwaffe ground crews, coastal artillerymen, seamen and even members of the Labour Service, all of whom were handed weapons and directed into the fight as they arrived. The second division, Brigadier General Heinz Harmel's 10th SS Panzer Division, was to go south to Nijmegen, but here a problem arose. In the normal way the division would simply have driven across the Arnhem rail and road bridges, but the former had been blown almost as soon as the British entered the town and Frost's group, holding the northern end of the latter, were handing out a fearful beating to anyone who came near them, and had mined the bridge-deck as well. The only alternative was for Harmel to pass his division across a vehicle ferry at Pannerden, several miles upstream, an agonizingly slow process which meant that it would be committed piecemeal to the fighting.

Simultaneously, Model had summoned reinforcements from Germany, including a battalion of Tiger tanks, and he ordered counter-attacks to be mounted into the flanks of the long corridor now held by 82nd and 101st Airborne Divisions, hoping to sever it. His intention was to inflict a decisive check on Montgomery at Nijmegen, where elements of 10th SS Panzer Division were already establishing a strong defensive perimeter around the southern ends of the rail and road bridges over the Waal. Such was his confidence after having so easily removed 1st Airborne Division from the Allied order of battle that, while the Nijmegen road bridge, incorporating the longest span in Europe, was partially prepared for demolition, he rejected suggestions that it should be blown on the grounds that it could well be used to mount counter-attacks to the south.

Meanwhile, spearheaded by the Guards Armoured Division under Major General Allan Adair, XXX Corps was fighting its way slowly but steadily northwards form the Dutch–Belgian border. During the after-noon of 18 September the Guards reached Taylor's 101st Airborne, which had captured bridges over the Wilhelmina Canal at Zon and the Zuit Willemsvaart Canal at Veghel. By the morning of 19 September the tanks had broken through to Gavin's 82nd Airborne, which had captured the bridge over the Maas at Grave.

Gavin's division consisted of the 504th, 505th and 506th Parachute Infantry Regiments, plus the 325th Glider Infantry Regiment and supporting arms. The glider troops were still in England, fog-bound, and their absence was keenly felt at a time when the division was simultaneously required to clear Nijmegen, capture its bridges and fend off counter-attacks on its eastern perimeter, mounted from the nearby Reichswald forest on the German border. Gavin believed that on the afternoon of the 17th the bridges would have been his for the taking but now, as a result of Model's prompt counter-measures, all approaches to them were strongly held. Altogether, some 500 panzergrenadiers, commanded by Captain Karl-Heinz Euling, had taken up positions in Huner Park, in a ruined medieval fort known as the Valkhof and on a large traffic roundabout, all covering the approach to the road bridge, and in houses, a small park and on the embankment leading to the railway bridge. In support of Euling's troops were a number of self-propelled guns, automotive multiple flak mountings and anti-tank guns.

The task of opening up the bridge approaches was clearly beyond the capacity of the fully extended and lightly equipped 82nd Airborne, but the arrival of the Grenadier Guards, Adair's leading battlegroup, changed the situation somewhat. Gavin was able to spare one battalion, Lieutenant Colonel Ben Vandervoort's II/505, and two combined task forces were set up to fight their way through with the assistance of guides provided by the Dutch Resistance. The stronger or eastern task force consisted of most of No. 3 Squadron 2nd Grenadier Guards, No. 2 Company 1st Grenadier Guards (a motorized battalion) and Companies 'E' and 'F' II/505. Moving off at 16.00, it easily secured its first objective, the post office in the centre of the town, incorrectly stated by the Dutch to house the enemy's switchboard for the demolition charges on the road bridge. However, as the Shermans approached the roundabout leading to the bridge itself one was hit by an 88mm anti-tank round and set ablaze, and another was knocked out as it tried to edge past. The infantry, unable to get forward because of intense automatic weapon fire from the Valkhof, trenches in the park and loopholed houses, became involved in fierce house-to-house fighting which lasted until nightfall.

Simultaneously the smaller western task force, consisting of five Shermans from No. 3 Squadron, one platoon of 1st Grenadiers in carriers and Company 'D' II/505, had been expertly guided to a point 200 yards west of the southern end of the railway bridge. As dusk was approaching it was decided to attack at once but two tanks were immediately knocked out by anti-tank guns firing from across the river and the infantry assault stalled under fire from the railway embankment and surrounding houses. The task force pulled back a little way and took possession of several houses, where it remained for the night, anticipating that it would be attacked. No such attack materialized because on this sector the panzergrenadiers, unsettled by the arrival of enemy tanks and infantry behind their lines, were more concerned that they should not be cut off from their escape route across the Waal. In fact, after setting a number of buildings ablaze to provide illumination in case the task force renewed its own attack, the Germans in the immediate vicinity withdrew into a contracted perimeter around the railway bridge.

'Market Garden' was now falling badly behind schedule. According to the master plan, the Guards should have reached Arnhem that afternoon, just 48 hours after the operation began, yet they were still south of the Waal and the Nijmegen bridges were still in enemy hands. Browning, the commander of I Airborne Corps, desperately worried that the bridges would be blown at any moment, called a conference during the evening to plan for the following day. Present were Horrocks, Adair, Gavin, the commanding officers of the Guards units, Colonel Reuben Tucker, commander of 504th Parachute Infantry, and senior staff officers. It was now common knowledge that things had gone disastrously wrong at Arnhem. The immediate priorities, therefore, were to relieve the embattled 1st Airborne Division and, if possible, to effect a link with Frost's small group, still tenaciously maintaining its grip on the northern end of the Arnhem road bridge. Speed had to be the primary consideration for, isolated and lacking heavy weapons, Urquhart's men could not be expected to hold out for much longer. British and American officers alike were therefore agreed on the absolute necessity of capturing the Nijmegen bridges quickly and intact. Strategic considerations aside, the British motivation was intense and the reasons for it obvious; so, too, was that of the Americans, inspired by fellow feeling for paratroopers who had passed through a gruelling selection procedure similar to their own and who shared the same dangers as themselves.

It was, in fact, Gavin who produced an original and daring plan for the capture of the Nijmegen bridges. If the Allies were simply to go on battering at the southern approaches, he pointed out, it would be a time-consuming process which, even if it succeeded, could still end in the enemy blowing the bridges. The correct solution, he felt, was to attack both ends of the bridges at once. While every effort was maintained to eliminate the enemy defending the southern approaches, the 504th would make an assault crossing downstream and, once ashore, they would attack the northern end of the bridges. As soon as these had been secured the Guards would charge across. Inevitably, the crossing would incur heavy casualties but in the long term lives would be saved. Browning approved of the idea but commented that no assault boats were available. Horrocks was able to tell him that his engineer stores convoy included three lorries loaded with a total of 32 assault boats and orders were given for these to be driven to Nijmegen throughout the night. Because of the congested road conditions along XXX Corps' axis it was known that this would take time so H-Hour for the crossing was set at 13.00 next day, 20 September.

At 08.30 the Grenadiers and II/505 renewed their attack on the approach to the road bridge. This time it was decided to advance northwards from the traffic roundabout in the centre of the town, the Keizer Karel Plein, towards the river, then attack the heart of the German defences from the west. Pressure was also maintained on the roundabout near the bridge, the Keizer Traianus Plein, while targets in Huner Park and elsewhere were brought under artillery and mortar fire. The smaller western task force was instructed to clear the area around the railway bridge approach, in which the enemy rearguard was still putting up a stiff fight. While this methodical progress continued, major counter-attacks were launched on Gavin's eastern perimeter by Lieutenant General Eugen Meindl's II Parachute Corps. With the assistance

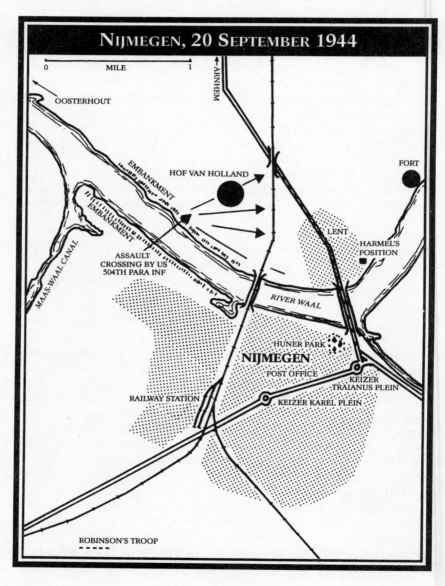

of 1st Coldstream Guards' Shermans these were contained by nightfall but at one time the Germans came dangerously close to breaking through into Nijmegen itself.

Farther west, the morning was spent making preparations for the assault crossing by Colonel Tucker's 504th Parachute Infantry. Tucker fitted his countrymen's concept of a tough paratroop leader perfectly. Always helmeted and armed with a revolver and trench knife, he was generally to be found chewing a cigar and expectorating the result, provoking slightly raised eyebrows among the Guards officers with whom he was to work. Notwithstanding this and a manner of speech blunt to the point of rudeness, he was a very capable officer who willingly committed his regiment to an extremely dangerous operation mounted for the benefit of fellow paratroopers in a very tight spot. The 504th contained numerous veterans of the fighting in Sicily, Salerno and Anzio, and had sustained such serious casualties at the last that it did not take part in the 82nd Airborne's night drop on the eve of D-Day. On 17 September it had captured the bridge over the Maas at Grave in a model operation, accepting the high risk of accidental injuries when it deliberately jumped into a built-up area close to the objective.

Tucker decided that the first wave of the assault crossing would consist of Major Julian Cook's III Battalion, followed by I Battalion under Major Willard E. Harrison. After a suitable launching site had been found a half-mile downstream from the railway bridge Cook, a graduate of the West Point class of 1940, climbed to the roof of a nearby power station with Lieutenant-Colonel Giles Vandeleur of 2nd Irish Guards, whose Nos. 2 and 3 Squadrons would be providing direct gunfire support for the crossing with their Shermans. Examining the terrain through binoculars, Cook was horrified by what was demanded of his men. First came the Waal itself, some 400 yards across and flowing with a ten-knot current. Then came a flat featureless shoreline varying in width between 200 and 800 yards, bounded inland by a sloping dyke twenty feet in height with a road running along the top. Behind the dyke was a scattering of houses and approximately 800 yards further inland was a low moated structure named Fort Hof Van Holland, referred to in some accounts as Fortress West. Enemy positions could be clearly identified on the embankment and there was also activity around the fort.

Cook was told that 30 minutes prior to H-Hour rocket-firing Typhoons would strafe the entire area, which would then be bombarded for fifteen minutes by the Irish Guards and 100 British and American artillery weapons. Shortly before H-Hour the tanks would switch to smoke rounds, building up a screen behind which the crossing would commence. When Cook briefed his men they were reassured by the support they would receive but still intimidated by the width of the river. Seeking to make light of the danger, he announced that he would emulate the famous painting of George Washington crossing the Delaware during the War of American Independence, standing erect in the prow of his boat. There was, however, no sign of the three lorries carrying the assault boats. This was hardly surprising when some 20,000 vehicles belonging to XXX Corps and I Airborne Corps were all attempting to use the same road, on which movement was regularly being disrupted by enemy counter-attacks and air strikes. Where it was moving at all the traffic was grinding along at a mere ten miles per hour, with constant arguments as officers claimed priority for their own convoys. Even with absolute priority the assault boat lorries were having extreme difficulty threading their way through the tangle and at length H-Hour was postponed from 13.00 until 15.00. This was hard on Cook and his men, who were keyed up and ready to go, although in the overall context it was of some benefit for, while the attacks on the bridge approaches were making steady progress, they had not yet gained sufficient ground to rush the bridges themselves.

Promptly at 14.30 a formation of Typhoons roared overhead, peeling off in succession to batter the German positions with their rockets and cannon. At 14.40, while the Irish Guards' tanks were moving into position on the southern embankment, the assault boat convoy arrived. One lorry, approaching the launching site along the embankment, became an immediate target for the enemy and was hit, the effect being to reduce the number of boats available from 32 to 26. Few of Cook's men had any experience of small boats. None had ever handled such a craft before and in the time available there was very little that the Royal Engineers could teach them. The boats were of collapsible wood and canvas construction, were nineteen feet long, weighed 200 pounds and had been designed to carry thirteen fully equipped infantrymen and three engineers; each boat should have been equipped with eight paddles but some had only two and would have to be propelled by rifle butts. At 14.45, while they were being assembled, the artillery opened up, firing smoke against the far bank then switching to high-explosive to engage targets further inland while the tanks continued to thicken up the smoke-screen.

Cook only had room for Companies 'H' and 'I' and his battalion headquarters group in the first wave. As the tank and artillery fire rose to a crescendo they stood waiting by the gunwales of their boats until, at 15.00, Cook shouted 'Go!' The boats were carried bodily down the embankment at a run and launched. As the men scrambled aboard some grounded in the mud and had to be pushed out into deeper water. Already the enemy, understanding the significance of the smoke, had begun to fire into it with rifles, machine-guns, mobile flack mountings, mortars and artillery. Then, as the smoke was dispersed by the wind, the group of labouring craft was exposed for all to see. Instantly the river was torn by automatic fire and its surface was blasted into foam and spray by exploding mortar and artillery rounds. Grimly, the paratroopers pressed on through the curtain of fire. Behind them the tanks had expended their smoke rounds and switched to high-explosive ammunition to engage any target which presented itself. Fort Hof Van Holland, on the roof of which were 20mm anti-aircraft guns and other automatic weapons, received particular attention.

From the roof of the power-station the crossing was watched in silence by Browning, Horrocks, Tucker and Giles Vandeleur. Some boats were being blown apart, some were sinking, some were drifting helplessly downstream with their occupants dead, some were limping slowly with obvious casualties aboard, but the rest were still moving forward. Through binoculars it was possible to see paratroopers using their helmets, and even their hands, to paddle their way furiously towards the slowly approaching shoreline. In Vandeleur's mind the words 'Horrible, horrible', kept repeating themselves. In the boats men crouched as low as possible, feeling completely naked on the open surface of the river. Cook was shouting 'Keep going! Keep going!' as the paddles flayed the water. Some found themselves almost paralyzed by their terror while others were physically sick. In their different ways they spoke to their Maker, perhaps for the first time in their lives. Then, unbelievably, they grounded on the far shore and began scrambling out. The watchers on the power-station saw them, now reduced by distance to the size of dots, running steadily across the open ground towards the embankment, leaving a still figure here and there, until they vanished beyond.

Browning turned to Horrocks and said quietly, 'I have never seen a more gallant action.' Chester Wilmot, the distinguished Australian war correspondent, described the crossing as 'a most brilliant and courageous feat of arms'. It was not, however, over just yet. Hardly able to believe his eyes, Vandeleur watched the three-man Royal Engineer crews of the assault boats, those of them that survived, push off from the far shore to collect the next wave. Only thirteen boats remained, but they continued to cross and re-cross as long as they would float and there were crews to man them. Tucker had already left the roof, intending to join his men on the far bank.

The effect on Cook's troops of reaching the shore was dramatic. They could not imagine anything more terrible than the crossing they had endured. They had seen comrades blown apart at close quarters or shot dead beside them yet somehow they had survived. Now, like the Prussian Guard released from its ordeal on the slopes below St-Privat, they wanted their revenge and, like the 8th Argylls on Longstop Hill, they closed with their enemy in a blind rage, apparently quite oblivious to fear and not inclined to give quarter. Within thirty minutes the embankment and nearby houses had been cleared of defenders, some of whom were boys of fifteen while others were men in their sixties.

Altogether, the assault boats made six more trips to ferry the rest of Cook's battalion and then Harrison's battalion into the beach-head. Under Tucker's direction the 504th fanned out to the north-east and east, those on the left heading for Fort Hof Van Holland and those on the right for the northern end of the railway bridge. Tucker had asked the Irish Guards for constant fire support, which he received to the extent that the tanks' Browning machine-guns began to 'run away' as rounds cooked off in the overheated chambers.

Fort Hof Van Holland surrendered when several paratroopers swam the moat, climbed the walls and began dropping grenades down the ventilation shafts. At the rail bridge Captain Karl Kappel's Company 'H' was at first pinned down, but something like a panic broke out among the defenders who, still under pressure from within the town, now saw their escape route directly threatened. Abandoning their heavy weapons, they simply fled across the bridge in a mob, to be cut down by the waiting American guns. Some 260 bodies were counted on the bridge, plus numerous wounded; when the firing ceased, many others stood up to surrender. A search for demolition charges revealed nothing and, at Tucker's urging, Company 'H', together with Captain Moffatt Burriss' Company 'I', pressed on towards the road bridge, having dispatched a message that the Guards' tanks should commence their attack from its southern end.

The time was now approximately 17.00 and at this point an excited Irish Guards officer began shouting into his radio 'They're on the bridge! They're on the bridge!' Unfortunately, he did not say which bridge and no clarification was forthcoming. The Americans confirmed that they were now in control of the northern ends of both bridges, which was only true in the sense that the 504th had secured a third bridge, carrying the railway across the main Nijmegen–Arnhem highway, north-east of Fort Hof Van Holland. Another widely reported but unverified story has it that an American flag was seen flying from the northern end of the rail bridge, which was somehow mistaken in the smoke and confusion for the road bridge. The truth was that the northern end of the road bridge was still very firmly in German hands.

It had taken all day for the Grenadiers and II/505 to overcome the defenders of the bridge approach. At 17.30 a concentric attack commenced, overrunning the last of Euling's panzergrenadiers at the Valkhof, the bridge roundabout and Huner Park. Those involved had no doubt at all who held the northern end of the bridge, but despite this a small force had been detailed to fight its way across. This was drawn from Major John Trotter's No. 1 Squadron 2nd Grenadier Guards and consisted of No. 1 Troop under Sergeant Peter Robinson. At the briefing Trotter had told Robinson that the Americans had crossed the river to the west and, while the situation was unclear, they were now believed to be somewhere in the area north of the road bridge. The troop's task, therefore, was to rush the bridge, contact the Americans and form a bridgehead with them. Captain Lord Peter Carrington, the squadron's second-in-command, would follow immediately behind in his own tank and co-ordinate the operation. Also forming part of the force was a scout car carrying a Royal Engineer officer, Lieutenant A. C. G. Jones, whose task was to locate the German demolition charges on the bridge and neutralize them. Shaking hands with Robinson, Trotter told him not to stop for anything, as the bridge *must* be taken.

Robinson, a veteran of Dunkirk, had four tanks in his troop. Three were standard Shermans armed with a 75mm gun, but the fourth, in which he intended to lead the attack, was a Firefly, that is, a Sherman armed with a British 17pdr gun which gave it approximate parity with the German Panther. At 18.13 he led his troop from the roundabout on to the bridge approach ramp, conscious of drifting smoke from the burning buildings all around and an eerie silence. This was suddenly broken when an 88mm anti-tank gun, sited in a sandbagged emplacement 100 yards north of the bridge, opened fire as the tank turrets appeared above the crest of the ramp. The shot ricochetted off the road in front of the Firefly, sheared through an upper track idler and then the radio went dead. Throwing out smoke grenades, Robinson ordered his driver to reverse. The gun switched its attention to Lance-Sergeant Billingham's tank, next in line, but its muzzle flash had been spotted beside a burning building. After a brief duel, in which Billingham was joined by Sergeant Charles Pacey, the eighty-eight fell silent.

The troop reversed a little way down the ramp and Robinson changed tanks with Billingham, aware of tracer slashing past as he did so. Slipping on the headset, he could hear Trotter ordering the attack to continue at all costs. Sergeant Charles Pacey's tank roared past and Robinson followed. As the troop entered the bridge's main span it came under fire from what seemed every direction. Up in the girders of the great arch German troops were firing panzerfausts (bazookas), flinging grenades and sniping at the tank commanders. Putting their co-axial machine-guns at full elevation, the tank gunners sprayed the girders as they went, watching the dead and wounded tumble into the roadway below. Robinson was also aware that the tanks were under fire from anti-tank guns on the north bank, three to the east of the bridge and two to the west. What he did not know as he passed the halfway mark was that he and his entire troop had just escaped being blown into eternity.

When, at approximately 16.00, Brigadier General Heinz Harmel, commander of 10th SS Panzer Division, had been informed of the American assault crossing of the Waal, he had immediately left his headquarters at Doornenburg and driven to the village of Lent, just upstream from the Nijmegen road bridge, to assess the situation for himself. It was here, hidden close to a bunker on the roof of which he stood watching the fighting, that the main demolition switchboard was located. Harmel no longer felt bound by Model's decision to leave the bridges standing and, in the climate of suspicion which had existed in Germany since the failure of the July Bomb Plot against Hitler, he had no intention of being arrested and shot out of hand for dereliction of duty. All around, troops were pulling back to fresh positions and a final message from Euling, now encircled in Nijmegen with his last few men, convinced him that the great road bridge must be destroyed. His engineers assured him that everything was in place but he decided to wait until Allied troops were actually on the bridge. At length Sergeant Robinson's Shermans appeared and when they reached the central span he gave the order for the charges to be fired. Nothing happened. The reserve circuits were closed but still nothing happened. Hardly had Harmel absorbed this shock than he was told that the railway bridge was also intact and in Allied hands. He immediately gave orders that a defensive front was to be established on the Nijmegen–Arnhem highway and informed Bittrich at II SS Panzer Corps that the Allies were across the Waal. No satisfactory explanation has ever been given for the failure of the demolition charges, although an unproven theory suggests that the cables may have been cut by a young Dutch Resistance fighter, Jan van Hoof, who was captured and killed later in the battle.

Meanwhile, Robinson's tanks were approaching a roadblock at the northern end of the bridge. This consisted of heavy concrete blocks arranged in the form of a chicane and was covered by an anti-tank gun some 50 yards beyond. Pacey halted to engage the gun while Robinson tore past and through the chicane. As the Sherman emerged Robinson's gunner, Guardsman Leslie Johnson, got off three rounds of high explosive, wrecking the anti-tank gun. Nearby, some infantry broke and ran, only to be cut down by the tanks' machine-guns. The tanks were now roaring down the northern approach ramp. 'Come on, come on!' yelled Robinson into his microphone. 'Close up and get a move on!'

As his tank entered a wide boulevard it was engaged by a self-propelled gun near a bend in the road. Robinson recalled two explosions, one of which blew off his steel helmet, but no serious damage was sustained. Johnson fired several rounds and the enemy vehicle began to burn, as did a nearby house. In the gathering dusk the flames illuminated German infantry in position around a church opposite. This was also set ablaze and the infantry faded into the shadows. The advance continued until, after a further three-quarters of a mile had been covered, Robinson passed under a bridge carrying the railway across the road. Two grenades were thrown at his tank and he briefly opened fire with his Browning at some infantry in a ditch before realizing that they were wearing American helmets; fortunately, neither side did the other any damage. While the Americans, who belonged to Company 'I' III/504, swarmed joyfully over the tanks, Captain Burriss told Robinson, 'You guys are the most beautiful sight I've seen in years.' Only Robinson and

Pacey had got through, so the jubilation of the British crews was tempered by the knowledge that two of their tanks had been lost.

The troop's luck in its run across the bridge had indeed been too good to last. The two rearmost Shermans had been hit on the northern ramp and one was burning fiercely. The survivors of both crews baled out and most were taken prisoner by German infantry who had surfaced after Robinson and Pacey disappeared and were now pulling back. The exception was Lance-Sergeant Knight, shamming death in a ditch into which he had rolled. When all was quiet he emerged, bruised from interrogative kicking, and climbed back aboard his tank. To his surprise, he discovered that it was still mobile and, alone, drove on to rejoin Robinson where the presence of the vehicle could at least provide moral support.

On the bridge itself Lieutenant Jones had followed the Shermans closely until the roadblock was reached. There he left his scout car and, despite the attention of snipers, coolly proceeded to cut wires, remove detonators from demolition charges and deactivate mines until he was able to declare the bridge safe. Later, his troop arrived and in the course of their continued search discovered 81 Germans hiding in chambers built into the tops of the bridge piers.

While Jones was working, Lord Carrington drove across the bridge and halted at the far end, attracting fire from such Germans as remained in the area. Apart from the burning Sherman there was no sign of Robinson's troop, nor of any American paratroopers. For the next 45 minutes, until two companies of Irish Guards appeared, his solitary Sherman was the only obstacle in the path of an enemy counter-attack on the bridge, had Harmel chosen to make one. Once the infantry had deployed he was released and went on to join Robinson and establish a defence for the night.

The courage displayed by all concerned in the capture of the Nijmegen bridges deserved a better reward than it received. Arnhem lay only eleven miles distant and neither Tucker nor his men could understand why an armoured column had not been dispatched imme-diately to the relief of 1st Airborne Division. Tucker was almost incoherent with rage that his regiment's sacrifice had apparently been for nothing. Cook's two leading companies had sustained the loss of 134 men killed, wounded and missing, more than half of those involved in their assault crossing, yet seemingly no further move was contemplated. Given the chance, Tucker would personally have led the 504th towards Arnhem. Gavin fully understood the reasons for his anger and was sympathetic, but he was aware of the overall situation and its increas-ingly grim overtones.

The essence of the problem was that, for the moment, the resources simply did not exist to mount such a drive – and, although no one was aware of the fact at the time, it would have failed to produce the desired results even if it had been made. Horrocks had only the 82nd Airborne and Guards Armoured Divisions at his disposal and, as bad weather had further delayed the arrival of Gavin's glider infantry regiment, both were now under strength and overstretched. At dawn on 21 September most of 82nd Airborne and the Coldstream Guards' tank/infantry group were still engaged in keeping open communications south of the Waal, while within the Nijmegen bridgehead there were only the Grenadier and Irish Guards' groups and Tucker's depleted regiment. The bridgehead was itself vulnerable to counter-attack and in the circumstances Horrocks did not feel justified in dispatching the Guards on a thrust to Arnhem until they had been relieved by infantry from Major-General G. I. Thomas's 43rd (Wessex) Division. Unfortunately, this division's progress had been badly delayed by enemy action and the tangled traffic on the corps axis and its advance guard was only just crossing the Maas.

There was, too, the question as to where Horrocks should apply his strength when the moment came. Up to this time there had been no direct communication with 1st Airborne Division and it was uncertain where Urquhart's troops were located. At 09.00, however, a good radio link was established. Urquhart said that heavy fighting was still in progress at Arnhem road bridge and that the main body of the division was at Oosterbeek, west of the town, where it was under severe pressure but retained control of the Heveadorp–Driel ferry across the Lower Rhine. The message was based on out of date information, for Urquhart had lost contact with Frost, whose troops had fought so stubbornly to retain control of the bridge. The tragedy was that while Cook's battalion were making their crossing the previous afternoon, Frost and his men were fighting to the bitter end and the bridge was now in German hands. Early on the 21st, an RAF reconnaissance aircraft reported a column of German tanks moving south from Arnhem along the Nijmegen road, tanks which had almost certainly crossed the road bridge, and that the enemy was establishing defensive positions astride the road. For planning purposes, therefore, it was safest to assume that all of Arnhem, including the bridge, was in the enemy's possession, despite Urquhart's message.

Nevertheless, the information gave Horrocks something on which to work. If the Guards were checked on the main road to Arnhem, a second thrust on a north-westerly axis would establish contact with Major-General Stanislas Sosabowski's 1 Polish Parachute Brigade, which was to be dropped that afternoon near Driel. With control of both ends of the ferry site, it would be possible for the engineers to put in a bridge and continue with the drive northwards.

At 11.00 on 21 September No. 1 Squadron 2nd Irish Guards, commanded by Captain Roland Langton, left the Nijmegen bridgehead with orders to break through to Arnhem along the main highway. The mission was nothing more than a forlorn hope, for the road ran along the top of a causeway bordered by deep, water-filled ditches which permitted no room for manoeuvre whatsoever. Just south of Elst, less than halfway to Arnhem, the leading troop was knocked out by a self-propelled gun. There was no way round, and the cab rank of Typhoons circling overhead could not be brought into action because of a radio failure. While the Guards were stalled on the Arnhem highway the Poles dropped at Driel. However, by the time they had fought their way to the south bank of the Lower Rhine the ferry had been sunk and Heveadorp, its northern terminal, was in German hands. During the evening 43rd Division reached Nijmegen and began crossing into the bridgehead.

Early on the 22nd armoured cars of the 2nd Household Cavalry slipped out of the bridgehead to the west and, by-passing German positions in a heavy mist, broke through to the Poles along secondary roads. Later that morning 43rd Division attacked on a two-brigade frontage, securing the village of Oosterhout, two miles beyond the western perimeter of the bridgehead. During the evening Thomas sent a column through the village and this, following the route taken by the armoured cars, reached the Poles after dark, having ambushed and destroyed five enemy tanks along the way. Later an entire infantry brigade was pushed along this axis and the route between Nijmegen and Driel was secured. To some extent this success was balanced by the need to dispatch the Guards' infantry south into 101st Airborne's sector, where the enemy had temporarily cut the line of communications.

Support from XXX Corps' artillery was now available to 1st Airborne Division, as was a limited amount of re-supply and reinforcement by assault boat, which eased its situation somewhat. However, the perimeter held by Urquhart's men was now only 2,000 yards deep and 1,000 yards across and could not be expanded without a major assault crossing of the river, for which resources were not available. With great reluctance, therefore, Horrocks agreed with Browning that a bridgehead could not be secured at Arnhem and, in the circumstances, 1st Airborne Division should be withdrawn. Under cover of an artillery bombardment some 2,100 of Urquhart's men, all that remained of the original ten thousand, were ferried in assault boats to the south bank of the Lower Rhine during the night of 25/26 September. They had been expected to hold their ground for two days, or four at the most, but they had held on for nine.

Curiously, while Montgomery had been defeated at Arnhem, Model had been defeated at Nijmegen largely because of what took place at Arnhem, for the two battles had become tactically interlinked. Thanks to Frost having denied him the use of the Arnhem road bridge at what, to him, was the critical period of the battle, Model was unable to provide adequate reinforcements for his troops at Nijmegen, where the courage and determination of the Guards Armoured and 82nd Airborne Divisions had deprived him of two bridges he had been confident of holding.

Just one final act remained in the drama of Nijmegen. On the night of 28/29 September a dozen German frogmen, armed with explosives, slipped into the Waal five miles upstream of the bridges. Allowing the current to carry them, they reached both bridges, fixed their charges to the piers, then carried on down-river until they reached German-held territory. At the road bridge the charges were placed in too shallow water and although the explosion blew a hole in the decking this was soon repaired. At the rail bridge the charges were correctly placed and the central span was brought down. By then the bridge had lost much of its earlier importance and there were plenty of powered rafts and Dukws available to make good the deficiency.

10
JUMP ON CORREGIDOR
February 1945

Corregidor Island, shaped like a tadpole, dominates the entrance to Manila Bay and its possession is therefore essential to anyone wishing to use Manila harbour or the nearby naval base of Cavite. Only 3½ miles long and 1½ miles across at its widest point, the island was garrisoned by the US Army almost as soon as the USA became involved in the affairs of the Philippines following the Spanish–American War of 1898.

By the outbreak of the Second World War Corregidor had become a purely military installation, bristling with coastal artillery guns, anti-aircraft batteries and defence works. Some considered the defences to be so strong that the island was named the Impregnable Rock, and indeed the first obstacle any attacker would have to overcome was the strong tidal race which scoured the entrance to the bay. The tadpole's tail, or eastern end of the island, consists of sandy, wooded terrain rising to a maximum height of 150 feet above sea level and on this an airstrip known as Kindley Field had been constructed. At the base of the tail Malinta Hill rises steeply to an elevation of 350 feet, penetrated by the Malinta Tunnel complex, containing headquarters, signal, logistic and hospital facilities. Beneath the western slopes of the hill lies the waist of the island, named Bottomside, with small docks to the north and south and the remains of San Jose, a former fishing village. From Bottomside the ground rises gently through Middleside to the much steeper Topside, which forms the tadpole's head, then drops sharply away to the sea on three sides. Other than through Middleside, the only approaches to the 500-ft summit of Topside are up the James Ravine to the north, the Cheney Ravine to the west or the Ramsey Ravine to the south-east, all of which are easily defended. From Topside it is possible to dominate the entire island and the approaches to all possible landing sites.

When the Japanese invaded Luzon in December 1941 General Douglas MacArthur withdrew his troops into the Bataan Peninsula, forming the northern arm of Manila Bay where, despite their lack of air cover, reduced rations, widespread sickness and dwindling ammunition supplies, they continued to offer determined resistance. However, the damage inflicted on the US Pacific Fleet at Pearl Harbor meant that, for the moment, no relief could be expected. On 11 March, in reluctant obedience to a direct order from President Roosevelt, MacArthur left the Philippines for Australia, handing over his responsibilities to Lieutenant

General Jonathan M. Wainwright. During the first week of April the Japanese broke through the last defence line on Bataan and the Luzon campaign was effectively over. Only Corregidor and a few smaller islands in Manila Bay continued to resist.

Regular air attacks on Corregidor had begun in December. In March they were supplemented by artillery fire. The American gunners fought back, downing aircraft, destroying two artillery batteries, an ammunition dump and a tank park. However, while the Japanese were able to use observation balloons to control the fire of their guns, the Americans could only rely on direct observation from Topside and shoot from the map. After the Bataan fighting had ended the Japanese were able to concentrate the fire of one regiment of 240mm howitzers, forty-six 150mm guns, twenty-eight 105mm guns and thirty-two 75mm guns against The Rock. On 29 April, Emperor Hirohito's birthday, the air and artillery bombardment rose to a crescendo. When, on 2 May, a Topside ammunition bunker was penetrated, so great was the explosion that at first the Japanese thought the whole island had gone up; 13-ton mortars were torn from their mountings and flung 150 yards through the air, and the severity of the shock wave was such that, even three miles away, it induced bleeding from the ears and nose. On 5 May it became apparent that the Japanese intended effecting a landing as their fire was obviously being directed at specific shore defences, moving gradually towards the tail of the island.

Superficially, Corregidor presented a scene of devastation, although comparatively few of its defenders had been killed. Altogether, there were 15,000 people on the island, occupying accommodation designed for 6,000. This total included naval personnel from the abandoned base at Cavite, administration and headquarters troops, the Filipino government and its retinue, wounded from the fighting on Bataan, and a large contingent of nurses, the majority living a troglodyte existence below ground, mainly in the Malinta Tunnel complex. Wainwright's major problems were that, apart from his artillerymen and the 4th Marines, he had relatively few first line combat troops, and deploying these where and when they were needed would prove difficult because most of his communications had been destroyed.

At 22.30 on 5 May the landing craft carrying the leading elements of the Japanese 4th Division closed in on the northern shores of the island. The intention was to effect a landing as close as possible to the Malinta Tunnel, but the strength of the inwards tidal race had been under-estimated and the craft were swept eastwards, many of them being shot to pieces by the beach defences. At first it appeared as though the landing had failed, but by 23.30 part of the 61st Regiment, commanded by the energetic Colonel Gempachi Sato, had secured a small beach-head to the north of Kindley Field. Although he had only 1,000 men ashore, Sato quickly expanded this and began advancing towards the Malinta Tunnel.

A counter-attack was promptly ordered by Colonel Samuel Howard, commanding 4th Marines, but the troops involved had to force their way through the packed tunnel and by the time they emerged the Japanese had consolidated their position. As the night wore on Sato was reinforced with some light artillery and three tanks. The arrival of the latter was decisive, for at 10.00 the following morning they broke through the hastily formed American defence line near the eastern entrance to the tunnel complex. Wainwright, wishing to spare the women, civilians and his wounded the orgy of rape and massacre which had followed recent Japanese victories, ordered a white flag to be run up and opened surrender negotiations.

Lieutenant-General Masaharu Homma, commander of the Japanese Fourteenth Army, aware only of the 4,000 casualties inflicted by the beach defences on his men, believed that the landing had failed and had only recently been informed of the progress made by Sato's small force. He was openly contemptuous of Wainwright when they met, insisting that his surrender must include all American troops still active in the Philippines. Wainwright insisted that he would only surrender Corregidor. In that case, said Homma, hostilities would continue until his terms were accepted. In the circumstances, Wainwright could only comply.

Naturally, the episode left the bitter taste of humiliation in the mouths of the American military and public so that, when MacArthur's troops returned to Luzon in January 1945, for many of them the recapture of Corregidor held a far deeper significance than the purely military considerations of opening Manila Bay to Allied shipping. Planning the operation had already occupied the staff of General Walter Krueger's Sixth Army for some time, and it had reached the conclusion that the cost of a conventional amphibious landing would be prohibitive, opting instead for an airborne assault to be reinforced by sea. In reaching this conclusion the planners had evaluated the risks on the basis that the Japanese garrison of The Rock numbered no more than 850 men; in fact, the correct figure was in excess of 5,000, all but 500 of them naval troops, under the overall command of Captain Akira Itagaki of the Imperial Japanese Navy. Curiously, Itagaki had been warned by Tokyo to prepare for an airborne assault, although in 1942 the Japanese had themselves considered the idea too risky. Itagaki also considered that the island was too small and its terrain too rough for the prospect of a large-scale parachute drop to be taken seriously and he ignored the advice; instead, he concentrated on strengthening his beach defences.

The troops detailed for the operation, known collectively as Rock Force, included the 503rd Parachute Infantry Regiment, the 3rd Battalion 34th Infantry Regiment, the 462nd Parachute Field Artillery Battalion, one company of the 161st Parachute Engineer Battalion and supporting units. In overall command was the 503rd's commanding officer, 33-year-old Colonel George M. Jones, who had served with the regiment throughout the New Guinea campaign of 1943–4. At Noemfoor Island he jumped from the leading aircraft at an altitude of only 175 feet and, despite being stunned by a heavy landing on a compressed coral runway scattered with the wreckage of enemy aircraft, quickly recovered and led the regiment during what was described as a 'colourful' two months of jungle fighting.

D-Day for the assault on Corregidor was set for 16 February. Jones was given adequate warning of what was required of his men and on 6 February he accompanied a bombing raid to carry out a personal reconnaissance of the terrain. There was little sign of enemy activity, which apparently confirmed Sixth Army's estimate of the Japanese strength, but the only drop zone remotely worthy of the name was the overgrown Kindley Field. When he suggested this to Krueger, however, the general ruled it out immediately, first because the airstrip could be dominated by fire from higher ground and therefore offered little improvement on an amphibious assault, and secondly because it would take too long for the paratroops to secure Topside, the island's most important feature. In view of these considerations, the only alternative was to accept two minuscule areas on Topside itself, one a parade ground 325 yards long and 250 yards wide, the other a small sloping golf course 350 yards long and 185 yards wide. Both were already pock-

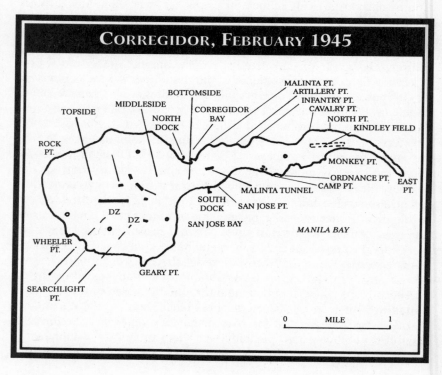

CORREGIDOR, FEBRUARY 1945

marked with bomb and shell craters and surrounded by tangled scrub, shattered trees, ruined buildings and general debris, while nearby the ground fell sharply away in steep slopes or cliffs.

As if the physical difficulties presented by the drop zones were not enough, there was also the wind to consider. A steady easterly wind was expected, approximately in line with the longer axes of the zones, and its speed was anticipated as being between fifteen and twenty-five miles per hour with the possibility of stronger gusts. Each transport aircraft would be over its drop zone for a mere six seconds, and as the drop would be made from an altitude of 400 feet it was calculated that during the twenty-five seconds of his descent each paratrooper would drift 250 feet westward, leaving a safety margin of only 100 yards. Human error, or a fluctuation in wind speed or direction, would result in paratroopers being dragged over the surrounding cliffs.

It was decided, therefore, that the transports would approach in two columns, one for each drop zone. Just sufficient time was available for each aircraft to drop a stick of six, after which it would turn away and attach itself to the rear of its column to make another pass, and so on. Altogether, it would take an hour to put 1,000 men on the ground. The transports would then return to their base and pick up the second wave of the 503rd's airborne assault. Planners normally allowed for 20 per cent jump casualties in airborne operations, but in this, the most difficult and dangerous drop of the war, Jones believed that the figure could be as high as 50 per cent, and that before the Japanese had even fired a shot. The result could be triumph or tragedy, but if the paratroopers cleared Topside they would certainly succeed in drawing the enemy's attention away from the follow-up amphibious landing, which was to be made on the southern shore of Bottomside and had Malinta Hill as its objective. Once a beach-head had been secured it would be possible to re-supply the 503rd by sea and evacuate its casualties.

Corregidor had been under air attack since 22 January and by D-Day had been battered by 3,125 tons of bombs, the most concentrated aerial pounding of any invasion target in the Pacific theatre of war. On 13 February the island also came under the fire of five light cruisers and nine destroyers, augmented two days later by three heavy cruisers and a further five destroyers. In reply the Japanese gunners sank a mine-sweeper and damaged two destroyers before they were silenced. Early on 16 February twenty-four B-24 Liberators bombed known gun emplacements while eleven B-25 Mitchells concentrated on eliminating anti-aircraft positions and thirty-one A-20 Bostons strafed and bombed the interior of the island. Simultaneously, the cruisers and destroyers bombarded the southern beach defences of Bottomside and the nearby Caballo Island, which also came in for its share of air attacks. Fast PT boats shot up coastal batteries with their heavy automatic weapons then moved into position to rescue any paratroopers unlucky enough to drop in the sea. Everything possible had been done to ensure the success of the landing and, even as the long columns of C-47s came into view, carrying the 503rd's first lift, seventy more A-20s roared in to savage the eastern half of Corregidor.

The 503rd was flying in from the island of Mindoro, to the south. The final briefing, held the previous evening, left the men in no doubt as to the dangers they faced. The first wave, consisting of Lieutenant Colonel John L. Erickson's reinforced 3rd Battalion, was in sober mood as it ate its pre-embarkation breakfast, disinclined to respond to the humourists' traditional references to the Last Supper; one man at least had an uneasy premonition that he would never leave Corregidor.

Approaching the island, the pilots of the leading aircraft adjusted their course to pass directly over the tiny drop zones, then the first sticks of six were tumbling out. At 08.33, just three minutes after the planners had intended, their boots were crunching into the rubble, and they were hauling in and divesting themselves of their 'chutes, snatching their weapons and heading for their assembly points. Behind came more and more sticks as each aircraft passed overhead and turned to repeat the process. Surprise was almost complete and the few Japanese who opened fire with rifles or light machine-guns were quickly eliminated. However, jump casualties amounted to 25 per cent, partly because the wind was blowing from the north instead of the east, and partly because the first drops were made from 550–600 feet instead of the designated 400 feet. Most men missed the drop zones and were carried into areas of ruined buildings and broken trees; others were dragged over the edge of the plateau and some landed on the beach below.

Nevertheless, luck was with the Americans. Some thirty men carried over the cliffs near Breakwater Point found themselves under fire from an observation post as soon as they touched down. Responding with the aggression instilled by their training, they overran the post. Among those killed in the skirmish was Captain Itagaki, the garrison commander. This left the Japanese leaderless, although the extent to which Itagaki could have directed the subsequent battle is questionable as the landline communications of his Topside command post were sketchy in the extreme. By 09.45 the first lift had been completed and Erickson's men had established complete control over the drop zones. The landing craft of the amphibious assault force, consisting of the 3rd Battalion 34th Infantry and supporting arms under the command of Lieutenant Colonel Edward M. Postlethwait, had left Mariveles harbour, at the southern tip of Bataan, at 08.30 and sailed round the western end of Corregidor. Two hours later, those paratroops manning the south-eastern sector of the perimeter on Topside had a grandstand view as they closed in on the southern beaches of Bottomside. The Japanese, already taken aback by the airborne drop and lacking orders, suddenly found themselves facing a fresh threat from the sea and, racked by indecision, failed to react positively against either. Incredibly, though vehicles were immobilized by mines in the shallows, the first four waves landed unopposed. The fifth wave attracted machine-gun fire from Ramsay Ravine, Breakwater Point and San Jose Point, but by 11.00 the summit of Malinta Hill had been secured at a total cost of two killed and six wounded. Effectively, the defences of Corregidor had been cut in two.

Back on Topside, Jones, who had jumped with his command group in the first lift, was approached by several officers who felt that conditions were too hazardous for further drops. However, the second lift, consisting of Major Lawrence B. Caskey's 2nd Battalion 503rd, was already on the way. This time the drop, commencing at 12.40, was made from the correct height with due allowance for the wind and the majority of the men landed safely on the drop zones. The drop, in fact, was so successful that the overall jump casualty ratio fell to 14 per cent, well within acceptable limits. Twenty men had been killed by ground fire or impact with buildings, fifty had been wounded by ground fire and 210 had sustained injuries on landing. Nevertheless, at this point Jones decided to cancel the third lift, involving Major Robert H. Woods' 1st Battalion 503rd; instead, the battalion was put ashore by landing craft at Bottomside the following afternoon.

Thus far, Jones had every reason to feel satisfied. Together, the boldness of the plan and its execution had secured the Topside landing zones, Malinta Hill and the Bottomside beach-head. The next phase would involve 3/34th Infantry containing the enemy to the east of Malinta Hill while the 503rd mopped up on Topside and Middleside; finally, the tail of the island was to be cleared. In the event, it took ten days of hard and bloody fighting to achieve this. The nub of the problem was that, while the Americans controlled the surface of the island, the Japanese controlled the network of tunnels and caves below. Again, since the Japanese believed that the worst disgrace that could befall them was to be taken alive by the enemy, they invariably fought to the death, as they had in every other action of the Pacific War. Nor was it apparent until the fighting had been in progress several days that the Japanese garrison outnumbered the Americans by a wide margin.

On 17 February the 503rd began a slow, methodical clearance of enemy-held strongpoints, bunkers and caves on Topside while 3/34th Infantry did likewise on Malinta Hill. Depending on its accessibility, the objective was pounded by naval gunfire or air strikes, the latter employing napalm as well as high-explosives, and the infantry would close in as soon as the covering fire lifted. If this failed to dislodge the occupants they would be brought under open-sights fire by the 75mm pack howitzers of 462nd Parachute Field Artillery and other weapons, while infantry-escorted flame-thrower teams crawled forward. The flame-throwers would then project unignited fuel into the objective and toss in a white phosphorus grenade to set it ablaze. If the cave or passage were long enough for those inside to escape incineration, and they still refused to give up, engineers used demolition charges to seal up the entrance.

Sometimes, the Japanese isolated themselves inside the deeper installations by closing the steel blast doors. In such circumstances, the only way they could be eliminated was by dropping explosive devices down the ventilator shafts. One such device, put together by Lieutenant William Blake, the 503rd's demolition officer, consisted of eight white phosphorus grenades and four blocks of dynamite taped to a jerrican of napalm, detonated by a 15-minute fuze. Blake realized that if the device were simply dropped down a shaft the Japanese would have ample time to dismantle it, so he solved the problem by tying it above the mouth of the shaft with primer cord which was exploded three seconds early, allowing the main charge to fall. On one occasion, while tackling a magazine, he was warned in English by a voice below that, as it contained 80,000 pounds of dynamite, he would blow himself up as well. Blake told the Japanese to come out; when they refused he completed the setting of the charge and withdrew to a safe distance. The tremendous roar, followed by an immense quantity of debris and smoke sent hurtling skywards, confirmed what the Japanese had said.

By these methods more than 1,000 of the defenders were eliminated on the 17th and 18th, at a cost to Rock Force of 30 killed and 110 wounded. The Japanese, however, were evidenctly aware that Itagaki was dead for local commanders on Topside were preparing a counter-attack. At about 02.00 on 19 February they blew up an ammunition bunker to the north of Breakwater Point, killing or injuring a score of paratroopers in a building directly above. The explosion was evidently intended to serve simultaneously as a diversion and a signal for the counter-attack force, approximately 400 strong, to issue from its tunnels at Cheney Ravine and Wheeler Point and assault the summit of Topside. Throughout the remaining hours of darkness the Americans attempted to fend off waves of screaming attackers. Company 'D' was overrun but survived savage hand-to-hand fighting which claimed the lives of thirteen of its members, including the company commander, Lieutenant Turinsky. Company 'F' managed to hold, but even so approximately one hundred of the enemy managed to break through into the barracks area on Topside. This brought Colonel Jones and his deputy, Lieutenant Colonel Jack Tolson, out on to the balcony of their command post, where they used their carbines to pick off attackers who reached the parade ground.

Dawn found most of the Japanese on Topside concentrated in a concrete building 200 yards north of the barracks, tenaciously resisting every attempt to winkle them out. Captain Henry Gibson, commanding Battery 'B' of the 462nd, moved two of his howitzers to an exposed knoll nearby and began blasting the building with high-explosive and incendiary rounds. When the return fire had been silenced the infantry closed in on the smoking ruin to find that all 85 of its occupants were dead. However, Gibson's part in the fighting was not quite over. A concealed machine-gun began raking the parade ground while troops were trying to gather recently dropped re-supply bundles from the drop zone. At length the weapon was located but as none of Gibson's 75mm pack howitzers could reach it he had one of them dismantled and moved to the porch of what had been the old officers' quarters. Here a parachute dangling from the roof blocked his line of sight and the Japanese, aware of what was going on, began raking the building. Despite this, Private First Class John P. Prettyman leaped on to the balustrade, seized the 'chute and heaved with all his strength, bringing it down, but was mortally wounded in the process. The howitzer then opened fire, destroying the machine-gun.

Another hero of the night's fighting was Private Lloyd G. McCarter of Company 'F'. McCarter was a company commander's nightmare, a hard case who was more or less permanently in trouble, but in action he changed completely. On the 16th he had personally stalked and killed six snipers, and during the night attack he had clearly been possessed by the joy of battle, inspiring others by his leadership. When most of his squad had been killed or wounded, he crawled forward to obtain a better shot at the enemy, despite being wounded repeatedly. Using first a Thompson submachine-gun, then a Browning automatic rifle, then a Garand M1 rifle, he personally accounted for 37 of the attackers, breaking up their assault on Company 'F'. Although no longer able to stand, he refused assistance until he fainted through loss of blood. Coming to in the aid station he saw a military policeman standing guard by the door and, despairing of his relationship with the Army, asked 'Good God, what have I done *now*?' Neither of them knew it at the time, but he had just won the Congressional Medal of Honor.

When mopping-up had been completed American losses were assessed as 33 killed and 76 wounded. Rock Force returned to the laborious business of clearing Topside, Middleside and Malinta Hill, further irked by the Japanese habit of emerging at night to re-occupy positions that had been subdued during the day. In the main this was tolerated as the key to these had been discovered during the first attacks and the result was that the new occupants could be eliminated at little or no cost. There was, however, another cause for anxiety. Jones had acquired Japanese documents revealing that, on the eve of the landing, the island's underground magazines and tunnels contained 35,000 artillery rounds, 80,000 mortar rounds, 93,000 grenades, two million rounds of small-arms ammunition and hundreds of tons of dynamite. As enough of this remained to turn Corregidor into a gigantic bomb, he decided to confine the knowledge to his immediate staff. In fact, the troops, now weary and showing the strain of several days' continuous combat, had already formed an accurate picture of the situation, and it was not a comfortable feeling to know that, if the Japanese chose to blow themselves and the island skywards, taking much of Rock Force with them, they had the power to do so, at any time they chose.

At 21.30 on 23 February the thought became a reality. A shattering explosion took place beneath Malinta Hill, causing flames to erupt from tunnel entrances. Rocks and debris were flung far and wide, fissures opened in the surface, men were thrown off their feet and six were buried alive by a landslide on the southern slopes of the hill. Shortly afterwards 3/34th beat off a weak counter-attack from the east and several hundred more of the enemy were seen escaping towards the tail of the island. For the remainder of the night further explosions shook the interior of the hill, though none was as severe as the first. Later, one of the few prisoners taken explained the sequence of events. The Japanese intention had been that, under cover of a controlled explosion designed to distract the Americans, the counter-attack force was to emerge from the tunnels and overrun Malinta Hill while the rest of the occupants made for the eastern end of the island and prepared for a last stand. The explosion, it seemed, had not been adequately controlled and it had killed many of the 2,000 men known to be in the tunnels. The subsequent explosions evidently marked the suicides of the trapped survivors.

Jones now felt that Topside, Middleside and Malinta Hill were sufficiently secure for him to pass two battalions of the 503rd through 3/34th and advance down the tail. Woods' 1st Battalion crossed its startline at 08.30 on 24 February, followed by Erickson's 3rd Battalion. The paratroops advanced behind a rolling barrage provided by the 462nd's pack howitzers, firing wheel to wheel from the Topside parade ground, while on either flank destroyers and PT boats hammered cave entrances and probable defended areas. Overhead flew a cab-rank of Thunderbolts, ready to pounce on any Japanese who showed themselves. Resistance was encountered at Engineer Point and again at Infantry Point, but when Woods halted for the night his troops were only 3,000 yards from the end of the tail. At about 21.00 he summoned his company commanders to brief them for the next day's advance. Before they could arrive Japanese mortars opened fire, killing Woods with a direct hit on the bomb crater which was serving as his command post; Major John Davis, his executive officer, assumed command of the battalion. Nearby was Staff Sergeant Andy Amaty, the battalion's senior signals NCO. Knowing that a mortar barrage generally preceded a Japanese attack, Amaty used his initiative and asked a supporting destroyer to fire illuminating rounds. After one round, which bathed the tail in an eerie glow before dying, the destroyer ceased firing. Amaty asked why and was told that the captain wanted to conserve his flares for the following night. Livid with rage, Amaty ordered his opposite number to fetch the captain *immediately*, adding 'We may not be around tomorrow night!' Unwilling to confront so obviously a senior officer, the captain resumed firing.

By the light of the flares Davis observed some 600 Japanese forming up on a feature known as Water Tank Hill, and called in the 462nd's howitzers. Shells began bursting in the packed ranks, which were further thinned by the 1st Battalion's own weapons. Undeterred, about half the enemy force launched a suicidal charge down the hill. Unable to penetrate the American lines after an hour and a half's fierce fighting, the survivors faded away.

Next day 1/503rd took Water Tank Hill and, beating off local counter-attacks, by evening had reached an approximate line between Monkey Point and Cavalry Point, occupying a low ridge overlooking Kindley Field. During the afternoon, and throughout the next day, some of the defenders attempted to escape by swimming to Caballo Island or Bataan, but most were intercepted and killed if they refused to surrender. On the morning of the 26th, therefore, there were grounds for believing that the battle for Corregidor was all but over. Only 1,000 yards of the tail remained to be covered and Davis reported that resistance was fading. However, the enemy was not prepared to let the island fall without making one last defiant, self-sacrificial, spectacular gesture. Beneath Monkey Point was a large tunnel in which tons of explosives were stored and at 11.00 they detonated this in one gigantic blast which, in its effects, dwarfed anything that had gone before. Rocks, rubble, broken concrete, and earth were hurled more than a mile distant; 2,000 yards offshore a destroyer was struck by a flying boulder. Those men closest to the explosion were literally blown apart and scattered across the landscape; elsewhere, they lay without a mark, killed instantly by the blast wave; some disappeared without trace, buried under tons of earth and rocks.

This would have been the moment for the Japanese to counter-attack, had there been enough of them; fortunately there were not. While the dazed survivors of the battalion did what they could for their injured comrades, Staff Sergeant Amaty advised Jones of the scale of the disaster. The latter ordered Erickson's 3/503rd to pass through and clear the remainder of the tail, then left his command post to see what help he could give. Monkey Point presented a scene of carnage and desolation. In place of the hillock which had marked the site of the tunnel was a crater torn from the living rock, 150 feet long, 75 feet wide and 32 feet deep. Nearby, men were working to free the seized hatches of a Sherman tank which had been thrown 50 yards through the air; ultimately, the task required an acetylene cutter borrowed from the Navy, but only one of the crew had survived the severe internal impacts. When, at last, the stretcher-bearers ceased coming in with their broken burdens it became clear that Davis' battalion had sustained 196 casualties, including 52 dead; some 200 Japanese had been killed instantly by the explosion. For

Captain William McLain, the battalion surgeon, reaction set in quickly: 'As soon as I got all the casualties off, I sat down on a rock and burst out crying. I couldn't stop myself and didn't even want to. I had seen more than a man could stand and still stay normal. . . . When I had the cases to care for, that kept me going; but after that it was too much.'

Meanwhile 3/503rd had fought their way the length of Kindley Field and by 16.00 had reached East Point at the island's tail. A few individuals and small groups of Japanese remained to be hunted down in tideline caves and other hideouts, but the battle for Corregidor was over. With the exception of twenty prisoners, the entire garrison had been wiped out, either killed in action, walled up, drowned or dead by their own hands. The cost to 503rd Parachute Infantry and its supporting units was 165 killed, 285 wounded and 330 injured, including jump casualties; 3/34th Infantry had 38 killed, 150 wounded, ten injured and five missing; 2/151st Infantry, which relieved 3/34th on 25 February, had seven killed and fifteen wounded. Overall casualties, therefore, amounted to approximately one quarter of those sustained by the Japanese in their amphibious landing three years earlier.

General Douglas MacArthur returned to Corregidor on 2 March. As he reached the parade ground on Topside, Colonel Jones stepped forward from the ranks of the 503rd to salute and make his formal report: 'Sir, I present to you Fortress Corregidor.' MacArthur addressed the troops then, observing that the old flagpole was still standing, ordered the Colours to be raised.

The last ghosts of the dark days of 1942 were exorcised some weeks later when 2/151st Infantry captured the remaining Japanese toeholds in Manila Bay, the small islands of Caballo, El Fraile and Carabao. The last was found deserted, but on Caballo and El Fraile, also known as Fort Drum or the Concrete Battleship because of its shape and long-silent naval gun turrets, the Japanese fought to the death; in each case, several thousand gallons of diesel fuel had to be pumped down ventilation shafts and then exploded. By then, Colonel Jones and his regiment had left Corregidor and were fighting on Negros in the Southern Philippines.

11
GOOSE GREEN
27–29 May 1982

For the Argentine junta that decided to invade the Falkland Islands in April 1982, the British decision to send a task force was a complete and extremely unpleasant surprise. The invasion had been mounted to bolster the junta's flagging popularity at home and, despite the unfavourable reaction of the United Nations, its leaders had no alternative other than to maintain their occupation of the islands if they wished to cling to power. This in itself presented serious problems as the garrison that was deployed to the islands under the command of Major-General Mario Menendez could not be strong everywhere and, after the Argentine surface fleet had retired to port following the sinking of the cruiser *General Belgrano* on 2 May, its links with the mainland were tenuous in the extreme; during the night of 10/11 May, for example, the supply vessel *Isla de los Estados* attempted to run the Royal Navy's blockade and was sunk in Falkland Sound by HMS *Alacrity*.

Presented with a difficult task, Menendez decided to concentrate on holding East Falkland, and specifically Port Stanley, the capital, establishing a three-ring concentric defence based upon the mountains to the west of the town. Yet, despite this sensible limitation, he detached the 5th and 8th Regiments to, respectively, Port Howard and Fox Bay on West Falkland, where they played little or no part in the conflict. More understandable was his decision to install a garrison at Goose Green, a settlement on the narrow isthmus connecting the northern and southern portions of East Falkland, since there was an airstrip there which could be incorporated in the overall defence plan for the islands.

The senior officer at Goose Green was Vice-Commodore Wilson Pedroza of the Argentine Air Force, who was responsible for running the base and its squadron of Pucara ground-attack aircraft. The airstrip, however, never having been designed for military use, presented operating difficulties and by the time it was assaulted its aircraft had been moved to Port Stanley, although the ground crews remained. The officer responsible for the defence of the base was Lieutenant-Colonel Italo Piaggi, who had at his disposal two companies from the 12th Infantry Regiment, one from the 25th Infantry Regiment and various attached units, producing the equivalent of an infantry battalion. Heavy weapons capable of supporting the defence included three 105mm pack howitzers, six twin-20mm and two twin-35mm anti-aircraft guns and six

120mm heavy mortars. Altogether about 1,000 men were available, including air force personnel who could serve in the infantry role.

Piaggi's troops were representative of the Argentine Army as a whole. The officers and NCOs were regular soldiers, and many of them were personally courageous and professional in their outlook. It did not, however, help to create any sort of bond between the leaders and the led when officers received such privileges as special ration packs, nor that some officers and NCOs failed to regard their men's welfare as an essential part of their duties. The rank-and-file were either young conscripts who had barely completed their basic training or reservists recalled to the Colours after completing their twelve months' service. Their standard of training was not such that they could be trusted to press home a counter-attack, although they were quite capable of holding prepared positions. To many the beloved Malvinas, as the national tradition had taught them to call the Falklands, were a dreadful disappointment; most came from a warmer northern climate and the endless dreary peat-bog, lowering grey skies, rain squalls and constant cutting wind eroded their motivation and morale. They were, however, adequately equipped with warm clothing and their boots were of a far superior design to those of their British opponents, which let in water.

A further problem was that Argentina had not fought a foreign war for a century so that, with the exception of counter-insurgency operations, her army was completely lacking in experience of modern warfare. Consequently, it was forced to operate by the manuals and purchased experience at the price of casualties. Nevertheless, Piaggi succeeded in establishing a formidable series of defensive positions in depth on the Goose Green isthmus and sited his howitzers expertly in a depression near the settlement where they were extremely difficult to detect. It was later found that preference for six-man trenches, instead of the two-man slits preferred by the British, had been a contributory factor in the high Argentine losses. In Goose Green itself the civil population was not harmed, although it was detained under guard in the community hall, but stores and other facilities were located among the houses in the belief that, in order to avoid loss of life among their own people, the British would not bombard the settlement.

When, during the night of 20/21 May, Brigadier Julian Thompson's reinforced 3 Commando Brigade (40, 42 and 45 Royal Marine Commandos, 2nd and 3rd Battalions Parachute Regiment) secured a beach-head around San Carlos Water, to the north of Goose Green, Piaggi had two standing patrols in the area. These managed to shoot down two light helicopters but were only able to offer a token resistance and, after reporting the landing, most of the men made their way eastward across the island towards Port Stanley rather than attempt to reach Goose Green, from which they were now cut off.

During the next few days both sides sustained serious losses in a furious battle between the Royal Navy's supporting warships and Argentine aircraft flying from the mainland. This did not disrupt the build-up within the beach-head, although on 25 May the Argentines scored a major success when the container ship *Atlantic Conveyor* was set ablaze and sunk by an Exocet missile, taking three large Chinook and six Wessex helicopters to the bottom with her. This left Thompson critically short of helicopter lift in extremely difficult terrain, and as Menendez was also suffering from the same problem it determined the course of the campaign.

Once the Argentine Air Force had been defeated in its attempts to stop the landing, the next logical step would have been to await the arrival of the second echelon of British ground troops, the 5 Infantry Brigade, before breaking out of the beach-head and advancing on Port Stanley. In London, however, the government was eager to announce a victory and Thompson was under immense pressure to start moving. With comparatively few helicopters this would not be easy; indeed, Menendez did not believe it was possible, and for this reason had not reacted to the landing. Yet Thompson had a priceless asset at his disposal, and that was the superb fitness of his commandos and paratroopers. Like all the British armed services they were professionals, but they were also élites into which entry was eagerly sought. Their selection procedures and training methods tested candidates' strength, stamina, determination, nerve and aggression to the limit so that only the best were accepted. Conscious of their ability and knowing that both commandos and paratroopers had trained regularly in harsh moorland conditions similar to those on the Falklands, Thompson decided that they would march to Port Stanley, leaving the helicopters free to haul guns, ammunition and heavy equipment; in the event, some men carried loads of 140 pounds.

Thompson's plan was that while the brigade commenced its advance on 27 May, 2nd Battalion Parachute Regiment, commanded by Lieutenant-Colonel Herbert Jones, would march south from its position on Sussex Mountain, on the southern edge of the beach-head, and attack Goose Green. This would serve the dual purpose of removing an enemy force from the brigade's right flank and simultaneously providing the politicians with the victory they wanted. The idea of a raid on Goose Green had been discussed for some days, although as everyone would be on foot and the distance between Sussex Mountain and the settlement was fourteen miles the word raid was not entirely appropriate. In the final analysis the operation was planned to eliminate the enemy presence on the isthmus, and since this would be the first major encounter between British and Argentine troops the outcome would be of immense importance to both sides.

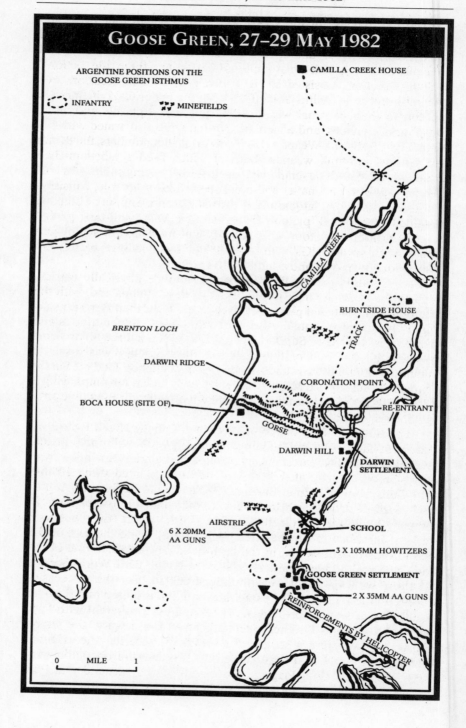

GOOSE GREEN, 27–29 MAY 1982

ARGENTINE POSITIONS ON THE
GOOSE GREEN ISTHMUS

INFANTRY   MINEFIELDS

CAMILLA CREEK HOUSE

CAMILLA CREEK

BURNTSIDE HOUSE

BRENTON LOCH

TRACK

DARWIN RIDGE

CORONATION POINT

BOCA HOUSE (SITE OF)

RE-ENTRANT

GORSE

DARWIN HILL

DARWIN
SETTLEMENT

AIRSTRIP

6 X 20MM
AA GUNS

SCHOOL

3 X 105MM HOWITZERS

GOOSE GREEN SETTLEMENT

2 X 35MM AA GUNS

REINFORCEMENTS BY HELICOPTER

0   MILE   1

The organization of Jones's battalion consisted of four rifle companies, a support company and a headquarters company. Three of the rifle companies, 'A', 'B' and 'D', contained a company headquarters and three platoons each with a platoon headquarters and three rifle sections. Each rifle section consisted of eight men and, on this occasion, two General Purpose Machine-Guns (GPMGs); the majority of riflemen, in addition to their personal weapons, carried high-explosive and white phosphorus grenades, and a large proportion were also armed with the 66mm Light Anti-tank Weapon (LAW) or, in smaller numbers, the 84mm Carl Gustav anti-tank weapon, both of which fired a tube-launched round which could be employed against the enemy's bunkers. 'C' Company, somewhat smaller and more specialized in its role, consisted of a Reconnaissance Platoon and a Patrols Platoon. Support Company contained an anti-tank platoon armed with six Milan anti-tank guided weapons, a mortar platoon with eight 81mm mortars, a machine-gun platoon with six GPMGs with tripods and sustained-fire barrels, an assault pioneer platoon and a sniper section.

Because almost everything would have to be physically carried, Jones decided that the men would take two days' rations and, with the exception of the medical personnel, they would leave their Bergen packs behind on Sussex Mountain. Also left behind would be the tripods and sustained-fire barrels of Support Company's GPMGs, three Milan firing posts and all but two of the 81mm mortars. Priority was given to ammunition and mortar rounds, so that as the battalion filed off Sussex Mountain at dusk on 26 May it was very heavily laden. Accompanying it was a small commando/artillery detachment armed with Blowpipe anti-aircraft missiles.

At 07.00 on 27 May the column reached Camilla Creek House, an abandoned farm with out-buildings lying in a hollow, approximately three miles from the nearest enemy position and almost nine miles from Goose Green. Shortly after first light helicopters lifted three 105mm Light Guns from '8' (Alma) Battery, 29 Commando Regiment RA, into position a little to the north, together with their ammunition supplies. 'C' Company sent out patrols to Camilla Creek, where they obtained excellent information on the enemy's positions, while the rest of the battalion lay up and rested in the farm buildings. At 10.00 one of the radios at battalion headquarters was tuned to the BBC World Service and those within earshot were thunderstruck to hear the newscaster proudly announce that '. . . a parachute battalion is poised and ready to assault Darwin and Goose Green'. Jones, almost incoherent with fury, spoke of suing the Defence Secretary and, if necessary, the Prime Minister, for permitting so grave a breach of security, the criminal stupidity of which could have compromised the entire operation with heavy loss of life. Both Piaggi at Goose Green and Menendez at Port Stanley were advised of the content of the broadcast, but neither of them believed that the British were capable of such idiocy; rather, they believed the report to be a bluff designed to divert attention from operations elsewhere and, at that stage, no steps were taken to reinforce the garrison of Goose Green. The leak was later traced to Downing Street, where eagerness to report progress had somehow become divorced from reality. That, however, does not exonerate the BBC which, heedless of the possible consequences, blandly ignored the cardinal rules of war reporting, namely that information which is of use to the enemy or which can place one's own troops in jeopardy must not be released until the situation has been resolved.

Not long after the broadcast the paratroopers had the satisfaction of drawing first blood, snapping up a commandeered civilian Land Rover which drove up the track from the south. It contained the commander of Piaggi's reconnaissance platoon and three soldiers, one of whom was wounded before they surrendered. During the battle the vehicle was put to good use hauling ammunition forward.

Jones spent the day working on his plan of attack. He was faced with a long narrow isthmus which permitted no room for manoeuvre. This meant that his battalion would be committed to a series of frontal assaults against defences constructed in depth. The enemy was known to have at least one company in position in the Low Pass/Burntside House area at the northern end of the isthmus, the presence of further troops was suspected at Coronation Point on the eastern shore, and a line of trenches could be seen on Darwin Ridge, which crossed the isthmus from the tiny Darwin settlement to the western shore. South of this, near the western shore, a platoon position had been identified near the site once occupied by Boca House. Beyond this, details were unclear, although due allowance was made for a further two infantry companies, one of which was in reserve at Goose Green while the other was in position at the southern end of the isthmus. Prepared positions would certainly exist at Goose Green and its airstrip, and these would be covered by the enemy's anti-aircraft guns firing in the ground role. Little was known of Piaggi's artillery, and nothing of its location, which was actually in a depression on the northern outskirts of Goose Green.

The battalion would be attacking over open heathland against an enemy who had had ample time in which to prepare his defences. Normally for such an undertaking the attacking force should have a numerical superiority in the ratio of 3:1, but in this case it was itself outnumbered by 2:1. It would, however, have the support of '8' Battery's three guns and the frigate HMS *Arrow*, lying in Grantham Sound, whose 4.5in gun could fire one 55-pound shell every two seconds. Unfortunately, because of air attacks from the Argentine mainland, *Arrow* would have to leave the area at 04.30 in order to reach the comparative security of San Carlos Water at first light. After dawn, Jones could call on air support, although this would be contingent upon the ability of Rear-

Admiral Woodward's aircraft carriers to fly off and recover their Harriers in the uncertain weather conditions. It was thus necessary to make the greatest possible use of darkness not only to eliminate the disadvantages of the open terrain but also to gain the maximum benefit of *Arrow*'s presence. Jones's plan, as finally drafted, contained six consecutive phases, the first of which would consist of the battalion's approach march from Camilla Creek House to its start-lines at the northern end of the isthmus. Phase II, the first in which the enemy positions would be assaulted, was to commence at 02.00 on 28 May and would be followed in succession by Phases III, IV and V as the battalion fought its way down the isthmus. Phase VI, the capture of Darwin and Goose Green settlements, would not begin until 06.30 and was intentionally timed to take place in daylight in order to minimize civilian casualties.

In the event, the time required to complete the operation was seriously under-estimated. Somewhat over-estimated, by both sides, was the effect their field artillery would have on the fighting, for not only did a high wind carry the shells off course, but when they did land they buried themselves deep in the peaty soil, which absorbed much of their explosive force. For the paratroopers, in the open, coming under artillery fire was still a serious matter, but for the Argentinians, sitting tight in their bunkers, it was less so, for only a direct hit was likely to prove fatal.

Jones held his final Orders Group during the last hours of daylight on the 27th and at 17.00 the battalion began to file away down the track leading from Camilla Creek House to Goose Green. In the darkness the march was extremely slow but when guides eventually led Major Dair Farrar-Hockley's 'A' Company to its Phase II start-line it was only 35 minutes behind schedule. The company, on the left of the battalion line, had as its objective Burntside House and another position nearby, which were to be assaulted from the east. The objectives were lit up by illuminating rounds fired by *Arrow* and raked with automatic weapons. When the assault went in the enemy was found to have fled, leaving behind two bodies. 'A' Company then advanced through steadily falling rain to Coronation Point, where at approximately 04.00 the reported Argentine position was found to be unoccupied.

On the right 'B' Company, commanded by Major John Crosland, had to wait on its start-line until 'A' Company had secured Burntside House, in order to avoid running into the latter's east-west fire. It began to move forward at 03.10 and four minutes later *Arrow* reported that her gun was temporarily out of action because of mechanical problems. This was a serious loss, but the company still had the support of '8' Battery's guns and Support Company's GPMGs, firing across Camilla Creek, and could also provide a limited amount of illumination for itself, using flares and its 2in mortars. Its advance took it straight towards the Argentine company position at the northern end of the isthmus. The battle began when a figure, thought to be a scarecrow, suddenly began moving, was challenged and, replying in Spanish, was shot dead. After that Crosland's platoons, now coming under fire from the enemy's artillery and mortars, fought their way through the position in what he describes as 'a violent gutter fight'. This involved some men concentrating their fire on trenches in succession while others crawled close enough to toss in a high-explosive or white phosphorus grenade. The reaction of the Argentinians was mixed. Some fought back, some ran off southwards in the darkness, and some hid beneath their blankets in the bottom of their trenches where, if they were not killed, they were winkled out at bayonet point.

One platoon commander commented that the capture of the position had an 'electrifying impact' on his men who, from that point onwards, believed themselves to be 'invincible'. This stemmed partly from the success of the attack and the knowledge that their trench-clearing methods were efficient, but other forces were at work too. From the onset, their training had emphasized aggression and the need to generate extreme violence in action yet, in contrast, whenever they had been employed in the internal security role, as in Ulster, it was essential that only the minimum necessary force was applied. Now, the presence of a visible enemy against whom no holds were barred must have provided a tremendous release. Again, every man in the battalion was subconsciously aware that he had inherited the traditions of the bridge at Arnhem and, having survived his baptism of fire, his morale soared with the knowledge that he could fight as well as his forbears.

Crosland rallied his scattered company at 05.00. 'D' Company, under Major Philip Neame, had come forward and was moving into the gap between 'A' and 'B' Companies when it became involved in a sharp battle which involved clearing an unexpected trench system. 'C' and Support Companies were following up but Jones was becoming concerned that his timetable was slipping further and further behind. At 06.30 he ordered Farrar-Hockley to leave Coronation Point and secure 'A' Company's next objective, Darwin settlement and, on the right 'B' Company resumed the lead and began advancing on Boca House.

Meanwhile, Piaggi had not been idle. Now fully aware that a full-scale attack was in progress, he sent platoons forward from Goose Green to man the trench line along Darwin Ridge, where they were joined by the fugitives from the company that had been overwhelmed during the night. On this, their main defence line, approximately 200 men awaited the appearance of 'A' and 'B' Companies in the half-light of dawn.

'A' Company's route took it beside a wide inlet to the north of Darwin. Farrar-Hockley detached his 3 Platoon along the northern shore of this to give fire support while the company assaulted the settlement from the west. His intended path would take him up a gorse-filled re-entrant – subsequently known as the gorse gully – to the south of the inlet, thence eastwards across the shoulder of Darwin Hill towards the objective. At 06.45 the Company was approaching the entrance to the gorse gully when three Argentinians were seen walking on the spur to the right. The leader platoon opened fire, dropping one, but heavy automatic weapon fire was immediately directed at the Company from enemy positions on the spur and the ridge to its right. Most of the Company managed to run forward and take cover in the gully, although those at the rear were forced to seek shelter in dead ground near the shoreline. Within the gully the enemy had dug trenches on the right-hand slope, but thanks to the initiative of the nearest junior leaders these were quickly cleared with GPMGs, grenades and 66mm LAWs. However, any attempt to move out of the gully or cross the spur to its right was greeted with a storm of fire and casualties began to mount. Farrar-Hockley was now in a very tight spot, being pinned down with about 60 men while the rest of the Company was scattered round the inlet, unable to assist.

At about the same time, 1,000 yards to the west, 'B' Company was advancing down the forward slope of a hill with two platoons forward and one back when it suddenly came under heavy machine-gun fire from Darwin Ridge to its left front and the enemy position at Boca House to its front. Crosland ordered his forward platoons to work their way down the slope into the belt of gorse which crossed the isthmus at this point, after which the rear platoon retired to the crest of the hill. Intensified mortar and artillery fire began to land among the troops, who were unable to make any further progress forward. By 07.30 the battalion's advance had been brought to a standstill. At this moment, and for several hours afterwards, it was vulnerable to counter-attack. Fortunately, Piaggi did not attempt such a move, largely because his men's training was unequal to the task. '8' Battery's guns and the two 81mm mortars did what they could to assist but made little impression on the defences. At about 08.00 three Pucaras attacked Camilla Creek House and the gun line without result; one was severely damaged by the explosion of a Blowpipe missile but managed to limp back to Port Stanley. No air support was available for the British as conditions at sea prevented the Harriers flying off.

For Jones the need to get the battle moving again held absolute priority. With his tactical headquarters he made his way forward under fire to 'A' Company and, collecting the stragglers on the shoreline, succeeded in reaching the gully at about 08.30. Here, with the gorse starting to burn, he could see Farrar-Hockley's problems at first hand. It might be argued that as the battalion's commanding officer he should not have allowed himself to become embroiled in a company commander's battle, but Jones habitually led from the front and his intention was to reinforce 'A' Company's will to win by his own presence. He believed that by sustained effort the Company would achieve a breakthrough which would enable it to roll up the rest of the Argentine defence line. So absorbed did he become in resolving this problem that when Neame suggested via the radio that he could outflank the enemy line by taking 'D' Company down the western shoreline of the isthmus, he rejected the idea with some asperity, perhaps because he was unwilling to commit his reserve at this stage of the battle and was unable to verify the feasibility of the plan himself. Likewise, when Major Hugh Jenner of Support Company came through just after 09.00 to suggest that the Milans be brought forward to engage the enemy bunkers, he refused permission.

Shortly after this he ordered Farrar-Hockley to take the spur on the right of the gully. The attack foundered on the crest in a storm of fire and the survivors pulled back into cover; among those killed were Captain Wood, the battalion's adjutant, and Captain Dent, 'A' Company's second-in-command. At 09.30 Jones decided that he would personally lead an attack round the base of the spur into the next re-entrant. As he climbed towards a trench on the left, covered by his bodyguard, Sergeant Norman, he was mortally wounded by a machine-gun firing from the opposite slope. Some accounts suggest that Jones's death marked the turning-point in the battle, while others express surprise that it did not break the back of the battalion's attack. Neither of these contradictory ideas bears close examination. As he intended, Jones had already reinforced 'A' Company's determination, emphasizing that the battle was a contest of wills in which that of the paratroopers would prove the stronger. Now, slowly but surely, Farrar-Hockley's men were gaining the upper hand in a bitter close-quarters brawl in which the 66mm LAW proved to be the critical weapon. Only ten minutes after Jones had been hit the machine-gun post responsible was blown apart. Thereafter, bunker after bunker was systematically eliminated until white surrender flags began to appear from the remainder. By 10.30 the ridge had been cleared. The position had actually contained 23 trenches held by 92 Argentinians; of these, eighteen, including one officer, had been killed and 39 wounded. The prisoners, beaten and cowed, were genuinely surprised to receive decent treatment from their captors; it was a point Jones had insisted upon. British casualties included three officers and three soldiers killed, plus eleven wounded. To these must be added one officer killed and one soldier seriously wounded when their casevac helicopter was bounced and shot down by Pucaras on its way forward.

Major Christopher Keeble, the battalion's second-in-command, was with the duplicate tactical headquarters some 1,500 yards to the rear when the news that Jones had been hit was received on the radio. He immediately spoke to each of the company commanders in turn. 'A' Company had just eliminated the enemy at the eastern end of the ridge but had sustained casualties and was still without No. 3 Platoon. 'B' Company, although not so severely hit, was still pinned down at the western end of the line. 'C' and 'D' Companies, however, remained uncommitted, as did the firepower of Support Company's Milans. It was a good inheritance which left plenty of clout at Keeble's disposal. The question of abandoning the operation did not arise and was therefore not discussed.

The next logical step was to eliminate the Argentinians still holding out at the western end of the ridge and in the area of Boca House. To achieve this Keeble adopted the suggestions already rejected by Jones, namely to take out the enemy bunkers with Support Company's Milans and pass 'D' Company down the shoreline where a limited degree of cover was available.

The Milan missile weighs 24 pounds and is effective to a range of 2,000 yards, being guided to the target by the operator keeping his sight trained on the target while infra-red sensors track the exhaust and transmit course corrections. Comparatively few missiles were needed to unlock the position, for the moral effect was as great as the physical. They penetrated the bunkers with pinpoint accuracy and exploded with devastating effect within; furthermore, the flaring exhaust was visible to the defenders as it streaked towards them, leaving no room for doubt as to their own vulnerability. Very quickly white flags began to appear and, covered by their own, 'B' Company's and Support Company's GPMGs, Neame's men moved along the shoreline to take possession of the Boca House area. Here twelve of the enemy had been killed and many of the fifteen prisoners were wounded; perhaps a dozen or so survivors were seen running off in the direction of the airstrip. This, the last position in the enemy's main defence line, fell shortly after noon.

The continual firing of guns and mortars outside his headquarters, added to the sustained roar of battle from Darwin Ridge, had told Piaggi that while his troops had managed, for the moment, to halt the paratroopers' advance, they had not repulsed the attack. Rather it could be said that the British had locked their teeth into his main defences and showed no signs of letting go. He asked Menendez for reinforcements and the latter scraped together what he could. At about the time Boca House fell a gaggle of helicopters put down briefly just south of Goose Green and 84 soldiers scrambled out. Piaggi pushed them into an inner defence line which he had been constructing as the situation deteriorated. This rested on a school building at the mouth of an inlet between Darwin and Goose Green, then extended westwards to the airfield and the gently rising ground in the centre of the isthmus.

Meanwhile, Keeble was restoring momentum to the battlefield and adapting the original plan to meet altered circumstances. 'A' Company was to remain firm on Darwin Hill. 'C' Company, commanded by Major Roger Jenner, was reinforced with 'A' Company's No. 3 Platoon and would fight as a rifle company, advancing down the forward slope of Darwin Ridge towards the airfield; Neame's 'D' Company would advance south-east from Boca House across the isthmus towards Goose Green; Crosland's 'B' Company, after moving down the western edge of the battlefield, would swing east and isolate the settlement from the south; and Support Company's Milans and GPMGs would come forward to the gorse line.

When 'C' Company began to move forward down the gentle forward slope of Darwin Ridge it immediately attracted heavy fire not only from the enemy's machine-guns and mortars, but also from his anti-aircraft guns on the airfield and the headland near the settlement. The volume of fire was described as incredible by those who experienced it, but in the circumstances it caused remarkably few casualties and most of the Company was able to take cover behind the bank of a shallow stream at the foot of the slope while the Milans and battalion mortars neutralized the anti-aircraft guns. The Company then moved down the stream towards the inlet and the school house. 'C' and 'D' Companies were actually on converging axes so that the left-hand platoon of the latter overlapped with the result that the defenders of the school were quickly driven out by a series of impromptu attacks delivered by elements of both companies.

On the airfield the remainder of 'D' Company had, in the meantime, become involved in the capture of several trench systems. It was becoming apparent that while some of the Argentinians were willing to continue the fight, the will of the remainder had been broken. This led to a controversial incident when, contrary to orders, a platoon leader went forward to accept an apparent surrender. The problem was that, while some of the enemy plainly wanted to give up, others, including their officer, did not. While discussion was taking place a GPMG crew back on the gorse line, seeing only distant figures which they understandably believed to be the enemy, put in a long burst. The Argentinians immediately opened fire, killing the platoon leader and two other men, and taking casualties in return. When a nearby ammunition dump exploded both sides pulled back. There was not, as was suggested at the time, treachery by either party.

Menendez continued to give Piaggi whatever support he could. At about 15.00 two naval Aermacchi jets came in from the south, strafing 'D' Company without result. A Blowpipe missile was fired prematurely from the gorse line and in his haste to avoid it one of the pilots lost control of his aircraft and it hurtled into the ground near 'B' Company. At 15.10 two Pucaras arrived from the north-west and 'D' Company was again selected as the target. The aircraft flew into a curtain of small-arms fire which damaged one so badly that its pilot ejected and it crashed near 'B' Company, showering the men with fuel from its ruptured tanks. The second was also seriously damaged but managed to drop two napalm containers before limping away; fortunately, these fell short.

Keeble had already told Neame to hold his position as, at last, the weather at sea had improved and a Harrier strike was on the way. This had as its target the 35mm anti-aircraft guns on the point near the settlement where, lying beyond the reach of the Milans, they were still active and engaging the school house. Two aircraft dropped cluster bombs slightly off target into the sea, where the water was churned into exploding foam by the hundreds of bomblets, but the third raked the position with rockets, causing a number of casualties. However, as a demonstration of what might be expected, the attack succeeded brilliantly in that it seems to have shattered what remained of the enemy's nerve. For the Argentinians, air attack was a new and very frightening experience; in the community centre the civilians could hear some of them screaming throughout the time the Harriers were overhead, although few were hurt.

The Argentinians, many of whom had abandoned their weapons, were now leaving their forward positions and trudging disconsolately into Goose Green. There had been killing enough and, for the most part, the paratroopers let them go. At last light another gaggle of helicopters put down just south of Goose Green, disembarking the last reinforcements Piaggi was to receive, 100 men of the 12th Regiment's 'B' Company. The helicopters quickly lifted off but as the troops began to converge on the settlement '8' Battery landed fifteen rounds squarely in their midst.

With the coming of darkness Keeble ordered his companies to pull back a little way. For most of his men this was to be their third night without sleep, and 'B' and 'D' Companies, being furthest from the source of supply, spent it without rations. To complete their misery, it snowed. This may have saved the lives of the wounded, British and Argentine, who had to wait many hours before being evacuated, as the intense cold helped staunch the flow of blood. Elation there was none; everyone knew that the battle would be renewed on the morrow. With this in mind, Brigadier Thompson gave Keeble permission to destroy the settlement if the need arose and undertook to fly 'J' Company 42 Commando and three additional guns to Camilla Creek House the following morning. Keeble, however, believed the enemy could be induced to surrender and sent in two captured NCOs under a flag of truce with an ultimatum. Pedroza, as the senior officer present, spoke with Menendez, telling him that he was now surrounded and, probably, that in the opinion of his officers, the troops would no longer fight. Menendez authorized him to surrender and the following morning, accompanied by Piaggi, he met Keeble and agreed terms. His own 250 Air Force personnel emerged first to surrender with much ceremony, then Piaggi led out some 800 soldiers to lay down their helmets and weapons. As a parting gesture, the latter thoroughly defiled the islanders' homes. Released from their captivity in the community hall, the people of Goose Green and Darwin greeted their tired liberators with mugs of hot tea, biscuits and sweets. For paratroopers and civilians alike it was a very moving and emotional moment.

At the time Two Para believed that they had killed 250 of the enemy and wounded 150 more. These figures are almost certainly too high and may have resulted from a contemporary mistranslation. On the other hand, the official Argentine figures of 55 killed and approximately 100 wounded seem somewhat low and the possibility exists that these are based on incomplete records. The battalion's own losses, including attached arms, amounted to eighteen killed and 35 wounded; significantly, those killed included no less than twelve officers and NCOs, proving the extent to which leadership had played a vital role in the fighting. Among the awards for the engagement was that of the Victoria Cross to Lieutenant-Colonel Jones.

The immediate consequence of the battle was that a British victory could be broadcast to the world. To reinforce Goose Green during the battle Menendez had taken troops from the Mount Kent sector, with the result that by 2 June the mountain was firmly in British hands. The outermost and potentially most formidable of the defence lines covering Port Stanley was therefore penetrated without the need for fighting. British confidence in the conflict's successful outcome was reinforced. Within the Argentine lines rumours of British ferocity abounded; one of the wildest stories circulating was that the 1st/7th Gurkha Rifles, who neatly rounded up fugitives from the Goose Green garrison in Lafonia, the southern portion of East Falkland, were cannibals. Such self-induced terror did nothing to maintain an already flagging morale. For the British, the lessons of Goose Green were quickly absorbed. All subsequent attacks were limited in their objectives, received adequate artillery and naval gunfire support, and were carried out at night. On 14 June Menendez surrendered and the Union Flag was once more flying over the Falkland Islands.

A POSTSCRIPT

In attempting to identify sources of motivation in the foregoing, I have selected the following five major headings; professionalism, including leadership, discipline, *esprit de corps* and tradition; success; the desire for revenge; survival; and self-sacrifice in what is believed to be an essential role. One, at least, of these elements was present in all of the episodes I have described.

Professional soldiers, in common with most of the population, believe they earn their pay and give good value for money. Time and again during the Falklands Conflict and Gulf War, we saw television reporters, anxious for a 'reaction' from private soldiers bound for the war zone, expertly swatted by the same simple straight-from-the-shoulder response: 'It's my job. It's what I do. That's why they pay me.' Naturally, the professional soldier has fears and anxieties, but he also has discipline, training, comradeship and a pride in his unit. He might fear death and disablement, but he is just as frightened of letting himself down in front of his comrades, and of letting his comrades down. The level of motivation in units fighting the first battles of a campaign tends to be high, since they are keen to prove themselves, are not always aware of the dangers, and have a high credit balance of courage.

This was certainly the case among British troops at Balaclava. The 93rd Highlanders knew exactly what was required of them and were only too eager to take the fight to the enemy. The Heavy Brigade, too, responded to its training for shock action and smashed into the mass of the Russian cavalry without hesitation, achieving an immediate moral ascendancy. The Light Brigade, already encouraged by the success of the Heavies, had a further source of motivation. They had played little or no part in the Battle of the Alma and they bitterly resented the infantry's comment that Raglan had deliberately 'kept them in a band-box'. Therefore, while fully conscious of the terrible dangers to which they were exposed, they accepted them and earned immortality.

It was *esprit de corps* and discipline which enabled the few surviving officers and senior NCOs to get the Prussian Guard up and moving again after it had sustained 8,000 casualties in twenty minutes on the slopes beneath St-Privat. Likewise, the reaction of 1 Army Tank Brigade's regular regiments at Arras was entirely professional. For days they had been mucked about, sent this way and that, been attacked from the air, all without the chance to hit back. Small wonder, then, that when the moment to counter-attack arrived it was more than welcome. At Goose Green 2 Para, selectively recruited, trained to the highest standards for a possible war against the Warsaw Pact, and conscious of the traditions of Arnhem, never even considered the possibility of abandoning the operation, despite the death of their commanding officer, grinding fatigue and the depth of the enemy's position.

The knapsacks of a fleeing enemy are the finest sight a soldier can behold, goes the old saying; or, as Lord Moran puts it, 'Achievement is a sharp tonic to morale.' This seems to be especially true in cases where training concepts are dramatically vindicated or equipment proves to be superior to that of the enemy. At Minden the deliberately aimed volleys of von Spoercken's regiments smashed up one French charge after another, and as each foundered the self-confidence of the British and Hanoverian infantry rose while that of their opponents fell in proportion. At Arras the Matildas' armour proved to be invulnerable to the German anti-tank guns. 'At that moment', recalled one of the tank crews, 'we did not see why we shouldn't go all the way to Berlin.' At Goose Green a paratroop officer observed that the success of the long-practised trench-clearing drill had an 'electric' effect on his men.

The desire for revenge, too, provides an extremely powerful source of motivation. It features prominently in survivors' accounts of Minden. Those besieging Delhi had terrible atrocities to avenge, including the massacre of women and children. The Prussian Guard at St-Privat had seen their comrades shot down in droves and were determined that the enemy would pay the price. On Longstop Hill 8th Argylls, enraged by the action of a prisoner who needlessly killed several men, stormed the bitterly contested summit of Djebel Ahmera in a mood of berserk fury and took it. The intensity of US III/504th Parachute Infantry's ordeal as it crossed the Waal generated so strong a sense of invincibility and a desire for revenge among the survivors that they overwhelmed the defences with little or no concern for their own safety.

Knowledge that the enemy will show no mercy is another factor which can reinforce a unit's morale at the critical moment. For the Desert Column sent to Gordon's relief there was the certainty that their bones would bleach in the sand if they lost their battles. Similarly, the US 503rd Parachute Infantry, having already made a hair-raising descent on to Corregidor, were aware that the Japanese would try to blow them to 'kingdom come' by detonating the island's huge subterranean ammunition stores, yet accepted the risks and numerous casualties sustained by this means in the knowledge that only by the enemy's total elimination could the situation be resolved.

Finally, the knowledge that others depend on a unit can stiffen its morale to the point of willing self-sacrifice. The Union defenders of Little Round Top, and in particular the 20th Maine, knew that the outcome of the battle depended on their ability to hold the vital ground. They were no braver than their Confederate opponents, who were not fully aware of the importance of the hill, but they were brave for a little longer, and that was sufficient to tilt the scales. The experience of the cavalry on both sides during the Franco–Prussian War was not a happy one. However, at Vionville von Bredow's cavalry brigade willingly and successfully sacrificed itself to prevent the German flank being decisively turned. The Arras Counter-Attack was, in simple terms, a Death Ride similar to von Bredow's, and also produced results which benefited the whole army. The Waal crossings by the Guards Armoured and US 82nd Airborne Divisions were made in a desperate attempt to break through to the British 1st Airborne Division, surrounded and under constant attack at Arnhem; those involved were unaware that, that very afternoon, the situation to the north had changed radically for the worse.

The reader will doubtless be able to supplement these few thoughts with some of his own. In operational analysis, which is one of the major functions of military history, the moral factors are as important as any other.

SELECT BIBLIOGRAPHY

Adkin, Mark. *Goose Green – A Battle is Fought to be Won*. Pen & Sword Ltd, 1992

Anon. *The Operations of the Allied Army under the Command of His Serene Highness Prince Ferdinand, Duke of Brunswick and Luneberg*. London, 1764

Atteridge, A. Hilliard. *Famous Land Fights*. Methuen, 1914

Barthorp, Michael. *The British Army on Campaign 1882–1902*. Osprey, 1988

Bentley, Nicolas (ed.). *Russell's Despatches from the Crimea*. Andre Deutsche, 1966

Bormbaum, Friedrich. *Die Schlacht bei Minden und das Gefecht bei Cohfeld am 1 August 1759*. Bruns' Verlag, Minden

Breuer, William B. *Retaking the Philippines*. St Martin's Press, New York, 1986

Catton, Bruce. *Glory Road – From Fredericksburg to Gettysburg*. White Lion Publishers, 1977

Churchill, Winston S. *The River War*. Landsborough, 1960

Devlin, Gerard M. *Paratrooper*. Robson, 1979

Duncan, John, and Walton, John. *Heroes for Victoria*. Spellmount, 1991

Edwardes, Michael. *Battles of the Indian Mutiny*. Batsford, 1963

— *Red Year: The Indian Rebellion of 1857*. Hamish Hamilton, 1973

Ellis, Major L. F. *Victory in the West*. Vol II, HMSO, 1968

Falk, Stanley. *Liberation of the Philippines*. Macdonald, 1970

Fontane, Theodor. *Der Krieg gegen Frankreich 1870–1871*. Manesse

Forbes, Archibald, (*et al*) *Battles of the Nineteenth Century*. Cassell, 1896

Frost, Major-General John. *2 Para Falklands*. Buchan & Enright, 1983

Grossen Generalstabe, Kriegsgeschichtliche Abteilung I. *Der 18 August 1870*. Mittler & Sohn, Berlin, 1906

Harris, John. *The Gallant Six Hundred*. Hutchinson, 1973

Hobart, F. W. A. *Pictorial History of the Machine Gun*. Ian Allan, 1971

Horrocks, Lieutenant-General Sir Brian. *A Full Life*. Collins, 1960

Howard, Michael. *The Franco–Prussian War*. Routledge, 1988

Hughes, Major-General B. P. *Honour Titles of the Royal Artillery*. Royal Artillery Institution

Katcher, Philip. *The American Civil War Source Book*. Arms & Armour Press, 1992

Leasor, James. *The Red Fort*. Werner Laurie, 1956

Liddell Hart, Captain B. H. *The Tanks – The History of the Royal Tank Regiment*. Vol II, Cassell, 1959

McGuffie, T. H. (ed.). *Rank and File – The Common Soldier at Peace and War 1641–1914*. Hutchinson, 1964

McKee, Alexander. *The Race for the Rhine Bridges*. Souvenir Press, 1971

Macksey, Kenneth. *Crucible of Power – The Fight for Tunisia 1942–1943*. Hutchinson, 1969

Moran, Lord. *The Anatomy of Courage*. Constable, 1945

Pearson, Hesketh, *The Hero of Delhi – A Life of John Nicholson*. Penguin, 1948

Pemberton, W. Baring. *Battles of the Crimean War*. Batsford, 1962

Perkins, Roger. *The Kashmir Gate – Lieutenant Home and the Delhi VCs*. Picton Publishing, 1983

Perret, Bryan. *Desert Warfare*, Patrick Stephens, 1988

— *Through Mud and Blood – Infantry/Tank Operations in World War II*. Robert Hale, 1975

— *Weapons of the Falklands Conflict*. Blandford, 1982

Pfanz, Harry W. *Gettysburg – The Second Day*. University of South Carolina Press, 1987

Playfair, Major-General I. S. O. (*et al*). *The Mediterranean and Middle East*. Vol IV, HMSO, 1966

Priesdorf, Kurt von. *Soldatisches Führertum Teil 9 & 10*. Hanseatische Verlagsanstalt, Hamburg

Rutherford, Ward. *Fall of the Philippines*. Pan/Ballantine, 1972

Ryan, Cornelius. *A Bridge Too Far*. Hamish Hamilton, 1974

Scales, Robert H. Jr. *Firepower in Limited War*. National Defense University Press, 1990

Schmid, E von. *Das Franzosische Generalstabswert uber den Krieg 1870/71. Heft 7. Schlachten vor Metz*. Friedrich Engelmann, Leipzig, 1907

Scott, Lieutenant Colonel Robert N. *The War of the Rebellion – A Compilation of the Official Records of the Union and Confederate Armies*. Series I Vol XXVII Part II, Washington, Government Printing Office, 1889

Seymour, William. *Yours to Reason Why – Decision in Battle*. Sidgwick & Jackson, 1982

Sichart, Lieutenant-General L. von. *Geschichte der Königlich–Hannoverschen Armee*, Hanover, 1870

Smith, Robert Ross. *Triumph in the Philippines*. Center of Military History US Army, Washington, 1963

Swinson, Arthur. *North West Frontier*. Hutchinson, 1967

Thomas, Donald. *Charge! Hurrah! Hurrah! A Life of Cardigan of Balaclava*. Routledge, 1974

Thompson, Julian. *No Picnic – 3 Commando Brigade in the South Atlantic 1982*. Leo Cooper, 1985

Tilberg, Frederick. *Gettysburg National Military Park*. National Park Service, US Department of the Interior,

Washington, 1962

Warner, Philip. *Dervish – The Rise and Fall of an African Empire*. Macdonald, 1973

Whiting, Charles. *First Blood – The Battle of the Kasserine Pass 1943*. Leo Cooper, 1984

Wilmot, Chester. *The Struggle for Europe*. Wm Collins, 1952

Woide, Lieutenant-General von. *Die Ursachen der Siege und Niederlagen im Kriege 1870*, Mittler & Sohn, Berlin, 1897

Woodham-Smith, Cecil. *The Reason Why*. Constable, 1953

' "Celer et Audax". The Minden Rose', in *British Army Review*, No. 95, August 1990

'Minden' in *Royal Hampshire Magazine*, August 1914

Irwin, Colonel A. S. H. 'Metz, a Marshal and a Miscalculation' in *British Army Review*, No. 99, December 1991

INDEX